Frontiers in African Business Research

Series Editor

Almas Heshmati, Jönköping International Business School,
Jönköping, Sweden

This book series publishes monographs and edited volumes devoted to studies on entrepreneurship, innovation, as well as business development and management-related issues in Africa. Volumes cover in-depth analyses of individual countries, regions, cases, and comparative studies. They include both a specific and a general focus on the latest advances of the various aspects of entrepreneurship, innovation, business development, management and the policies that set the business environment. It provides a platform for researchers globally to carry out rigorous analyses, to promote, share, and discuss issues, findings and perspectives in various areas of business development, management, finance, human resources, technology, and the implementation of policies and strategies of the African continent. Frontiers in African Business Research allows for a deeper appreciation of the various issues around African business development with high quality and peer reviewed contributions. Volumes published in the series are important reading for academicians, consultants, business professionals, entrepreneurs, managers, as well as policy makers, interested in the private sector development of the African continent.

More information about this series at http://www.springer.com/series/13889

Thomas Kigabo Rusuhuzwa

Monetary Policy in Rwanda

1964—Present

Springer

Thomas Kigabo Rusuhuzwa
College of Business and Economics
University of Rwanda
Kigali, Rwanda

ISSN 2367-1033 ISSN 2367-1041 (electronic)
Frontiers in African Business Research
ISBN 978-981-33-6745-6 ISBN 978-981-33-6746-3 (eBook)
https://doi.org/10.1007/978-981-33-6746-3

This Springer imprint is published by the registered company Springer Nature Singapore Pte Ltd.
The registered company address is: 152 Beach Road, #21-01/04 Gateway East, Singapore 189721, Singapore

Foreword

Professor Thomas Kigabo, 1963–2021

Professor Thomas Kigabo was an economist with more than 13 years of expertise in economic policy formulation and implementation both in Rwanda and in the East African Community and in economic research and analysis mainly as the Chief Economist of the National Bank of Rwanda (Central Bank). Professor Kigabo was also an active and known researcher and academic—Associate Professor—at the University of Rwanda and a member of different economic research institutions and thinktanks in Africa (e.g. the African Economic Consortium and the Macroeconomic and Financial Management Institute of Eastern and Southern Africa).

It was with great sorrow that we learnt that Professor Thomas Kigabo passed away on 15 January 2021. He leaves behind a wife and five children.

When Professor Kigabo's book *Monetary Policy in Rwanda* is released it will provide more evidence of his strong commitment to Rwanda and underline his legacy as a well-renowned academician, besides his undisputed importance as a leading promoter of the development of Rwandan macroeconomic policies.

Thomas Kigabo was born in Kabara in the Democratic Republic of Congo (DRC) on 2 December 1963. In 1987, Thomas Kigabo completed his bachelor's degree in

Mathematics from the Institut Supérieur Pédagogique in Kisangani, DRC. In 1996, he earned his Master's degree in Applied Mathematics from the Université Nationale du Bénin in Porto-Novo, Benin and in 2005 he successfully defended his PhD thesis titled "Integration, cointegration with structural break: application to the estimation of a money demand function: cases of Rwanda and Burundi," at the University Lyon 2, in Lyon, France.

Thomas Kigabo joined the National Bank of Rwanda in 2007 as Chief Economist and in this position, he played an important role in the formulation and implementation of the monetary policy in Rwanda and the Government of Rwanda's economic policies as well as the development of the financial sector. He also played an important role in negotiations for policies with different stakeholders including the International Monetary Fund and the World Bank. Thomas Kigabo also headed a high-level taskforce on the East African Monetary Union and acted as Rwanda's chief negotiator.

Alongside his professional career at the National Bank of Rwanda, Professor Thomas Kigabo was also engaged with higher education institutions as a teacher and researcher, most recently at the University of Rwanda; he was also engaged with the Jomo Kenyatta University and Kigali Independent University. Thomas Kigabo had extensive experience in research in different areas including monetary policy, financial inclusion, issue related to financial sector development, development economics, and regional integration.

Among his latest research contributions is 'Financial Inclusion under the Microscope' (2018), an IMF working paper and articles in the *Rwandan Handbook of Economic and Social Policy* (2019). Professor Kigabo supervised and co-supervised PhD students in Rwanda and Rwandan PhD students in different universities in Europe.

Besides Professor Thomas Kigabo's professional achievements he will also be remembered for his generous and humble personality as seen by numerous colleagues and friends in Rwanda and abroad.

February 2021

Almas Heshmati
Lars Hartvigson
Jönköping International Business School
Jönköping, Sweden

Preface

Monetary policy in Rwanda has undergone profound changes since the establishment of the National Bank of Rwanda (NBR) in 1964. For a period of 26 years, the NBR conducted direct monetary control before shifting to the use of indirect monetary policy instruments following the advent of free-market economic policies. Between 1964 and 1990, the direct monetary policy regime in Rwanda was characterized by a system of credit ceilings and sector credit allocation, a subsidized and regulated interest rate, exchange rate controls as well as import licensing. After the creation of money market in 1997, the NBR implemented a monetary targeting policy regime using reserve money as an operational target and broad money as an intermediate target, with the objective of achieving price stability between 1997 and 2018.

During that period, NBR introduced a number of innovations aiming at modernizing the monetary policy. They include flexibility in reserve money programme implemented during a period of 22 years; building the capacity of staff in modelling and forecasting as well as in liquidity forecast and management; development of money market, particularly interbank market; the development of a clear communication strategy to increase transparency and accountability of the bank; and the improvement of the decision-making process by establishing an information-inclusive strategy. Achievements in those areas made easier for NBR to adopt a new monetary policy framework in Jan 2019, that is the price-based monetary policy, which took into consideration changes in the Rwandan financial system.

This book documents the NBR's experience in managing its monetary policy from 1964 to date and the bank's significant contribution to supporting the government's development agenda by maintaining inflation low and stable, implementing monetary policy to support the financing of the private sector by the banking sector and limiting the impact of different shocks to the economy. Chapter 1, we describe the development in the Rwandan financial system which is the key for understanding the extent to which monetary policy actions are transmitted to aggregate demand and ultimately to prices, through various channels.

Chapter 2 describes the evolution of monetary policy implementation in Rwanda from the era of direct control to the adoption of indirect monetary policy instruments as well as the impact of NBR monetary policy on economic growth in the two periods. Chapter 3 presents the development of the monetary policy frameworks in Rwanda from the monetary targeting regime to price-based monetary policy. In Chap. 4, we examine different channels of monetary transmission mechanism, their characteristics such as time of propagating NBR actions and their development over time. The last chapter describes NBR communication journey to ensure transparency, openness, and accountability, which are critical for the efficiency of monetary policy.

This book is a contribution to central bankers' efforts in understanding how monetary policy is formulated and implemented in different stages of development, particularly in countries with a less developed financial system. It also presents empirical analysis of key factors that affect monetary policy efficiency in developing countries such as the stability of money multiplier and money demand, as well as the assessment of channels of monetary transmission mechanism and actions to make them more active. This is also a contribution to central bankers' further enlightenment on the way key features of monetary policy in developing countries are assessed and how their developments are linked to changes in financial system and in economic conditions.

Kigali, Rwanda Thomas Kigabo Rusuhuzwa

Contents

Chapter 1
Financial System Development and Monetary Policy

1.1 Introduction

Understanding how fast and to what extent changes in the central bank's policy instruments affect aggregate demand and inflation through their influence on investment and consumption decisions of firms, households, and financial intermediaries is crucial for monetary policy formulation and implementation. The extent to which channels through which monetary policy actions are transmitted to variables that affect conditions in non-financial sector such as deposit rates and lending rates, to aggregate demand and ultimately to prices, varies across countries due to differences in financial system development and structural economic conditions prevailing in the economy (Cecchetti 1999; Bondt 2002; Mishra et al. 2012).

The financial system has a broad scope and is generally composed of: (1) all financial intermediaries and financial markets, and their relations with respect to the flow of funds to and from households, governments, business firms, and foreigners, and (2) the financial infrastructure, which is the set of institutions that enable effective operation of financial intermediaries and financial markets including such elements as payment systems, credit information bureaus, and collateral registries (Mishkin 2004; Haan et al. 2015).

The main role of the financial system is to channel funds either directly or indirectly from sectors that are in surplus to sectors that are in shortage of funds. Firms and governments with a shortage of funds can directly borrow from others with surplus funds through a financial market (bonds or equity markets) or indirectly from a financial intermediary like a bank, which obtains funds from savers and uses the savings to make loans to a sector in need of finance (Madura 2010; Mishkin 2004). By performing these functions, the financial system contributes to reduction in information and transactions costs, and facilitates the trading, diversification, and management of risks, including liquidity and idiosyncratic risk (Allen and Gale 2000; Levine 1997, 2005).

T. K. Rusuhuzwa, *Monetary Policy in Rwanda*, Frontiers in African Business Research, https://doi.org/10.1007/978-981-33-6746-3_1

For the central bank, a good understanding of the structure and the development of the financial system is crucial for the design and implementation of monetary policy because the efficiency of transmission channels of monetary policy in a country depends on the extent of financial intermediation, the size, concentration, and health of the banking system; the development of financial markets; and structural economic conditions. For example, in a country with undeveloped financial market (money market and/or capital market), economic agents will not have much opportunities to save their money and borrow to finance their investment in addition to the use of commercial banks and non-bank financial institutions. Thus, the demand for deposits and loans will be less sensitive to changes in deposits and lending rates resulting from central bank actions. The same will happen if the banking sector is less competitive (Hannan and Berger 1991; Weth 2002). In a non-competitive banking sector, an increase in the supply of loanable resources resulting from easing monetary policy may not necessarily lead to a reduction in the cost of finance for the non-bank sector or to an increase in credit to the private sector. In addition, how the aggregate demand in an economy is influenced by the change in deposit and lending rates will highly depend on the characteristics of the financial system such as the degree of monetization of the economy, the size of the formal financial sector, and payment system, in addition to the general macroeconomic environment of the country (Mishra and Montiel 2010).

The role of competition in the banking sector in economic development is largely discussed by both researchers and policymakers. It is believed that large banks that have monopolistic power in the market charge higher loan interests from the firms, which limit innovation as most of the businesses avoid undertaking risky business projects. In addition, financial institutions will not be stimulated to do research and development activities which will limit the creation of new technologies and products. Though competition may be needed to boost market efficiency, policymakers and researchers often stress that there may be a trade-off between competition and stability in the banking industry. Competition may reduce the banking system stability by squeezing profits, lowering bank valuations, and encouraging bankers to make riskier investments.

There are two major schools of thought regarding banking competition and its stability: the competition fragility theory and the competition stability theory (Koetter et al. 2012). On one side, the first theory supports the negative relationship between banking competition and its stability considering that high level of competition among banks reduces market power and margins of profit, leading banks to make risky decisions. The competition stability theory, on the other side, supports increased competition among banks that leads to banking stability; as a result, reduction in interest rates resulting from competition will lead to more loans by decreasing default rates of loans which ensures the stability of banks. While this competition-fragility perspective is not universally accepted, there is a need for policymakers to decide about the degree of competition that appropriately balances the efficiency benefits and the fragility costs of competition, and also use supervisory, regulatory, and monetary policies to mitigate the fragility repercussions of competition.

Financial intermediation may be carried out either inside or outside of the formal financial sector. Informal finance may involve transactions between related parties, reliance on specialized money lenders, or the use of informal credit cooperatives and plays an important role in performing financial intermediation in developing countries due to low levels of formal financial sector development and intermediation (Demirguc-Kunt et al. 2017). In those countries, the capacity of monetary policy to influence inflation is reduced because formal financial sector variables, such as lending and deposit rates, tend to have weaker effects on aggregate demand. Comparing the levels of monetization and financial intermediation by group of countries, Montiel et al. (2010) show that those levels are very low in developing countries compared to advanced countries. For example, in 2005, the ratio to GDP of assets held by banks and other formal financial institutions in advanced countries was 1.24, while in low-income countries it was only 0.32. This explains why channels of monetary transmission channels are operational in developed than in developing countries.

As pointed out however, the economic benefits of financial sector deepening need to be weighed against the risks to financial stability as pointed out earlier. Excessive credit growth can lead to financial risks and is considered today as one of the most robust predictors of banking and currency crises. This is particularly important in an environment of rising interest rates as it would affect the affordability of variable interest rate loans, the cost of rolling over fixed term debt, and it could entail risks for financial institutions with maturity mismatches (Klemm and Herman 2017). In addition, financial deepening as measured by credit to private sector ratio to GDP does not necessarily imply access to loans by many individuals and businesses. This explains why channels of monetary transmission may be weak even in countries with high level of financial deepening. The financial depth, indicating how economic sectors and agents are able to use a range of financial markets and financial intermediaries for savings and investment decisions, is another aspect of financial system linked to the effectiveness of monetary policy (King and Levine 1993; Rajan and Zingales 1998; Chami et al. 2009; Goswami and Sharma 2011). One approach to analyse financial deepening is to consider both the banking sector and capital markets, and expand the range of actors to include non-bank financial intermediaries in addition to households and firms. Indeed, different actors bring different preferences for financial exposure and different attitudes about risk, which creates opportunities for gains from trade. For example, while banks transform maturities (borrowing on short-term basis and lending on long-term basis), pension funds and insurance companies invariably match maturities (borrowing and lending on long-term basis), making them natural buyers of long-term bonds and facilitating the development of markets.

The degree of financial deepening, generally measured by credit to the private sector as percentage of GDP and reflecting levels of intermediation, is also an important determinant of monetary transmission mechanism. In countries with high degree of financial deepening, generally defined as an increase in the size of the financial system and in its role in the economy, changes in central bank rate are more rapidly transmitted to the whole term structure and more generally to financial assets prices.

This affects the economy through the cost of investment and the return on saving as firms can exploit a wider range of financing opportunities. and households' portfolios are more diversified.

1.2 Financial System and Monetary Policy

In this subsection, we present key aspects of financial intermediaries, financial markets, and financial infrastructures, which are important for monetary policy efficiency.

1.2.1 Financial Intermediaries

A financial intermediary, such as a commercial bank, is an institution playing the "intermediary role" between the savers and the borrowers and helps to transfer funds from one economic agent to another. Financial intermediaries play an important role in transmitting resources between lenders and borrowers and in creating multiple layers of financial derivatives that deepen the financial system and reinforce the multiplier of credit growth. Financial intermediaries fall into three main categories: (i) depository institutions, such as banks, that accept deposits from individuals and institutions and make loans; (ii) contractual saving institutions, such as insurance companies and pension funds, that acquire funds at periodic intervals on a contractual basis and can predict with reasonable accuracy how much they will have to pay out benefits in the coming years. They tend to invest their funds primarily in long-term securities such as corporate bonds, government bonds, and stocks because they do not have much liquidity problem[1]; and (iii) investment intermediaries, such as finance companies, mutual funds, and money market mutual funds.[2]

In different countries, financial intermediaries are the main source of financing the private sector (individuals and corporations) for different reasons, including financial markets which are either undeveloped, inexistent, or atomic. This makes financial intermediaries important for monetary policy management. In the case of atomic financial markets, markets face a free-rider problem, contrary to the baking sector, limiting the identification of innovative projects which are key for sustainable economic growth. Because banks provide a range of financial services to their clients, they end up building long-run relationships with them and acquire more information that is used to make investments without revealing their decisions in public markets. In addition, clients with long-term relationships with banks can access bank loans at low prices than new borrowers (Rajah 1998).

[1]In countries with less developed financial markets, those institutions are important depositors in the banking sector.

[2]For more details on investment intermediaries, see, for example Mishkin (2007).

Financial intermediaries also play an important role in the development of financial markets, though the two are complementary in providing financial services to the economy. Financial intermediaries not only participate in the markets on day-to-day basis but also reduce the cost of learning about how to effectively use financial markets compared to households. Different researches show that the increase in the breadth and depth of financial markets is linked with greater use of those markets by intermediaries and firms and not by individuals (Allen and Santomero 1997). Corporate markets and stock markets can also complement banks by offering alternative ways of financing investments by the private sector which improves the efficiency of monetary policy. Borrowers can use capital markets rather than banks to raise funds, reducing the potential negative impact of excessive bank market power. In addition, financial markets can offer alternative opportunities to consumers to invest in government and private bonds and stocks rather than depositing their money in the savings accounts only.

A financial system in which banks and capital markets offer different opportunities of raising funds to finance the private sector is crucial for the efficiency of monetary transmission channels, as pointed out earlier. It provides the possibility of substituting bank deposits by money market funds such as investment in treasury bills and loans by equity and corporate bonds, which improves interest rate pass-through, that is the link between market rates (deposit rates and lending rates) and money market rates such as interbank rates and treasury bill rates.

1.2.2 Financial Markets

A financial market, which is a market where securities (debt securities and equity securities) and derivatives are traded, is composed of money and capital markets. Well-functioning money markets, foreign exchange markets, and secondary markets for government securities are crucial for the efficiency of monetary policy and central bank financial stability objective, and broadly it should benefit economic development. For central banks using price-based monetary policy, well-functioning money markets increase the efficiency of monetary policy by facilitating the transmission from central bank rate to other money market rates such as interbank rates, T-bill rates, and interest rates on repo operations. Liquid foreign exchange markets can help to limit the exchange rate pass-through by stabilizing the exchange rate and reducing transaction costs in cross-border trade and transfers. The development of these markets supports the introduction of more financial products such as repo and derivatives, which should in turn contribute to the improvement of risk management by financial institutions and their stability. A well-functioning and liquid money market with stable short-term interest rates support market-making, help to reduce the cost of issuance for the government and other fixed-interest issuers, and contribute to the development of the secondary market for government securities which may promote the development of a wider fixed income securities markets and its yield curve serving as the benchmark for the pricing of the private sector credit.

To raise funds in a financial market, a firm can issue a debt instrument such as a bond or a mortgage or issue an equity such as common stock. A debt instrument is a contractual agreement by borrower to pay the holder of an instrument a fixed amount at regular intervals of time until the maturity date when the final payment is made. Short-term debt instruments such as treasury bills (maturity less than one year) are traded on the money market while long-term debt securities such as bonds are traded on the capital market. Another way of raising funds on the financial market, specifically on the capital market, is by issuing equities such as common stock, which are claims to share in the net income of a business. Equities are considered as long-term securities because they made periodic payment, called dividends, and do not have maturity date. Because the corporation must pay all its debt holders before it pays its equity holders, the corporation's equity holder is a residual claimant. However, contrary to debt holders for whom the payment is fixed, equity holders benefit directly from any increase in the corporation's profitability or asset value due to ownership rights on the equity holders.

Another aspect of financial markets to be distinguished here and linked to the efficiency of monetary policy is the categorization of the market into primary and secondary market. A primary market is a financial market in which new issues of securities are sold to initial buyers while on the secondary market securities that have been previously sold on the primary market can be sold. For some securities, their secondary markets are more active and are therefore more marketable than others. This feature of securities is key for investors who consider the probability of selling securities prior to their maturities and helps central banks to conduct monetary policy through open market transactions in liquid secondary markets.

Indeed, while the development of the secondary market may be facilitated by effective monetary policy implementation through the adequate provision of liquidity to market makers and stable short-term rates, deep and liquid secondary market of government securities also ensures proper implementation of monetary policy. By reducing day-to-day fluctuations in short-term rates and credibly signalling its monetary policy stance, the central bank contributes to increase in liquidity in the secondary market and investors' confidence in long-term securities, and promotes maturity transformation by financial intermediaries. More investment in securities with long-term maturity reduces the frequency of new issuance and contributes to the improvement in the government planning process. By reducing the need for monetization of government deficits, the independence of the central bank is enhanced, which is crucial for effective monetary policy. In addition, if the secondary market is liquid, purchases and sales of government securities for liquidity management purposes may be executed quickly and without unjustifiably changing the yield of these instruments.

Understanding the nature and categories of instruments that are used to raise funds on the financial market as well as the participants on that market is crucial for better formulation and implementation of monetary policy by central banks. For example, operation of monetary transmission channels highly depends on the extent to which banks and capital markets offer different opportunities of raising funds to finance the private sector as seen before. This shows the role of corporate bond markets and equity bond markets in monetary policy management. One of the main factors explaining why channels of monetary transmission are functioning in developed countries than in developing and emerging countries is the differences in capital market development, particularly corporate bond and equity markets development Mishra and Montiel (2012). Though corporate bonds markets are rarely the first or the only source used by companies to finance their operations and growth, and many companies may never require any form of capital-markets financing, they play an important role in meeting the funding and risk-management needs of many corporates as they evolve to become larger, more mature, and complex organizations (Allen and Gale 2000).

1.2.3 Financial Infrastructure

Financial infrastructure is the set of institutions that enables effective operation of financial intermediaries and financial markets, including such elements as payment system, credit information bureaus, and collateral registries. A payment is a transfer of money between economic actors, for example, between a consumer and a merchant to pay for a good or service using cash and non-cash money. For cash payment, there is no need for a settlement system because when bank notes and coins are handed over, the settlement is done on spot. For a non-cash payment however, such as a transfer from a bank account, a system for settlement is needed because one bank account has to be debited and another account has to be credited. The payment system is required to ensure that the transfer is completed in a safe and efficient manner.

A payment system can be defined as a combination of technical, legal and commercial instruments, rules, and procedures that ensure transfer of money between banks. Two categories of payment systems can be distinguished: Retail payment systems and wholesale payment systems. Retail payment systems are used for transaction, clearing, and settlement of relatively low value and non-time-critical payments initiated through payment instruments such as cheque, credit transfers, direct debits, and payment cards. Those payments are generally made by many economic actors and typically relate to the purchase of goods and services in both the consumer and business sectors. Wholesale payment systems facilitate large value and/or time-critical fund transfers and are made between financial institutions within the system for their own account or for their customers (BIS 2003).

Thus, the payment and settlement systems are a key part of the infrastructure needed for the development of market. Banks use wholesale payment systems to make transfers on behalf of customers (e.g. tax payments and payment for securities); and they make transfers on their own behalf which will often be more time-critical because they are related to liquidity management. In transfers involving securities instruments which are often in dematerialized form, payment and settlement systems must have certain features. To serve the development of the market, users of the systems must trust the operator and regard it as efficient because risk of loss or delay will discourage some trades. On the side of central banks, they have strong interest in the development of sound payment and settlement systems to achieve their monetary and financial stability goals. By securing interbank lending via securities repo or collateralized lending as well as central bank lending to the banking system, payment systems facilitate the central banks' monetary policy and liquidity management operations, as well as supporting financial stability.

Modern payment systems have developed large value transfer systems (LVTSs) to clear and settle time-critical and large payments that require a high degree of security and reliability, such as those generally associated with money market and securities operations, which are key for the implementation of monetary policy by central banks. For central banks, reliable real-time gross settlement system is an important prerequisite for the efficient functioning of financial markets, and thus, effective implementation of monetary policy. As lender of last resort, central banks could provide credit facilities as part of its payment services, especially in connection with an LVTS, to facilitate a smooth flow of settlements in the payment system as long as these credit operations do not reduce its control over liquidity management.

The instruments and operations of monetary management, the institutional arrangements for money markets, and aspects of the payment systems are closely linked. The interbank market, which is important for settlement balances, is a component of money market, whose features are themselves strongly influenced by both payment system design and the monetary operations framework. Central banks play an important role in the development of payment systems by establishing a legal framework to ensure appropriate institutions, organizational structure, and monetary policy environment; facilitating payments finality; regulating private agents in the payment system; administering as owner/operator of various payment services; and providing credit for participants in the payment system, especially in LVTSs.

The development of real-time gross settlement (RTGS) systems and the dematerialization of securities contributed to a reduction of risk related to transfers. RTGS systems are wholesale payment systems that settle in central bank money continuously throughout the day, with direct access normally restricted to banks. Through these systems, payment notifications from the payer occur when the transfer is considered as legally final; this means notification is received only if fund transfer has taken place across the central bank's books. This will avoid any intraday settlement risk. The rapid and reliable settlement of securities also promotes trading and so liquidity in the market because, for example, a market maker can take a short position by selling a security to a customer even if it does not hold that security in its portfolio, provided it can be purchased in the market, and expects to take delivery in time to pass on to its customer. In addition, the dematerialization or immobilization of securities not only eliminates the risk (and cost) of handling paper securities, by allowing book-entry transactions, but it also permits the introduction of delivery versus payment (DvP) which is a mechanism that permits simultaneous exchange of value in the system so that one side only delivers value, the security for example, when the other side makes the payment. Thus, the design of payment systems affects the conduct of monetary policy, the soundness of financial institutions, and the functioning of the economy as a whole.

A well-functioning financial system also needs a robust legal framework to ensure protection of property rights and enforcement of contracts. Property rights refer to control of the use of the property, the right to any benefit from the property, the right to transfer or sell the property and the right to exclude others from the property. Absence of secure property rights and enforcement of contracts severely restricts financial transactions and investment, thereby hampering financial development. A robust legal framework provides rules on how financial market function. By providing market participants with some legal certainty that the validity of trades will be upheld in the court of law, the legal framework contributes to the market development. This framework composed generally of regulations or market standards should include authorization from the government to borrow as well as the standards on how that borrowing is to be conducted, rules on secondary market trading, as well as regulations defining the legal properties of government securities and their use as collateral in transactions such as repo. While the legal system provides framework for risk management, it has to be flexible by ensuring a balance between the need for control and the creation of an environment for market development.

Another element which is key for the development and functioning of the financial system is credit reporting system. It includes institutions, individuals, rules, procedures, standards and technology that enable information flows relevant to making informed decisions related to a credit agreement. Under the credit reporting system, banks and other lenders submit information about their borrowers to a credit bureau (CRB) to be shared with other credit providers. A credit bureau is a type of credit reporting system whose primary objective is to collect and store credit information received from creditors and other sources on individuals and entities with legal personality. It helps to produce credit reports and deliver other services to creditors and other persons engaged in providing goods and services subject to deferred payment. Thus, the credit reporting system eases access to finance, attenuates adverse selection, and alleviates information asymmetry between lenders and borrowers and can therefore increase lending and reduce default rates. Where the credit information is available, lenders are able to assess credit risk and make informed lending decisions.

1.3 Financial System Development in Rwanda

In this chapter, we describe the key aspects of financial system development in Rwanda linked to the functioning of monetary transmission channels such as development and structure of the banking sector, financial market development, and payment system development.

1.3.1 *Financial Sector*

The financial sector in Rwanda is composed of banking sector, insurance and pensions, microfinance institutions (MFIs), and non-deposit taking financial institutions (NDFIs). The number of commercial banks and insurance companies increased, respectively, to 16 and 14 as of March 2020 while it was 14 and 8 in December 2010. The number of MFIs is reduced to 457 from 524 in the period under review as some of them were merged. Furthermore, the country has 12 private pension funds and 4 non-deposit taking financial institutions (NDFIs) that are recently established. As a result, the number of financial institutions in Rwanda is 504 as of March 2020 and is 547 as of December 2020.

During the same period, the sector has grown tremendously in terms of size. Total asset of the sector increased by 340.7%, from FRW 1242 billion to FRW 5474 billion in the period under review, due to high increase in banks' assets (314%), insurance (477.2%), public pension (398.9%), and microfinance (265.3%). In terms of structure, the financial sector in Rwanda is dominated by commercial banks, representing 67% of total assets of the sector as of March 2020; however, reducing from 71% as of end December 2010, followed by pensions (17%), insurances (10%), and microfinance institutions (6%) (Table 1.1).

1.3.1.1 Non-bank Financial Institutions

Non-bank financial institutions (MFIs and pensions) play a crucial role in the development of banking sector and government security market in Rwanda. MFIs supplement

Table 1.1 Financial sector composition

	December 2010			March 2020		
	Number	Assets (FRW, billion)	% of Total assets	Number	Assets (FRW, billion)	% of Total assets
Banking sector	14	879	71	16	3643	67
Insurance	8	92	7	14	531	10
Pension	1	183	15	1	913	17
Private pension funds			0	12	49	1
MFIs	524	88	7	457	321	6
NDFIs			0	4	17	0
Total	**547**	**1242**	**100**	**504**	**5474**	**100**

Source NBR, Financial Stability Directorate

Table 1.2 MFI loans by sector of activities

Economic sector	Dec-14	Dec-15	Dec-16	Dec-17	Dec-18	Dec-19
Agriculture, livestock, fishing	12.1	19.2	20.0	22.3	24.9	64.2
Public works (construction), buildings, residences/homes	28.7	36.5	40.8	39.5	38.8	24.1
Commerce, restaurants, hotels	32.8	40.8	45.6	47.4	51.2	52.5
Transport, warehouses, communications	3.4	4.6	5.6	4.8	6.7	7.2
Others	12.9	15.4	22.1	24.3	42.5	35.2
Total	**90.0**	**116.6**	**134.0**	**138.3**	**164.0**	**183.2**

Source NBR, Microfinance Institutions Department

banks in providing financial services to individuals and firms and tailor their services to particular groups such as agriculture sector, and small and medium sectors which have limited access to bank credit due to different factors including lack of collateral. For households, in addition to the lack of collateral, lack of enough revenue, lack of adequate financial products in the banking sector, and complicated process to access bank loans are among constraints to the access on banks' loans cited by adults Rwandans. As a result, only 8% of adults borrowed from the bank in 2019, up by four percentage in 2016 (FINSCOP 2020). Between December 2014 and December 2019, 33.3% of loans disbursed by MFIs went to commerce, restaurants and hotels, followed by public works such as construction of residences and other buildings (26.5%), agriculture, livestock, fishing (8.5%), and other activities (17.8%) (Table 1.2).

In addition to extending loans to their clients, MFIs provide alternatives to transform the economy's savings into capital investment by collecting deposits from their members, making deposits in commercial banks, as well as investing in debt securities. In 2008, Umurenge SACCOs were established with the aim of boosting rural savings and providing Rwandans with loans to improve their earnings and enhance their livelihoods. Consequently, the number of Rwandan adults using formal financial institutions increased to 42% in 2012 from 21% in 2008. In just three years of existence, Umurenge SACCOs attracted over 1.6 million customers, and in six years of their existence, SACCOs and other MFIs served almost the same number of people as the entire banking sector (FINSCOP 2016).

As a result, MFIs size extended significantly between 2015 and 2019. Total assets of the sector increased by 53.5% from FRW 208.9 billion to 320.7 billion. Deposits in MFIs from their clients also increased by 45.1% in the period under review to FRW 170.2 million from FRW 117.3 million. MFI investments in government securities tremendously increased by 1081.4% to FRW 5.5 billion in 2019 from FRW 461.91 million in 2015. Deposits of MFIs in commercial banks also increased by 36.5% in the period under review amounting to FRW 101.5 billion from FRW 74.4 billion. For details on MFIs balance sheet, see Appendix 1.1.

Table 1.3 NBFI's deposits in commercial banks (percentage share)

	SSF	OFCs		SSF	OFCs	
	Share in total deposits		Total	Share in time deposits		Total
2015	15.8	9.3	25.0	32.3	15.4	47.7
2016	15.0	7.0	22.0	34.3	11.9	46.2
2017	17.3	7.6	24.9	32.7	12.7	45.5
2018	14.9	9.0	23.9	25.7	15.2	40.8
2019	14.1	10.0	24.1	30.4	16.5	46.8
Average	15.4	8.6	24.0	31.1	14.3	45.4

Source NBR, Financial Stability Statement
SSF: Social Security Fund
OFCs: Other Financial Corporations (Insurance companies, MFIs and SACCOs)

On the other side, because funds mobilized through contractual savings by pension and insurance institutions are of long term in nature, banks rely on deposits from those institutions to reduce the risk associated with maturity mismatches between long-term investment needs of businesses and short-term deposits mobilized by banks from the public. The analysis of the portfolio structure of insurance and pension shows that in 2020, 50% are deposits in commercial banks (38% as term deposits and 12% as demand deposits), 21% are investment in government securities, and 15% investment in equities. While the share of social security fund and other financial corporations (insurance companies, MFIs and SACCOs) deposits in the banking sector was 24% on average between 2015 and 2019, their share is very high at 45.4% of time deposits, which shows how the banking sector highly depends on the social security fund and other financial corporations to mobilize long-term deposits (Table 1.3).

In addition, non-bank financial institutions (NBFIs) significantly contributed to the development of the government's security market. As we will see later, while commercial banks in Rwanda reduced their holdings of government securities since 2014, NBFIs increased their investment for the same. Comparing the periods 2008–2014 and 2014–2019, the share of commercial banks' outstanding investment in T-bonds reduced by 52% from 83.2 to 40%, while NBFIs share increased by 277.7% from 14.4 to 54.4%. In terms of amount, the outstanding investment of commercial banks and NBFIs increased from FRW10.7 and FRW 1.9 billion to FRW 68.0 billion and FRW 103.5 billion, respectively, during the period under review (Fig. 1.1).

1.3.1.2 Banking Sector Development in Rwanda

The number of banks in Rwanda has been increasing over time, reaching 16 as of March 2020 from one commercial bank in 1964 after the establishment of the National Bank of Rwanda (NBR). The sector expanded significantly across the country during the last decades. The number of bank branches increased from 99 in

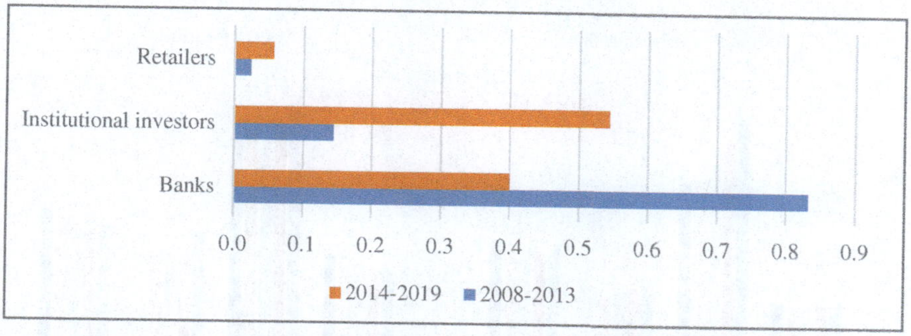

Fig. 1.1 Changes in shares of investment in T-bonds by category of investor. *Source* Our own calculations using data from NBR, Financial Markets Department

2010 to 522 in 2018 and 3780 bank agents exist today across the country. The expansion of bank branches and microfinancial institutions in unbanked areas, coupled with high and sustainable economic growth, showed a stable macro-economic environment characterized by stable and low inflation and stable FRW exchange rate, as well as the political stability of the country after the genocide against Tutsi in 1994, which contributed to a significant increase in deposits and credit to the private sector by the banking sector as well as in the size of the banking sector in Rwanda as measured by total assets. Deposits increased from FRW 90.3 billion in 2000 to FRW 2184 billion in 2019 while credit to the private sector increased from FRW 70.9 billion to FRW 2084 billion and total assets increased from FRW 879 billion to FRW 3476 billion during the period under review (Table 1.4).

The level of financial sector development and deepening has been also increasing though remain low, just like in other developing countries. Credit to private sector expressed as percentage of GDP has almost doubled, increasing from 10.3% in 2000 to 20.1% in 2019. The monetization of the economy accelerated during the period under review as the ratio of M3 to GDP increased from 16.5 to 26.3% and deposit to GDP ratio increased from 13.4 to 23.9%. However, the degree of monetization is evidently still low and this is one of the challenges to the well-functioning of the monetary transmission channels in developing countries. Low levels of financial sector development and intermediation imply that a small part of economic activities interact with the banking sector. Thus, the monetary policy actions on lending rates would have limited impact on aggregate demand and inflation. In EAC countries,

Table 1.4 Evolution of total assets, loans and deposits in FRW billion

	2010	2011	2012	2013	2014	2015	2016	2017	2018	2019
Total assets	879	1084	1248	1511	1803	2133	2380	2685	3091	3476
Total loans	456	583	775	881	1051	1269	1457	1646	1871	2084
Total deposits	536	651	741	866	1042	1418	1530	1723	1965	2184

Source NBR, Financial Stability Directorate

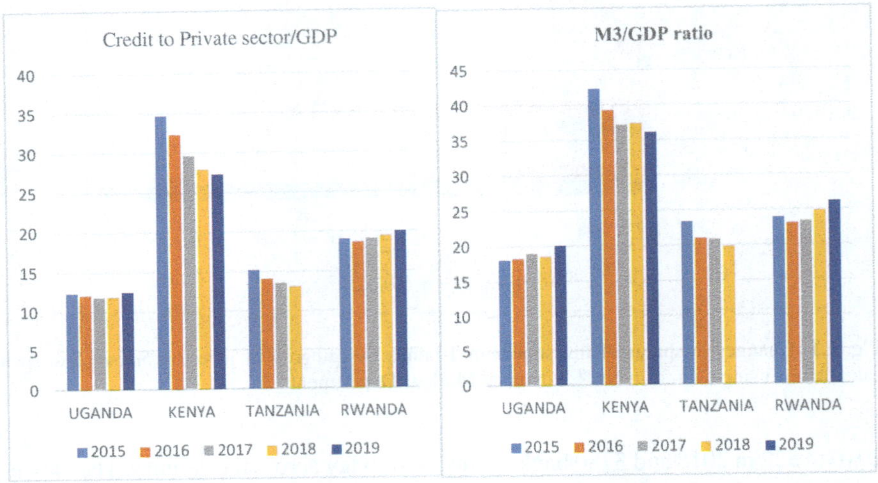

Fig. 1.2 Financial deepening indicators. *Source* East African Central Banks

the average credit to private sector to GDP ratio between 2015 and 2019 is 12.2% in Uganda; 30.4% in Kenya, and 14% in Tanzania.[3] The level of monetization of the economy measured by M3 as percentage of GDP is 18.9, 38.5, and 21.3% in Uganda, Kenya, and Tanzania, respectively.

One of the characteristics of financial system in developing countries is the large size of non-monetized sector, an indication of small size of financial sector. The implication is that the non-monetized sector has an important contribution to the overall economic growth in those countries in addition to the role played by monetized sector, whereas the mutual interaction between the two sectors and its implications on how monetary policy affects the real economy cannot also be overlooked. The term non-monetized comprises activities that do not involve the use of money such as subsistence, that is, goods produced and consumed at home. In other words, it means the production of goods and services which are subsequently found to have been directly used by their producers.

The distinctive characteristic of non-monetary economic activities is that the output is retained by producers for their own use, which may be final such as crops or livestock produced and consumed at home or intermediate such as the use of seed from the previous harvest or building materials from the farm. The level of monetization of an economy has important implication on the formulation and implementation of monetary policy, because monetization can affect money supply and velocity through the functions of money. In addition, lower levels of monetization, calculated as broad money ratio to GDP, indicates that a small part of economic activities interact with the banking sector, reducing the impact of monetary policy on the aggregate demand (Fig. 1.2).

[3]In Tanzania, data covers the period 2015–2018.

Another important aspect worth analysing is the competition of the banking sector in Rwanda. The fact that competition is a complex notion and therefore not directly observable has resulted in the development of different methods for its assessment and measurement leading to dissimilar inferences regarding competition. Empirical studies on that topic use two approaches to measure competition: the structural and non-structural approaches. The structural approach deduces the degree of competition from the structure of the market while the non-structural approach assesses the degree of competition by observing the behaviour of firms in the market.

The objective of structure–conduct–performance (SCP) paradigm is to explain aspects of the conduct and performance of firms taking into consideration the structural characteristics of the markets in which they operate. Those characteristics include the number of firms and their size, the entry and exit conditions, and the extent of product differentiation. The overall idea is that the structure of the market is expected to influence the conduct of firms, meaning the way firms define their strategic decisions about prices and organization of the market to influence their performance (Ergungor 2004). The most important perception of the SCP paradigm is that the more concentrated an industry is, the easier it is for firms to operate in an uncompetitive environment (Leon 2014). The concentration measure frequently used in empirical research is the Herfindahl–Hirschman Index (HHI) defined as follows:

$$HHI = \sum_{i=1}^{N} s_i^2 \quad \forall i = 1, \ldots, N \tag{1.1}$$

where N is the total number of firms in the market. The HHI index ranges between $1/N$ (for equal-sized firms) and 1 for monopolies. The banking industry is regarded to be unconcentrated if the HHI is less than 1500 (or 0.15). It is considered as moderately concentrated when the HHI lies between 1500 (or 0.15) and 2500 (or 0.25) and highly concentrated if the HHI is above 2500 (or 0.25). The HHI stresses the importance of larger firms by assigning them a greater weight than smaller ones, thus reflecting their relative importance. Under this approach, concentration increases when there is more collusion between banks and this resulted in higher prices and profits. We have computed HHI on banks assets, loans and deposits in Rwanda and the indicators show that the banking sector in Rwanda has been unconcentrated. However, since 2016, the sector became less competitive and the loan market became concentrated since 2018, indicating the increase in the loan market power of some banks (Fig. 1.3).

However, different empirical studies have challenged the SCP approach showing, for example, that even in a duopoly, price competition can occur (Bertrand equilibrium) and that in a concentrated market, an industry/firm can behave competitively if hurdles for entry and exit are low (Baumol et al. 1983). As a result, a new set of measures of competition were developed by directly observing the conduct of firms in the market. The most used indicator in this category is the Lerner index (or price–cost margin). In this approach, the market power of a firm is derived from the difference between the firm's price and its marginal cost, considering that in

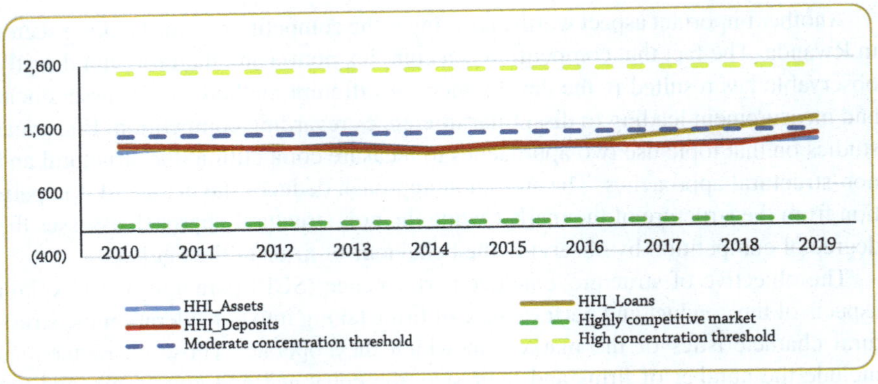

Fig. 1.3 Evolution of HHI on banks assets, loans and deposits. *Source* Our own computation using data from NBR, Financial Stability Directorate

perfect competition, the price and marginal cost should be equal and diverge in a less competitive environment. The Lerner index measures whether and how banks are able to set price above the marginal cost. In a perfect competition, price and marginal cost should be equal and Lerner index would be 0. In a less competitive market, there will be a price mark-up above the marginal cost. The index is computed as:

$$L_{it} = \frac{P_{it} - MC_{it}}{P_{it}} \tag{1.2}$$

where i denotes bank i, and t denotes period of time. P_{it} stands for price and is derived as the ratio of total income to total assets for bank i at time t, and MC_{it} is the marginal cost for bank i at time t. Figure 1.4 displays the evolution of average Lerner index in the banking sector in Rwanda. A lower Lerner index implies less market power to price above the marginal cost, hence more competition. The index shows that the competition in the banking sector in Rwanda has been increasing since 2012, although in the last two years (2018 and 2019) that trend has reversed and the market has become relatively less competitive as also pointed out by HHI.

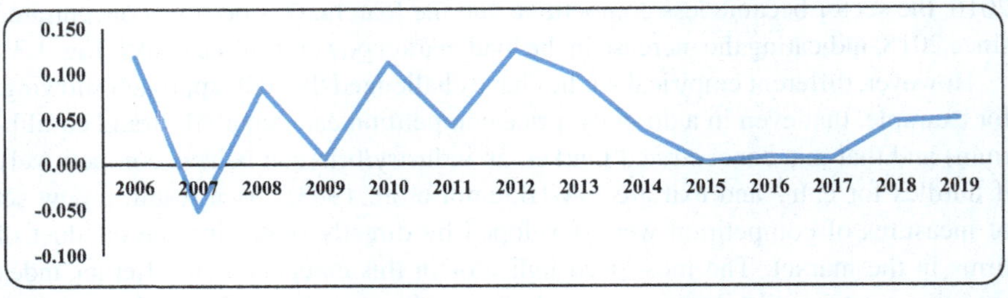

Fig. 1.4 Evolution of Lerner index. *Source* Our own computation using data from NBR, financial stability directorate

1.3.2 Financial Markets

In this subsection, we present the key development in financial markets in Rwanda, both money and capital markets, linked to the efficiency of the NBR's monetary policy formulation and implementation. The money market and capital market were established in 1997 and 2005, respectively, and significant progress has been achieved in the two markets, supported by good governance in Rwanda that created macroeconomic and financial sector stability and led to high credibility of the government as the government is the only issuer of debt instruments in the two markets. These factors are key prerequisites for the development of the government securities market. Indeed, to have an efficient government securities market, credible and stable government, sound macroeconomic policies (fiscal and monetary policies), effective legal, tax, and regulatory infrastructure, smooth and secure settlement arrangements, and a liberalized financial system with competing intermediaries are needed (IMF & World Bank 2011).

In addition, the coordination between monetary and fiscal authorities contributed to the development of money and capital markets in Rwanda. In practice, when the Ministry of Finance and Economic Planning (MINECOFIN) decides about the timing and amounts of government securities issuance, the needs of NBR's monetary policy are not taken into consideration. To avoid conflicts between government's debt/cash management and NBR's open market operations, the Treasury Management Committee (TMC) was created, co-chaired by MINECOFIN and NBR, and its members meet on quarterly basis. To ensure proper implementation of the decisions of the TMC, a small technical committee was established and members work together on regular basis. The debt management committee also formed by staff from the two institutions prepares the working documents, to support TMC decisions on liquidity management in the market.

Coordination between the two institutions is crucial for the better management of liquidity in the market. For example, the need of the government to issue securities may occur when the market is illiquid. Through the established coordination mechanism, NBR can choose whether or to what extent it will provide additional liquidity to the market and make it possible for the government to raise funds, or MINECOFIN may be able to adjust the timing and amount of funds to be raised from the domestic market to better adapt to the prevailing money market conditions.

1.3.2.1 Money Market

The money market in Rwanda was established in August 1997 by the regulation no. 02/97. Its establishment, two years after the adoption of indirect instruments of monetary policy and the recognition of NBR independence by law played a crucial role in the implementation of monetary policy. On the one side, the market provided an avenue for domestic funding of budget deficits by the government, putting an end on its monetary financing. On the other side, the development of the money market progressively enabled the use of market-based monetary policy instruments, strengthened the implementation of monetary policy, and improved the transmission mechanism of monetary impulses over time. Twenty-three years down the road, the market has reached a good level of development and has been one of the key foundations of monetary policy modernization in Rwanda and the development of the capital market as well as by increasing the liquidity of securities and making easier for commercial banks to cover short-term liquidity needs while investing in long-term securities.

In addition to the issuance of treasury bills, other instruments are used on the money market such as Repos and reverse repos. The NBR issues T-bills by auction on weekly basis with maturity dates of 28 days, 91 days, 182 days, and 364 days. The announcement to the public about issuance of T-bills is made each Monday via the NBR website and email group of investors. The announcement specifies characteristics of the bids such as amount of the bids and the corresponding maturities, mode of auction, as well as other criteria to be respected for bidding. To ensure transparency in its operations, tenders are publicly announced at least seven days before the tender date, informing the public about the characteristics of the issuance, namely, the tender date, the categories of bills (treasury bills or central bank bills), their maturities, the total amount of issuance, as well as the deadline for submission of bids. Under the current market practices, bids are classified as either competitive or non-competitive.

Competitive bids must be multiples of 50 million FRW and the bidders in this category must indicate the offered price (the interest rate), while non-competitive bids are those that are below 50 million FRW but with minimum FRW 100,000. For this category, the applied interest rate is the weighted average rate of the retained competitive bids. The market allocation is done following the Dutch method, where offers are retained starting from those with lower interest rates. Bidders are informed about market allocation on the same day and the transaction settlement is done the following day. The auction takes place on Thursday (T) while the settlements are done on Friday (T + 1). An example of public notice regarding the issue of treasury bills is given in Appendix 1.2.

To facilitate investments in T-bills, the NBR introduced a Central Security Depository (CSD) in 2011. The CSD holds, administrates, and enables securities transactions, both equities and debt instruments, to be processed in electronic form instead of high-risk physical certificates.

Given the accessibility and affordability of transactions brought by the CSD, there was increased opportunity for multiple small investors to participate in the market. Additionally, CSD incorporates the securities settlement function linked to real-time gross settlement (RTGS) for the compliance of the delivery versus payment (DvP) principle. Treasury bills commonly pay no explicit interest as they are sold at a discount, their yield being the difference between price and the par-value called redemption value. Thus, a discount bond, also called a zero-coupon bond, is bought at a price below its face value (at a discount), and the face value is repaid at the maturity date. Unlike a coupon bond, a discount bond does not make any interest payments; it just pays off the face value. For example, a treasury bill with a face value

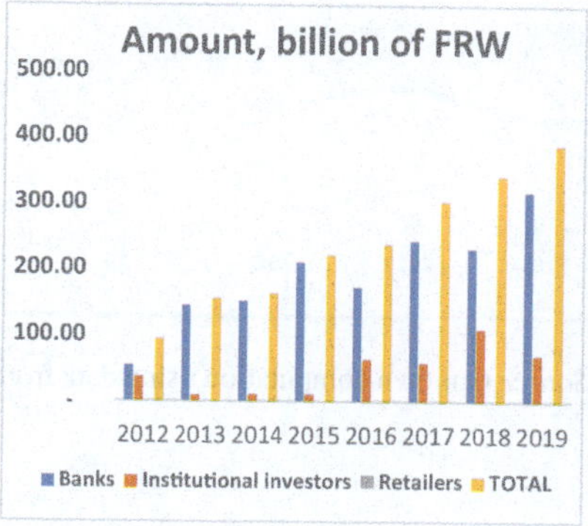

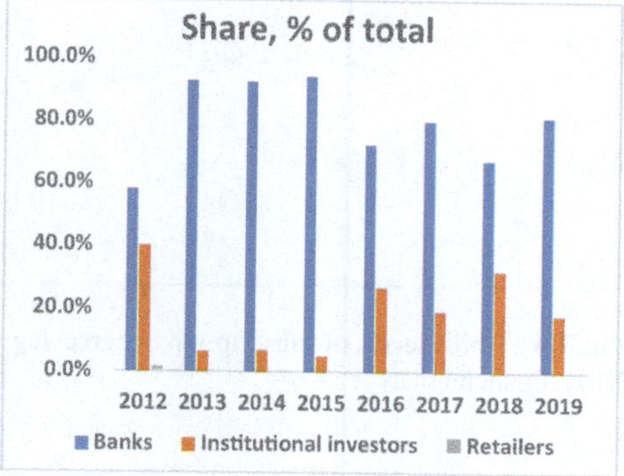

Fig. 1.5 T-bills outstanding by category of investors. *Source* NBR, Financial Markets Department

of FRW 100,000 might be bought for FRW 90,000 (interest rate of 10%) and in a year's time (maturity) the owner would be repaid the face value of FRW 100,000.

As in many developing and emerging markets, the T-bill market in Rwanda is dominated by commercial banks. Between 2013 and 2019, the share of commercial banks in outstanding Treasury bills investment is 83.2% against 16.7 and 0.1% for institutional investors and retailers, respectively. The dominance of commercial banks on the primary T-bills market is a limitation for the development of the secondary market as the banking sector in Rwanda has been characterized by structural short-term excess liquidity reducing the need for banks of selling securities before maturities (Fig. 1.5).

International experience shows that excessive reliance on the banking system as the main investors in government securities is associated with high costs for governments and investors (IMF & World Bank 2001). When commercial banks have market power, they tend to maintain a high margin between deposit rates and the risk-free return on government securities to compensate for maturity transformation, and it is crucial for banks which accept liquid deposits and invest in long-term assets. However, in countries where supply of treasury bills by the government is lower compared to its demand from the market, the capacity of banks to impose high costs on investors is reduced. In the case of Rwanda for example, the margin between deposit rates and the risk-free return on T-bill was very small, equivalent to 0.27% on average between 2005 and 2010, and the average level of subscription on T-bills was 144.9% between 2012 and 2019 (Fig. 1.6).

Another important component of the money market is the interbank market—the market for short-term lending between banks. Since 2010, the NBR devoted much efforts in building the capacity of its staff in monetary policy operation and liquidity forecasting aimed at developing the money market in Rwanda. The bank's interventions on the money market supported by well-improved liquidity forecasting played a crucial role in the development of the interbank market, which has been progressively providing incentives to banks to actively use the money market to manage

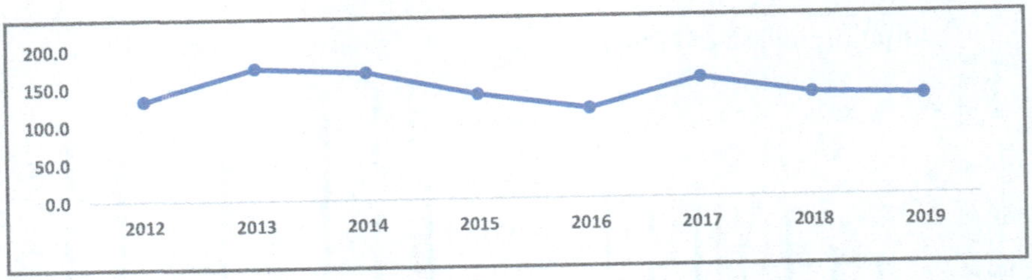

Fig. 1.6 T-bills levels of subscription in percentage. *Source* Our own computation using data from NBR, financial market

short-term liquidity risk. The value of transactions in interbank market significantly increased by 331.4% on average from FRW 188.6 billion in the period 2012–2015 to FRW 813.8 billion in the period 2016–2019.

1.3.2.2 Capital Market

The capital market in Rwanda was established in 2005 but officially launched in January 2008. The market currently has different participants, including investors, issuers, and intermediaries, which include the Rwanda Stock Exchange (RSE) officially launched in January 2011, licensed brokers, dealers, and sponsors. The Capital Market Advisory Council (CMAC) was created to put in place a legal and regulatory framework to regulate the market and operate it at the same time as an over-the-counter market (ROTC). An appropriate regulatory and legal framework is crucial for the development of capital market as it helps to provide market participants with the confidence to enter the market by providing them with clear legal guidance on how business is conducted and what will happen in cases of bankruptcy.

Market participants need to be also informed about accounting standards, disclosure, and other reporting requirements. In addition to the development of a regulatory framework, different strategies were adopted to develop the capital market such as financial education for the public; privatization of government companies; promotion of cross listings; mobilization of other private sector players; small and medium enterprises (SMEs) to utilize the stock market; and integration with other East African markets.

Financial education of both investors and issuers is important for the promotion of market participation. Issuers must understand the issuance process and the options available to them before deciding whether to issue financial products and investors must understand how financial markets function and the risk-return profiles attributed to different financial products. As a result of those different strategies to develop the capital market, good progress has been achieved in the nascent Rwanda stock exchange compared to other regional stock exchanges. Eight years down the road, nine companies (of which four are domestic) are listed and the RSE market capitalization stood at FRW 2893.55 billion ($3.6 billion), representing around 35.6%

Table 1.5 Comparison of regional stock exchange

Stock exchange	Start period	Listed companies	Operational period (years)	Market capitalization ($ bn.)	AV. listings per year
Nairobi Securities Exchange (NSE)	1954	65	66	20	0.98
Dar Es-Salaam Stock Exchange Plc (DSE)	1996	27	24	6.5	1.12
Uganda Securities Exchange (USE)	1997	18	23	4.9	0.78
Rwanda Stock Exchange (RSE)	2011	9	9	3.6	1
Stock Exchange of Mauritius (SEM)	1989	64	31	7.3	2.06
Nigerian Stock Exchange (NSE)	1960	145	60	34.8	2.41

Source RSE (2020)

of the Rwanda gross domestic product (GDP) and 41% when fixed income stock is added (Table 1.5).

Between 2008 and 2013, commercial banks were the main investors in government bonds with an average share of 83.2% of total outstanding investment. However, as a result of financial education supported by a stable macro-economic environment, high and sustainable economic growth, and confidence in the Government of Rwanda as the sole issuer on the primary market, the investors' base has been widening over time. The share of banks in T-bonds investment almost reduced by half to 40% between 2014 and 2019, while the share of institutional investors and retailers increased to 54.4 and 5.6%, respectively, in the period under review, from 14.4 to 2.4%, respectively, in the period 2008–2013. More details are presented in Appendices 1.3 and 1.4. The increased participation of institutional investors and retailers also contributed to the development of secondary market of government securities in recent years. The number of deals on the secondary market increased from 99 to 274 and the value of issued bills on that market increased from FRW 1634 million to FRW 19,874 million between 2016 and 2019 (Table 1.6).

To further develop the bond market, the Government of Rwanda in collaboration with the NBR has been publishing a quarterly bond issuance programme since February 2014. Currently, the government bonds of different maturities (2, 3, 5, 7, 10, 15 and 20 years) have been issued. In addition, to facilitate the trading of bonds in the secondary market, the NBR offered to rediscount the bonds as a last resort at 3% below the prevailing market yield or coupon rate upon written confirmation from the RSE that there is no available buyer. Furthermore, the Government of Rwanda

Table 1.6 Development in secondary market of T-bonds

	2016	2017	2018	2019
Number of deals	99	179	187	274
Value of the bonds in primary market (in FRW million)	1634	5121	9740	19,874
Value of the bonds in secondary market (in FRW million)	1680	5195	10,034	20,713

Source NBR, Financial Markets Department

has granted different fiscal incentives to attract more companies to participate in the capital market. Venture capital companies registered with the CMA in Rwanda benefit from a corporate income tax of 0% for a period of 5 years and capital gains in the secondary market transaction on listed securities is exempted from capital gains tax. The withholding tax on dividends and interest income on securities listed in capital markets and interest arising from investments in listed bonds with a maturity of 3 years and above are reduced to 5% lower than withholding tax of 15% on other payments (Fig. 1.7).

Though good progress has been achieved, there is still big room for improvement to further develop the capital market in Rwanda for it to play its role of pooling domestic savings and mobilizing foreign capital as well as availing these resources to the private sector to finance productive long-term investments needed for economic development. Experience shows that investors willing to participate in capital market often discover that offered securities are insufficient in volume to meet their investment needs. There is a clear need of attracting more issuers in the market to increase the benefit of capital market in financing the economy. For example, between 2014 and 2019, the level of oversubscription in T-bond investment was 180.3% on average. This situation is due to limited number of issuers in the market as currently, the Government of Rwanda is the only existing issuer (Fig. 1.8).

The current plan to develop a corporate bond market needs to be accelerated to support private sector financing by channelling the existing capital to productive investments and diversify the sources of credit and associated risk. In addition, a well-functioning corporate bonds market will contribute to the promotion of greater

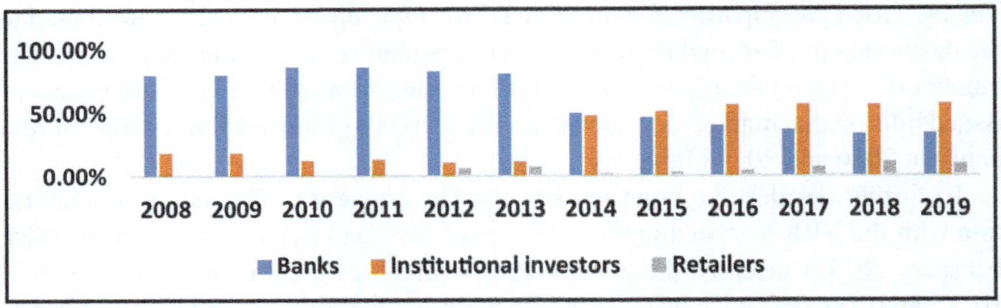

Fig. 1.7 Outstanding T-bonds investment by category of investors (share, %). *Source* Our own computation using data from NBR, Financial Markets Department

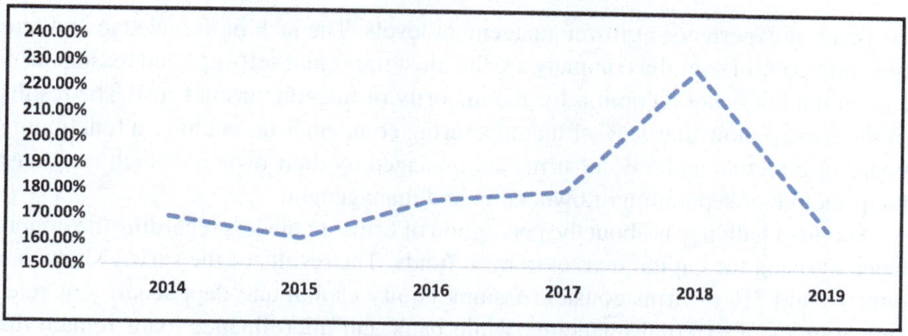

Fig. 1.8 T-bonds levels of subscription in percentage. *Source* Our own computation using data from NBR, Financial Markets Department

market discipline and transparency through information disclosure, greater corporate governance, and adherence to a uniform set of market standards.

In 2013, the RSE published special rules pertaining to the listing of small and medium enterprises (SMEs) and currently, a number of companies are under advisory process through the capital market investment clinic programme aimed at improving their financial records and strengthening their corporate governance as part of basic requirements defined by the RSA for listing on the bourse. Those requirements include: (i) quality governance, whereby a prospective firm should have an active board with a minimum of three members; (ii) the firm should have been in operation for the last two years, with books of accounts regularly reviewed by an external auditor; (iii) as legal status, firms must be registered as company limited by shares.

The results of a survey conducted by the NBR in 2019 on how the manufacturing sector in Rwanda sees the capital market as source of raising funds to finance their businesses show that manufacturing firms in Rwanda comply with a good number of RSA requirements. About legal status, 68% of firms were registered as companies, while 32% were enterprises (i.e. under sole proprietorship statute). In addition, companies have diverse ownership structure, with single investors owning around 33% of manufacturing firms; family-owned firms accounted for 15.5% of the total manufacturing sector; and about 24 and 21% of manufacturing firms were owned by groups of local and foreign investors, respectively. Concerning financial transparency, the RSA requirement is that prospective firms must have been in operation for the last two years, with books of accounts regularly reviewed by an external auditor as pointed out. The results of survey show that nearly 93% of firms were two years or older; nearly 81% of manufacturing firms were externally audited; and 79% of firms used the standard accounting software showing that financial opacity was not a hindrance to the financial disclosure required for participation of manufacturing firms on the bourse.

However, some challenges exist and need to be addressed to have more participation in the capital market. One of the challenges is about the governance. While only 29% of managers do not have the required qualifications, 71% of them hold undergraduate or postgraduate degrees and 73% of general managers have more than

10 years of experience at firm management levels. The lack of knowledge and fear of losing control over the company are the most important self-reported reasons why capital market is not an option for the majority of manufacturing firms. The results of the survey show that 16% of manufacturing companies do not have a functioning board of directors and 59% of firms are managed by their owners, which is against the principle of separation of ownership and management.

Another challenge is about the perception of firms' managers regarding the importance of using the capital market to raise funds. The results of the survey show that only 16 and 5% of firms consider issuing equity capital and debt security as relevant sources of external financing, while bank and microfinance loans remain the dominant source of external financing for manufacturers. The main reasons for that perception are: the limited knowledge of capital markets (49% of manufacturers); the fear of losing control over their firms (30%); and the perception that their businesses are too small to enlist on the bourse (17%). About 40 and 50% of managers, respectively, are uncertain as to whether issuing a debt security or equity capital would be easy for them to decide and would fit well to their corporate culture.

1.3.3 Financial Market Infrastructure Development

1.3.3.1 Payment Systems

The National Payment System in Rwanda was developed to respond to rapid economy-wide changes and development so as to provide the necessary infrastructure for smooth capital movement in both the public and private sector, allow broader access to financial services, and improve the mobilization of more long-term savings and financial investments. Before the adoption of indirect monetary policy instruments in 1997, Rwanda had a clearinghouse created in 1976 for clearing checks, debit notes, letters of credit, promissory notes, and bills of exchange and credit advices. Because the settlement was done manually and the clearinghouse is located in Kigali, the processing could take at least 3 days considering the time to receive payment of instruments from provinces.

As a result of financial liberalization, the banking sector has been progressively opened to foreign investors and transfer of funds were needed to support import/export activities. The use of SWIFT international network, introduction of Western Union money transfer services in 1996, and electronic payments using smart card in 1999 with the provision of debit card-based payments service through automated teller machines (ATMs) to its customers up to 2000, the NBR continued providing clearing service for interbank payment transactions.

In its efforts of having payment systems which meet international standards, the NBR in collaboration with commercial banks started a project in 2001 aimed at the establishment of the electronic money transfer, electronic clearing system, and real-time gross settlement (RTGS) system. In 2005, a bank card processing station was officially inaugurated and started its activities with the launching of the domestic debit card, interbank card transactions, and ATMs and POS. Between 2005 and 2008, the semi-automated clearing system was settling at T + 1 and cleared three instruments, namely, the cheques, credit transfers, as well as the debit cards operations. During that period, all interbank payment systems, clearing and settlement, were still semi-manually processed in paper form, and the settlement of clearinghouse balances was posted manually in the NBR accounting system. Cards transactions were cleared at SIMTEL and a settlement report was sent to the NBR system electronically.

In 2010, the Payment Systems law was passed by the parliament and a regulation governing the payment service providers was approved by the NBR's Board of Directors. To ensure that time-critical payments are settled in real time, the NBR started working on the implementation of a real-time settlement system, the Rwanda integrated payments processing system (RIPPS), encompassing the automated clearing house (ACH), the real-time gross settlement (RTGS), and the central securities depository (CSD), all three running on the same platform. To further enhance the developments in payment systems, NBR together with the Rwanda bankers' association, embarked on the cheque truncation project in 2010, the automated transfer system (ATS) and the central securities depository (CSD) were put in place in 2011, as components of RIPPS. On the debt side, the CSD handles repos, treasury bills, and treasury bonds, while on the equity side, it handles locally listed companies shares. The CSD-Rwanda is closely integrated with the RTGS and operated a settlement cycle of T + 2.

The ATS which started to be operational since February 2011 comprises the real-time gross settlement (RTGS) system function for large value and time-critical payments and the automated clearing house (ACH), which provides clearing and netting facilities for a range of low-value electronic instruments, including direct debits, direct credits, and cheques. This development contributed to the reduction in the payment lag. As of today, the process of a payment order takes a maximum of one day and a minimum of two hours for banks with a smoothly functioning interface compared to a minimum of three days for the beneficiary to obtain funds before the adoption of the RTGS. To facilitate cross-border payments in the East African Community (EAC) and Common Market for Eastern and Southern Africa (COMESA) regions, the Rwanda integrated payments processing system (RIPPS) was upgraded in 2012 to enable linkage to regional cross-border payment systems; the East Africa payment systems (EAPS), and the COMESA regional payments and settlement system (REPSS). Rwanda started operations with REPSS on 3 October 2012 and was officially launched at 18th COMESA central bank governor's meeting which took place on 10–11 December 2012 in Kigali, Rwanda. Retail payment system has also improved with two new systems, T24 core banking and enterprise resource planning (ERP) introduced in 2014. In 2015, mobile network operators (MNOs) in partnership with banks introduced innovative products such as mobile saving to promote financial inclusion and increase cashless payments.

It is in that line that new types of POS devices were introduced, including mobile POS and near-field communication (NFC). The enhancement of RIPPS with master card integration facilitated settlement of transactions by eliminating exchange cost and fastening payments for locally issued cards and the implementation of cheques truncation system (CTS) that enables electronic exchange of all files related to cheques. This has shortened significantly the clearing cycles and settlement of cheques by reducing time to the same day settlement (T + 0).

1.3.3.2 Credit Reporting System

As pointed out in the introduction of this chapter, a credit reporting system is very important in easing business as it facilitates access to finance, attenuates adverse selection, and alleviates information asymmetry between lenders and borrowers. In line with its objective of easing business, the Government of Rwanda established the credit reporting system framework in 2010, with the law governing it enacted in May 2010. Under that law, the first private credit bureau (CRBAfrica Rwanda Ltd) was licensed by the National Bank of Rwanda in July 2010, and taken over by TransUnion Rwanda in January 2016. As per the law, all licensed banks, microfinance institutions and SACCOs institutions granting student loans and insurance companies regularly share the required information with TransUnion. In order to produce a credit report and credit score for lenders and claim enabler report for insurance companies to help them assessing the risk, lending institutions submit information on the identification of borrowers and their loan payment history while insurance companies share policies and claims information. In addition to its support to financial institutions in their decision-making process, the credit reference bureau contributed to ease of doing business in Rwanda. Before having a loan clearance certificate from each lending institution was a requirement for loan applications. This is no longer a requirement because every lender gets online credit information about a borrower through the CRB system. Similarly, a borrower can access his/her credit information by requesting information to TransUnion office or using online service platform. This process of getting a loan clearance certificate from each lending institution was cited as one of the hindrances in the process of getting loans from banks as it was time-consuming and costly.

To increase the coverage of the CRB, a new law governing the credit reporting system was enacted in September 2018 in replacement of the one of 2016 to include telecommunication companies and utilities companies on the list of companies mandated to share credit information. As a way forward, the NBR is engaging lending institutions to consider credit scores when setting lending interest rates to ensure that borrowers with good credit score can get loans at lower interest rates and can be asked less-stringent collaterals. As of March 2020, TransUnion CRB had 506 subscribers, with a coverage ratio of 26.9, corresponding to 1,995,848 individuals and legal entities. The level of coverage is still low because a big part of adult population does not work with formal financial institutions. TransUnion CRB in collaboration with the NBR is trying to collect credit information from all sources, focusing on voluntary data providers (e.g. traders), aimed at increasing the CRB coverage ratio.

Subscribers to the CRB are institutions that have signed an agreement with TransUnion CRB to share and use their credit information according to the laws and regulations governing the credit reporting system. These institutions are data providers and data users and they are mainly lenders. In addition, there exist other institutions that only use CRB data and do not require to provide information to the system. As a result of the awareness about the use of credit reference bureau, not only by the lenders but also by the borrowers, the usage of the system has been generally increasing over time. Every month, TransUnion CRB publishes a report on data usage by each subscriber and this report allows NBR inspectors to know whether lending institutions are considering customer credit report while assessing requests for loans (Table 1.7).

The development of financial system is supported by legal rights and enforcement mechanisms of contracts, and research in that area shows that distinguishing countries by the efficiency of national legal systems in supporting financial transactions is more useful than distinguishing countries by whether they have bank-based

Table 1.7 Key CRB statistical information (The number of subscribers has slightly reduced since March 2019 as some MFIs have been merged or acquired)

Period	Number of subscribers to CRB	Number of inquiries made to CRB system/CRB usage	Number of individuals and companies included in CRB system	CRB coverage ratio (of adult population) in %
March 15	493	37,711	603,803	9.5
June 15	492	27,655	621,549	9.7
September 15	493	32,174	685,159	10.6
December 15	493	29,954	721,960	11.1
March 16	494	33,955	760,479	11.6
June 16	498	44,517	885,351	13.4
September 16	498	35,427	957,431	14.4
December 16	493	25,638	1,019,767	15.2
March 17	492	34,666	1,070,131	15.9
June 17	496	41,674	1,146,076	16.9
September 17	498	40,844	1,193,368	17.4
December 17	512	45,971	1,414,469	20.5
March 18	512	49,035	1,466,544	21.1
June 18	514	66,988	1,534,712	21.9
September 18	518	85,165	1,579,555	22.3
December 18	518	111,452	1,655,234	23.2
March 19	514	119,467	1,713,356	23.9
June 19	510	135,939	1,726,420	24.4
September 19	510	134,111	1,798,048	24.5
December 19	506	164,940	1,833,401	24.9
March 20	506	133,358	1,995,848	26.9

Source TransUnion CRB Rwanda

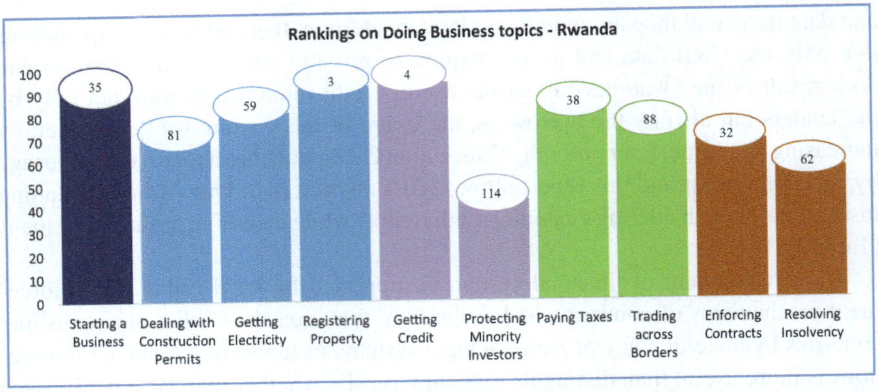

Fig. 1.9 Rwanda ranking in 2020 (Global). *Source* World Bank Doing Business Report (2020)

or market-based financial systems (Haan and Schoenmaker 2012). About regulatory environment, the World Bank Doing Business report which is published every year provides measures of business regulations and their enforcement across 190 economies. It provides quantitative indicators on regulation for starting a business, dealing with construction permits, getting electricity, registering property, getting credit, protecting minority investors, paying taxes, trading across borders, enforcing contracts, and resolving insolvency.

According to the World Bank (2020) report, Rwanda remains the second easiest place to do business in Africa and 38th globally. Rwanda ranked second in Africa after Mauritius and maintained first position in the East African Community (Fig. 1.9).

The indicator about the ease to get credit measures the strength of legal rights, the depth of credit information, the credit bureau coverage, and the credit registry coverage. For all four indicators, Rwanda is above the sub-Saharan Africa (SSA) level and in particular, the strength of legal rights Rwanda is highly ranked than OECD countries (only five countries are ahead globally). Note that the ranking of economies depends on the score which is the sum of the scores for the strength of legal rights index and the depth of credit information index (World Bank 2020).

The World Bank (2020) defines these indicators as follows:

- The indictor of strength of legal rights measures the extent to which rights of borrowers and lenders are protected by collateral laws and also protection of secured creditors' rights through bankruptcy law, both with the aim of facilitating lending.
- The depth of credit information index measures rules and practices affecting the coverage, scope, and accessibility of credit information available through a credit bureau or credit registry.
- Credit bureau coverage (% of adults) measures the number of individuals and firms listed in the largest credit bureau as a percentage of adult population, while credit registry coverage (% of adults) measures the number of individuals and firms listed in credit registry as a percentage of adult population (Table 1.8).

Table 1.8 Getting credit indicators

Indicator	Rwanda	Sub-Saharan Africa	OECD high income	Best regulatory performance
Strength of legal rights index (0–12)	11	5.1	6.1	12 (5 Economies)
Depth of credit information index (0–8)	8	3.9	6.8	8 (53 Economies)
Credit registry coverage (% of adults)	10.4	8.3	24.4	100.0 (2 Economies)
Credit bureau coverage (% of adults)	15.8	11.0	66.7	100.0 (14 Economies)

Source World Bank Doing Business Report (2020)

References

Allen F, Gale D (2000) Comparing financial systems. MIT Press, Cambridge, MA

Allen F, Santomero A (1997) The theory of financial intermediation. J Bank Financ Elsevier 21(11–12):1461–1485

Baumol WJ, Panzar J and Willig RD (1983) Contestable markets: an uprising in the theory of industry structure: reply. Am Econ Rev, 93(3):491–496

BIS (2003) The role of central bank money in payment systems. Bank of International Settlements, Basel

Bondt GD (2002) Retail bank interest rate pass-through: new evidence at the euro area level. European Central Bank (ECB), Frankfurt

Cecchetti SG (1999) Legal structure, financial structure, and the monetary policy transmission mechanism. Federal Reserve Bank New York Econo Policy Rev 5(2):9–28

Chami R, Sharma S, Fullenkamp C (2009) A framework for financial market development. IMF Working Paper No. WP/09/156, Washington

Demirguc-Kunt A, Klapper L, Singer D (2017) Financial Inclusion and inclusive growth: a review of recent empirical evidence. Policy Research Working Paper; No. 8040. World Bank, Washington, DC

Ergungor EO (2004) Market- vs. bank-based financial systems: do rights and regulations really matter? J Bank Financ Elsevier 28(12): 2869–2887

FINSCOP (2016) Financial inclusion in Rwanda. Access to Finance, Kigali

FINSCOP (2020) Financial Inclusion in Rwanda. Access to Finance, Kigali

Goswami M, Sharma S (2011) The development of local debt markets in Asia. IMF Working Paper No. WP/11/132, Washington

Haan JD, Schoenmaker D (2012) Financial markets and institutions: a European perspective, 2nd edn. Cambridge University Press, London

Haan JD, Oosterloo S, Schoenmaker D (2015) Financial markets and institutions: a European perspective. Cambridge University Press.

Hannan T, Berger A (1991) The rigidity of prices: evidence from the banking industry. Am Econ Rev 81(4):938–945

IMF & WorldBank (2001) Developing government bond markets: a handbook. International Monetary Fund/World Bank, Washington

IMF & WorldBank (2011) Developing government bond markets: a handbook. International Monetary Fund/World Bank, Washington
King RG, Levine R (1993) Finance and growth: schumpeter might be right. Quart J Econ 108(3):717–737
Klemm A, Herman A (2017) Financial deepening in Mexico. IMF Working Papers WP/17/19, Washington, DC
Koetter M, Kolari JW, Spierdijk L (2012) Enjoying the quiet life under deregulation? Evidence from adjusted Lerner indices for U.S. banks. Rev Econ Stat 94:462–480
Leon F (2014) Measuring competition in banking: a critical review of methods. CERDI Working papers No 201412
Levine R (1997) Financial development and economic growth: views and agenda. J Econom Literat 35(2):688–726
Levine R (2005) Finance and growth: theory and evidence. In: Aghion P, Durlauf S (eds) Handbook of economic growth. Elsevier, pp 865–934
Madura J (2010) Financial markets and institutions, 11th edn. Florida Atlantic University
Mishkin FS (2004) The economics of money, banking, and financial markets, 7th edn. Pearson, Addison Wesley, Boston
Mishkin FS (2007) Comment on "Monetary rules in emerging economies with financial market imperfections". NBER Chapters. In: International dimensions of monetary policy. National Bureau of Economic Research, Inc., pp 311–317
Mishra P, Montiel PJ (2010) How effective is monetary transmission in low-income countries? A survey of the empirical evidence. IMF Working Paper No. 12/143, Washington, DC
Mishra P, Montiel PJ (2012) How effective is monetary transmission in low-income countries? A survey of the empirical evidence. IMF Working Paper No. 12/143, Washington
Mishra P, Montiel PJ, Spilimbergo A (2012) Monetary transmission in low-income countries: effectiveness and policy implications. IMF Econ Rev 60(2):270–302
Montiel PJ, Spilimbergo A, Mishra P (2010) Monetary transmission in low income countries. IMF Working Paper No. 10/223, Washington
Rajah R (1998) The Malaysian financial crisis: capital expansion, cronyism and contraction. J Asian Pacif Econ 3(3):358–378
Rajan R, Zingales L (1998) Financial dependence and growth. Am Econ Rev 88(3):559–586
RSE (2020) Rwanda stock exchange. https://rse.rw/ Accessed on October 12, 2020
Weth M (2002) The pass-through from market interest rates to bank lending rates in Germany. Deutsche Bundesbank Discussion Paper 11/02, Frankfurt
World Bank (2020) Doing business report. World Bank, Washington

Chapter 2
Evolution of Monetary Policy Implementation in Rwanda

2.1 Introduction

Monetary policy in Rwanda has undergone profound changes since the establishment of the National Bank of Rwanda (NBR) in 1964. For a period of 26 years, the NBR conducted direct monetary control in the absence of a money market. In 1990, the bank shifted to the use of indirect monetary policy instruments following the advent of free-market economic policies, also known as the "Washington Consensus", such as the introduction of the Structural Adjustment Programs (SAPs), supported by the Bretton Woods institutions (BWIs).

With most African countries gaining independence in the early 1960s, there was increasing optimism that rapid economic growth and development could be attained across the continent, a view that was shared with the donor community. Since the private sector was non-existent in Africa at that time, economic growth and development in most African states had to be primarily government-driven. With the support of donors, governments in Africa invested in large state-run basic import-substitution industries, which were sheltered from competition via the enactment of protectionist regulations to control prices, restrict trade, and allocate credit and foreign exchange (Owusu 2003). They were further supported by substantial public investments in infrastructure such as roads, ports, telecommunications, and power generation; as well as in health and education. Initially, good economic performance was recorded in many African countries. For example, annual economic growth in sub-Saharan Africa averaged 3.4% between 1961 and 1980.

This good economic performance was however short-lived as poor growth of the productive sectors, a declining level and efficiency of investment, increasing debt, high population growth, and weak institutional capacity constrained the development momentum in the early 1970s. By the mid-1970s, economic performance was lagging behind that of other parts of the developing world, leading to high budget and balance of payments deficits and significant public debt (Calamitsis 1999; Heidhues and Obare 2011). For the donor community, the failure of African economies to realize sustainable development was attributable to their governments and the policies

T. K. Rusuhuzwa, *Monetary Policy in Rwanda*, Frontiers in African Business Research, https://doi.org/10.1007/978-981-33-6746-3_2

that they were pursuing, including weak resource management, inadequate exchange rate policies, excessive state intervention, and especially, the protection of inefficient producers, the unnecessary subsidization of urban consumers, and corruption. One of the macroeconomic policies used during that period in Africa was direct monetary policy used by central banks to support governments' economic development agendas.

Generally, a central bank implements monetary policy by directly using its regulatory powers through direct instruments, or indirectly using its influence on money market conditions. Direct instruments operate by setting or limiting either prices (interest rates) or quantities (amount of credit) through regulations. In that context, authorities directly influence balance sheets of commercial banks and financial market conditions that do not play any role in the determination of financial prices and allocation of credits as it would have been if indirect monetary policy instruments were used instead. The most common instruments in a directly controlled monetary policy regime are interest rate controls, credit ceilings, and lending at the discretion of the authorities, rather than for commercial reasons.

By using interest rate controls, a central bank can announce the minimum and maximum rates of interest and other charges that domestic banks may impose for specific types of loans, advances, or other credits and payments on deposits collected by commercial banks from the public. When a central bank uses credit controls as an instrument of monetary policy, it controls the volume, terms and conditions under which banks guarantee loans to the private sector, such as instalments of loans. In this regime, resources of the banking sector are also used to finance governments' deficits, contributing to crowding out of the private sector and encouraging the development of the informal financial system as was the case in different African countries in the years 1970–1980s.

As a response to the rising economic hardships, Structural Adjustment Programs (SAPs) by the Bretton Woods institutions (i.e. the World Bank and the IMF) were introduced across Africa in the 1980s and continued to operate throughout the 1990s. The SAPs involved a combination of free-market policies such as privatization, fiscal austerity, free trade, and deregulation. These policies were expected to lead to more open and efficient economies and ultimately contribute to the improvement of living standards and to the reduction of relative poverty.

As in other African countries, there was great need for rapid and sustained economic growth in Rwanda after the country gained its independence. However, as a result of lack of good governance and poor economic policies, weak economic development was recorded since the second half of 1980s with average economic growth progressively dropping from 4.4% in 1975–1980 to 2.5 and 2.4% in 1980–1985 and 1985–1990, respectively Ansoms (2005). Rwanda adopted the SAPs in November 1990, underlying the adoption of market-based principles in the management of the economy to determine different prices on various markets. Nevertheless, the move undertaken at that time was suspended, due to the war that started in 1990 and the genocide against the Tutsi in 1994.

In a context of lack of good governance and economic policy failure, the use of direct monetary policy instruments such as interest rate controls, credit ceilings, and direct lending at the directive of political authorities, based on other consideration rather than economic criteria, had exacerbated the economic problems. Therefore, the introduction of SAPs paved the way for shifting away from direct monetary control to an indirect approach, based on the use of market-based instruments to implement monetary policy. This chapter describes monetary policy instruments used in both directly controlled monetary policy and indirect monetary policy, and presents the key outcomes of the NBR monetary policy during the two separate policy episodes.

2.2 Era of Direct Control (1964–1990)

When Rwanda gained its monetary sovereignty in May 1964, the NBR adopted direct monetary control to support the government's objective of promoting rapid economic growth after the country gained its independence. This monetary regime was used in the context of a generally controlled economy by the government. Political authorities kept control on prices of goods and services as well as on labour market wages. At its inception, the NBR's mandate was to maintain monetary stability and implement credit and exchange rate policies to support the economic development of the country. The direct monetary policy regime in Rwanda was characterized by a system of credit ceilings and sector credit allocation, a subsidized and regulated interest rate regime and exchange rate controls, as well as import licensing.

2.2.1 Monetary Policy Instruments

During the period of direct monetary control, the NBR used credit and interest rates control, the refinancing facility, and reserve requirement to manage the amount of money in the economy. In the absence of financial markets, coupled with a rudimentary banking sector and limited skilled staff, this approach was relatively easy to implement and contributed to achieve government objectives of channelling resources to certain priority sectors of the economy as defined by the government. Below is a description of each of the monetary policy instruments mentioned above as well as the fixed exchange rate regime.

Credit Control

To implement its credit policy, an annual growth objective of the credit to the private sector to be provided by commercial banks was set by NBR at the beginning of each year and the set amount was distributed among commercial banks based on their respective deposits mobilized from the public and their net worth. In addition, the NBR had to determine the maturity and allocation of credit to specific sectors based on economic activities considered as priority by the government. To closely monitor the evolution of monetary growth, NBR had to authorize beforehand any credit granted by a bank to its customers exceeding a certain amount or defined a certain threshold of the total amount of credit granted to one customer by different banks.

This procedure was compatible with the set objectives of credit growth and control of the development in monetary aggregates on one hand. On the other hand, it was a way for NBR to help commercial banks reduce credit risk in a period when banks did not have capacity to assess risks associated to requested loans. Moreover, the country's judicial system was not well equipped to help banks pursue defaulting borrowers, including difficulties for commercial banks in bringing action against defaulting borrowers, complicated procedures for recovering loans, and serious shortage of judges in the country.

To incentivize banks to finance high-risk economic activities, particularly agricultural projects, a special guarantee fund was established and all banks were required to contribute 10% of their pre-tax profits to this guarantee fund. In addition, commercial banks had to ensure that all loan applications submitted for approval were backed by the required collaterals: for example, ensuring that land and houses used as collateral by individuals had formal titles. Also, commercial vehicles, equipment, and trade inventories were eligible to be used as collateral and the value of collateral had to cover 200–300% of the loan value.

Furthermore, the NBR required commercial banks to constitute provisions for doubtful loans or those under litigation with an equivalent of 100% of the value of such outstanding loans plus accrued interest. Additionally, from October 1987, commercial banks were strictly required to respect the solvency ratio of 10% when deposits exceed FRW 3 billion and 7% when deposits were less than FRW 3 billion to enhance their stability. The solvency risk is when a bank cannot meet maturing obligations, because the value of its assets is less than the amount of its liabilities. In order to avoid such a risk, banks need to keep an adequate buffer of capital, so that in case of losses, they can reduce capital accordingly and remain solvent.

Due to liquidity scarcity in the banking system, as banks could only mobilize limited and short-term deposits from the public, loans to the private sector by commercial banks and banques populaires were limited to short-term loans except for house loans for their employees. Only the Development Bank of Rwanda (BRD) had the capacity of providing long-term loans (over five years) for productive activities and short-term loans to its staff. At least three quarters of collected deposits from the public had to be devoted to financing short-term operations, generating benefit or maintaining the equilibrium of the balance of payments. Due to the limited level of deposits in the banking sector, the NBR used the discount window to facilitate the financing of commercial banks.

Between 1968 and 1979, on average, deposits represented 56.9% of the broad money M3 that amounted FRW 5.8 billion and currency in circulation representing 43.1%. Total deposits mobilized by commercial banks amounted only FRW 3.3 billion on average in the period under review of which 86.8% were demand deposits and only 13.2% were term deposits. Owing to limited and short-term deposits from the public, loans to the private sector by commercial banks was only FRW 7.9 billion in the period under review (Fig. 2.1).

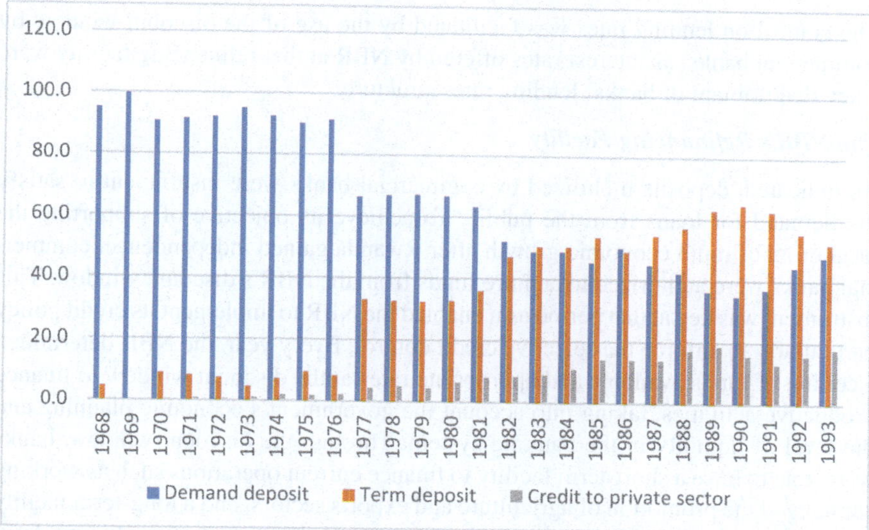

Fig. 2.1 Demand deposits and term deposits as percentage of total deposits and credit to private sector in FRW billion. *Source* Our own compilation using data from NBR, statistics department

Regulation of Interest Rates

The general conditions applied by banks with regard to interest rates and commission fees were also defined by the NBR. The government regulated interest rates considering the observed and projected economic developments and financial conditions in the country. Term deposit interest rates were supposed to attract savings from households and enterprises, but not so high to increase the lending rates at levels that would potentially constrain investors. About lending rates, they were divided into two categories. First, preferential rates for activities are considered to be of economic or social importance, such as export crop financing, agricultural production, and import of inputs for industry, and second, ordinary rates for non-priority activities, such as construction and personal loans.

The rationale for controlling interest rates was that credit had to be cheap so as to promote investment and support targeted borrowers. One of the challenges created by the control of interest rates was that the interest structure typically did not account for loan maturity or risk, and in fact created perverse lending incentives for banks, with riskier sectors such as agriculture being given a preferential rate. Furthermore, lending rates were sometimes too low to compensate for both risks and overhead costs associated with loans to privileged borrowers.

Between 1967 and 1987, term deposit rates increased from 1.0 to 3.0%, 2.0 to 3.3%, 2.5 to 4.0% and 3.5 to 4.5%, for 1, 3, 6, and 12 months maturity, respectively. Lending interest rates for sectors considered as priority by the government were kept constant at 9.0%, while for other sectors, it increased from 9.0% in 1967 to a maximum of 17.0% in 1979, before fixing the maximum rate at 12.0% in 1987.

The control on lending rates was facilitated by the use of the discount window by commercial banks, as interest rates offered by NBR at that refinancing facility were a key determinant of banks' lending rates structure.

The NBR's Refinancing Facility

As indicated, deposits mobilized by commercial banks were insufficient to satisfy the demand for loans from the public. To achieve its objective of supporting the promotion of rapid economic growth after Rwanda gained independence, commercial banks were authorized to acquire funds from the NBR's discount window. This instrument was key at that period as it enabled the NBR to implement its credit policy particularly to enforce the selective credit control. Every year, the NBR determined a ceiling of funds available and appropriate rates at the discount window to finance productive activities, taking into account the government's economic planning and the level of liquidity in the banking system. Through the discount window, banks were able to have a short-term facility to finance current operations such as working capital and the promotion of agriculture and exports sectors, and a long-term facility to finance investment. These special measures contributed to finance the modernization of the primary sector, particularly tea and coffee farming,[1] the production of minerals, the promotion of decentralization of economic activities, the promotion of international transport services, the building of the storage capacity of oil products, and the construction of local authority houses, to name a few.

Foreign Exchange Regulations

Between 1964 and March 1995, the exchange rate of the Rwandan Franc (FRW) was managed through a fixed regime, with the value of the FRW fixed by the President of the Republic after consultation with cabinet members and based on the NBR's recommendation, as indicated in the legislative decree number 06/81 of 6 February 1981 establishing the fixed exchange rate regime.[2] The foreign exchange transactions and capital account were fully centralized and controlled by the NBR. During that period, foreign reserves of the banking system were held by the NBR, which was also the sole institution authorized to carry out exchange transactions. Initially, the exchange rate was pegged to the Belgian Franc (BF), then to the American dollar (USD) and finally to the Special Drawing Rights (SDR).

From 1964 to March 1966, the FRW was fixed to the BF whereby one BF was exchanged against one FRW, before being pegged to the USD between April 1966 and 1973. In April 1966, the FRW was fixed to the USD at a rate of one USD equivalent to 100 FRW. The same rate was maintained up to 29 December 1971, before revising it to 92.11 FRW because of USD depreciation. In 1973, the FRW was pegged again to the BF at rate of 100 BF for 230 FRW, before being re-attached to the USD at a rate of one USD against 92.84 FRW in 1974. Between 6 September 1983 and March 1995, the FRW was fixed to the SDR at a rate of one SDR equivalent

---

[1]Between 1980 and 1990, the value of coffee and tea exports represented 83% of total export earnings. The share was 91% on average between 1986 and 1988.

[2]NBR, 25th anniversary, 1989.

to 102.71 FRW. Since 1995, foreign exchange transactions and the capital account were progressively liberalized, with the exchange rate framework shifting from a fixed regime to a more market-driven exchange rate regime.

Reserves Requirement

To ensure the stability of the banking sector in the country, all deposit-taking institutions were obliged to constitute 10% of their profits as legal reserves and 5% of profits when the reserve fund reached FRW 100 million. It is since August 1990 that the NBR adopted the reserve requirement system aimed at protecting depositors against liquidity and solvency risks of banks but also used as monetary policy instrument to regulate money supply. Initially, the reserve requirement ratio was fixed at 5% for all deposits in the banking sector before being revised down to 1% in December 1991. To take into consideration the prevailing banking liquidity conditions and to continue supporting commercial banks to finance the economic development, different amendments were introduced. In March 1992, the reserve requirement ratio increased to 5% of banks' current deposit, and remained at 1% for other deposits, before being increased to 7% of current deposit and 5% of other deposits in April 1994.

2.2.2 *Outcomes of NBR Monetary Policy Between 1964 and 1994*

As indicated above, most African countries and the donor community were optimistic for rapid growth and development after these countries became independent in the early 1960s. However, poor economic performance was recorded in those countries in the early 1970s due to different factors including bad governance and poor economic policies. After averaging at 4.4% in the period 1975–1980, Rwanda's economic growth slowed to an average of 2.5% in 1980–1985 and 2.4% in 1985–1990. In the context of weak governance and unsound economic policies, the use of direct monetary policy instruments such as interest rate controls, credit ceilings, and direct lending at the directive of political authorities exacerbated the economic problems across the African continent.

Direct monetary policy instruments created inefficiency in financial resource allocation by channelling loans at preferential rates to non-productive companies. In addition, they led to disintermediation and constrained the development of the financial sector by limiting competition in the banking sector and the entry of new banks in the country. Furthermore, prior authorization provided to banks for granting credit often led to lack of appropriate assessment of risks faced by banks (NBR at 50 anniversary and Journal official de la République Rwandaise du 1/10/1987). As a result, between 1980 and 1993, broad money and credit to the private sector as a percentage of GDP, two indicators of financial sector development, fluctuated between 12.2 and 17.1% and between 5.1 and 9.1%, respectively. Annual gross loans to the private sector were very low in the period 1980–1993, amounting to FRW 13 billion on average compared to FRW 622.3 billion in the period 2000–2019 and total deposits in the banking sector were 40 times lower than their 2000–2019 level.

2.3 Period of Market-Based Monetary Policy Instruments

Developed countries started to phase out the use of direct instruments in the 1970s. The adoption of indirect monetary policy instruments by central banks was in line with the general objective of improving market efficiency by enhancing the role of price signals in the economy. In the monetary sphere, indirect instruments, referred to as market-based instruments, are used to change the supply of base money and central bank monetary liabilities through the transactions of the central bank with banks and non-banks at market-based prices and on a voluntary basis (Balino et al. 1995).

Contrary to direct monetary control, monetary authorities influence the balance sheet of commercial banks by changing items of its own balance sheet such as reserve money. Using monetary policy instruments such as open market operations, central banks change the supply of reserves to the banking system which in turn affects the supply of money in the economy through the money supply process as explained in Chap. 3. These actions of central banks affect money market interest rates as well as deposit and lending rates. In turn, these changes in financial prices will lead to adjustment of the medium-term supply and demand conditions in the goods market, and therefore affecting the price levels. These transmission channels however depend on different factors including the structure and level of development of financial markets and the financial system in general, as described in Chap. 1.

The liberalization of the economy in Rwanda gradually took place since 1995 after the genocide against the Tutsi and the financial sector experienced significant changes as a result. These changes paved the way for the introduction of indirect instruments of monetary policy. Policy reforms included the removal of interest rate controls, requirements for banks to lend to specific sectors, and credit ceilings, and appropriate rules and regulations were enacted to strengthen bank supervision. While the direct control of credit was abandoned in 1992, interest rates were fully liberalized in 1996, with lending interest rates being liberalized sooner than deposit interest rates. The instruction No.2/95 of March 1995 liberalized all lending and deposit interest rates on operations made in FRW, except fixed-term deposit rates, which were liberalized later in 1996.

The reform of the exchange rate system began with the launch of the SAPs in 1990 and different measures were taken progressively. Residents were authorized to open accounts in foreign currencies in commercial banks. In 1995, the flexible exchange rate system was introduced and new regulations were put in place. The main features of these new regulations were the determination of the exchange rate by the market forces, the establishment of foreign exchange bureaus, the authorization of foreign direct investments (FDI) in Rwanda, and the transfer abroad of the returns on FDI. The current and capital account operations were fully liberalized in September 2010.

Allowing more flexibility in exchange rate in a stable macroeconomic and political environment contributed to more financial integration and progressive improvement in monetary transmission through exchange rate channel. The two factors, flexible exchange rate and financial integration, are among macroeconomic drivers of monetary transmission mechanisms. In a country with floating exchange rates, monetary policy is transmitted to aggregate demand through domestic interest rates and through the exchange rate, the latter affects the composition of absorption between domestic and foreign goods. In this case, as the degree of financial integration increases, the power of monetary policy to affect aggregate demand increases with it.

The reason is that increased integration implies a reduced scope for monetary policy to create rate-of-return differentials between domestic and foreign assets. A policy-induced change in the domestic interest rate must create a larger offsetting expected change in the exchange rate. As response to an increase in domestic interest rate, the domestic currency is expected to depreciate, and an appreciation is expected in response to a decrease in domestic interest rate. This shows how higher degree of financial integration is very important for the functioning of channels of monetary policy transmission. Indeed, the higher the degree of financial integration, the greater the extent to which exchange rate changes reinforce the effects of interest rate changes on aggregate demand, which improve the monetary transmission mechanism. As a result of fully capital account liberalization in Rwanda, more flexible exchange rate, strong macroeconomic fundamentals, and political stability, FDI in Rwanda increased over time (Fig. 2.2).

Regarding the sectors these flows are invested in, as at the end of 2018, ICT sector accounts for the largest share with 29.1% of the total, followed by the financial sector (19.3%), the manufacturing sector (13.4%), the electricity, gas and steam sector (11.0%), and other sectors (27.2%) (Fig. 2.3).

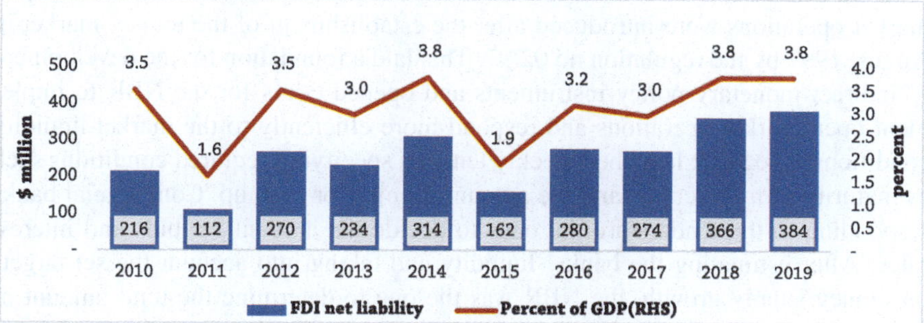

Fig. 2.2 Trend in Net FDI (2010–2019). *Source* NBR, statistic department

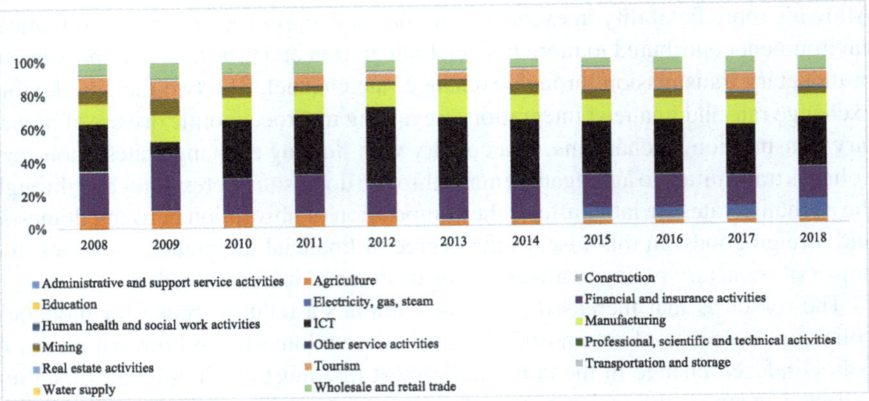

Fig. 2.3 FDI stock by economic sectors. *Source* NBR, statistics department

2.3.1 Monetary Policy Instruments

From 1997 to 2018, the NBR implemented a monetary targeting policy regime using reserve money as an operational target and broad money as an intermediate target, with the objective of achieving price stability as it will be presented in Chap. 3. Targets on reserve money were achieved by managing the banking system's liquidity using the following monetary policy instruments: open market operations; statutory reserve requirement; the standing lending and deposit facilities; the discount window; and foreign exchange market operations.

Owing to the absence of the money market in Rwanda, the reserve requirement system and discount window were the only monetary policy instruments used in Rwanda between 1995 and 1997 to regulate the banking system's liquidity. Open market operations were introduced after the establishment of the money market in August 1997 by the regulation no 02/97. This laid a foundation for the development of indirect monetary policy instruments and opened doors for the NBR to implement open market operations and respond more efficiently to the market liquidity conditions. The NBR launched weekly tenders, specifying required conditions such as maturity of transactions and the amount to inject or mop up. Commercial banks responding to the tenders are the ones to decide the amount for bids and interest rates. After estimating the banks' liquidity and taking into account the set targets on money supply growth, the NBR was the one to determine the total amount of liquidity to mop up or to inject in the banking system. Furthermore, transactions of short-term obligations such as treasury bills (T-bills) facilitated the mobilization and allocation of resources, and enabled the government to borrow from the domestic market instead of directly borrowing from the NBR. Prior to the establishment of the money market, 50% of annual government revenues were from the NBR. In 1997, direct lending to the government was prohibited with the objective of building the NBR's credibility, limiting pressures on inflation originating from fiscal policy and improving the effectiveness of monetary policy. The only possibility of addressing issues linked to cash management by the government due to tax revenue fluctuations is the use of the overdraft facility, not exceeding 11% of the state's current revenue collected during the previous year (article 49, NBR law, 2007).

Open Market Operations (OMOs)

Open market operations may be simply defined as central bank transactions with commercial banks at the central bank's initiative. Thus, an open market operation (OMO) occurs when a bank buys or sells government securities on the open market through auction. The usual aim of OMOs is to influence the short-term interest rate or the supply of reserve money and thus indirectly control the total money supply in the economy. When a central bank sells securities, it reduces domestic banks' reserves and as a consequence, reduces the monetary base. On the other hand, when it buys securities, it increases the monetary base. OMOs are implemented using different instruments such as repurchase agreement operations (repo and reverse repo), treasury bills, and central bank bills.

Since 2004, Rwanda's banking sector has consistently been awash with significant excess liquidity resulting from high public spending, especially backed by stable and huge aid inflows, high economic growth achieved in the last two decades averaging around 8%, and limited remunerative alternatives to money as the financial market was less developed. The structural excess liquidity has been a limitation to the use of OMOs in Rwanda, up to 2016. Between 2004 and 2016, the stock of broad money (M3) rose by around 19.5% a year on average and the banking reserves above the statutory requirement increased from 17% between 2004 and 2008 to 38% in 2009–2012 and 46% in 2013–2016. As shown by Gichondo et al. (2017), between 2004 and 2016, the optimal excess reserve was estimated to be around FRW 14.3 billion on average, which was far below the observed excess liquidity held by banks in Rwanda (Fig. 2.4).

Several authors have observed that abundance of liquidity is likely to have adverse consequences for the ability of monetary policy to influence demand conditions and, thus, to stabilize the economy (Agénor et al. 2004; Aryeetey and Nissanke 1998).

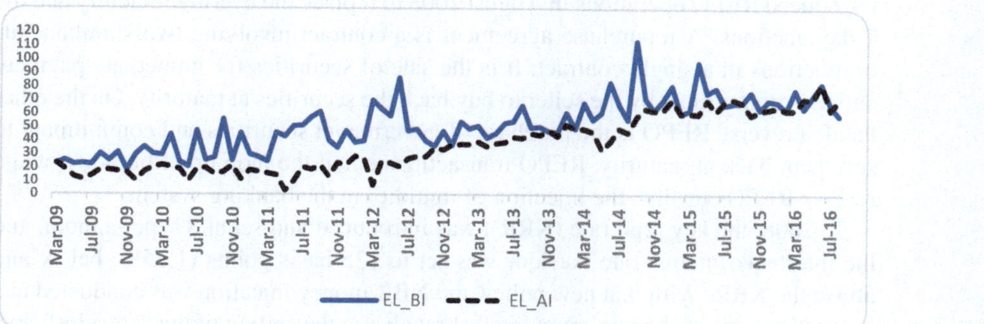

Fig. 2.4 Development in excess liquidity before intervention (EL-BI) and after intervention (EL-AI). *Source* NBR, monetary policy department

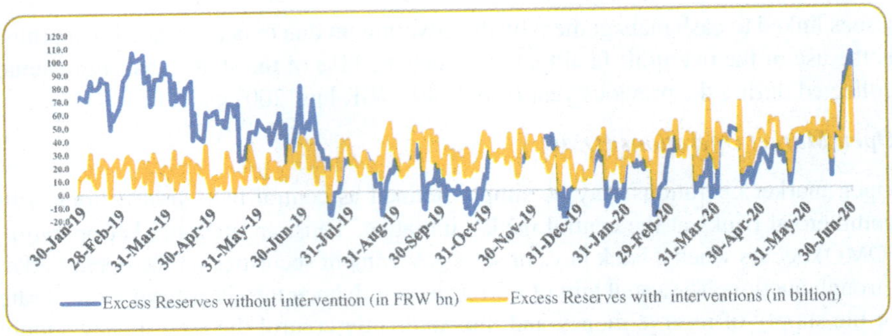

Fig. 2.5 Trend of excess reserves. *Source* NBR, monetary policy department

Indeed, if for example banks hold liquidity in excess of requirements, actions of the monetary authorities aiming at increasing liquidity in the banking sector and stimulate aggregate demand by increasing loan to the private sector will prove largely ineffective. Thus, one would expect excess bank liquidity to weaken the monetary policy transmission mechanism. As a result of high excess liquidity in the banking sector, the refinancing instruments and liquidity injection tenders were rarely used. Since then, the NBR focused on the development of liquidity mop up instruments to counteract prevailing liquidity conditions. Therefore, the NBR introduced an overnight facility and a 7-day auction before introducing the repurchase agreements and treasury bills for monetary policy purpose. However, due to improvement in liquidity forecasting and management, and development of money market, particularly interbank market which make it easy for banks to borrow in order to cover contingencies, excess liquidity reduced significantly since 2017 and NBR started to use reverse repo operations making the central bank rate cost of funds for banks an effective signal of monetary policy stance (Fig. 2.5).

Repurchase Agreement Operations (REPO and Reverse REPO)

In order to improve the management of the banking system's liquidity, the NBR introduced REPO operations in August 2008 to replace the overnight facility and the 7-day auctions. A repurchase agreement is a contract involving two simultaneous transactions in a single contract. It is the sale of securities for immediate payment and the commitment by the seller to buy back the securities at maturity. On the other hand, a reverse REPO is the purchase of government securities and commitment to sell them back at maturity. REPO transactions entail the mop up of liquidity, while reverse REPOs involve the injection of liquidity in the banking system.

In 2008, the key repo rate (KRR), was introduced and set at 8% per annum, and the interbank interest rate corridor was set to 125 basis points (1.25%) below and above the KRR. With that new policy, the NBR money injection was conducted at a competition basis, the minimum interest rate being the ceiling of the "corridor". In a similar manner, the bank absorbed excess funds on a competitive basis, the maximum interest rate being fixed at the floor of the "corridor".

In December 2009, the Monetary Policy Committee (MPC) decided to use the KRR only as a reference to borrow/lend liquidity from/to the market. It indicated the maximum rate at which the NBR mops up excess liquidity from the banking system and the minimum rate it injects liquidity in the banking sector. The KRR has been regularly reviewed by the monetary policy committee (MPC) based on the assessment of inflation outlook, as well as on the development in banking sector liquidity conditions. This policy instrument has progressively become a tool for signalling the NBR's monetary policy stance, and communicating with the market. In 2012, the NBR decided to use the KRR as a reference rate for its money market operations in order to induce the efficiency and development of the money market. Indeed, while the use of indirect monetary policy instruments is influenced by a country's financial system, the proper use of those instruments supported by appropriate liquidity forecasting also contributes to the development of the money market. It increases the efficiency of financial intermediation, and the level of competition in the financial sector. Repo and reverse repo transactions were fixed at only 7-days maturity, and operated within a corridor, the lower and upper limits being overnight deposit and lending standing facilities, respectively.

In December 2009, the MPC decided to cut the KRR from 9%, to 7.5% and set the discount rate at KRR + 4% and it was further revised down to 7% in March 2010, and to 6% in November 2010. Due to inflationary pressures experienced in 2011–2013, the MPC decided to raise the KRR to 6.5% and to 7.5% in October 2011 and May 2012, respectively. The NBR started to ease monetary conditions mid-2013 as the inflationary pressures were fading away. The KRR was cut to 7.0% in June 2013, to 6.5% in June 2014, to 6.25% in December 2016, to 5.5% in December 2017, to 5% in May 2018, and to 4.5% in April 2020 (Fig. 2.6).

Treasury Bills and Central Bank Bills

Generally, central banks use government securities and central bank bills as main debt instruments in their open market operations. The two securities have no credit risk, their maturities do not exceed one year and are at the bottom end of the return spectrum. Country experiences show that the choice between the use of the two securities depends more on country circumstances, the level of coordination between central banks and fiscal authorities, as well as existing legal guidelines on the matter.

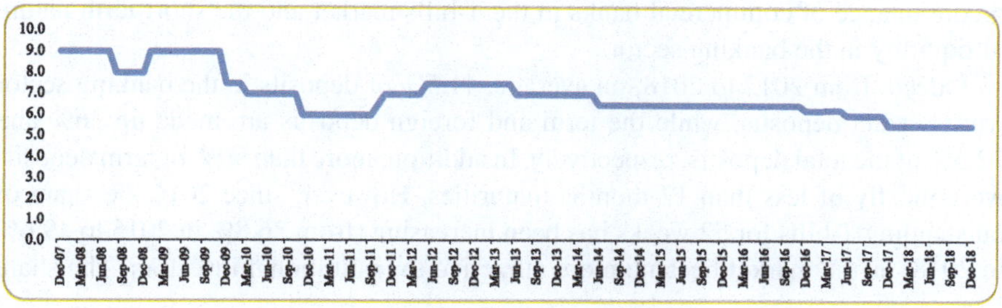

Fig. 2.6 KRR developments *Source* NBR, monetary policy department

Table 2.1 T-bills and central bank bills outstanding in FRW billion

	2012	2013	2014	2015	2016	2017	2018	Average
Treasury bills (TB)	95.2	156.5	163.9	222.5	238.8	303.7	343.2	217.7
Central bank bills (CBB)	7	11.5	21.2	13.5	4	6	14.2	11.1
Total Treasury bills and central bank bills	102.2	168	185.1	236	242.8	309.7	357.4	228.7
TB shares (in %)	93.2	93.2	88.5	94.3	98.4	98.1	96	94.5
CB shares (in %)	6.8	6.8	11.5	5.7	1.6	1.9	4	5.5

Source NBR, Financial market department

Furthermore, central banks normally use their own securities in situations where the market for government securities is undeveloped[3] or when securities issued by the governments and other monetary policy instruments are insufficient to absorb excess liquidity (Habermeier 2012).

For the case of Rwanda, the NBR decided to intervene on the money market by issuing T-bills with 28, 91, 182, 364 days maturity in accordance with provisions of the instruction no. 05/98 of 24 September 1997. While the use of T-bills was a way of limiting the inflationary pressures from the NBR's financing of the government, T-bills are also used for monetary policy purposes, to absorb liquidity from the economy. Later central bank bills (CB-bills) were introduced to sterilize excess liquidity whenever T-bills and other instruments failed to bring the reserve money to the targeted levels. During the period of 2012 to 2018, the average T-bills outstanding was FRW 217.7 billion, while the outstanding CB-bills amounted only to FRW 11.069 billion on average (Table 2.1).

The use of both central bank bills and treasury bills in Rwanda is facilitated by the NBR's transparency in the process of issuing bills, and good coordination between the NBR and the Ministry of Finance and Economic Planning (MINECOFIN).

While investments in central bank bills are restricted only to commercial banks, other financial institutions holding a current account with NBR as well as other investors, be individuals or legal entities approved by the NBR to bid through their banks, are free to invest in the T-bills on the primary market. As indicated in Table 2.2, investors mostly preferred short-term T-bills (4, 13, and 26 weeks) between 2012 and 2015, accounting for 83.5% of total outstanding T-bills. This is explained by the predominance of commercial banks in the T-bills market and the short-term nature of liquidity in the banking sector.

Indeed, from 2012 to 2018, on average, 41.5% of deposits in the banking sector were current deposits, while the term and foreign deposits are made up 36% and 22.5% of the total deposits, respectively. In addition, more than 90% of term deposits were mostly of less than 12 months maturities. However, since 2016 the share of outstanding T-bills for 52 weeks has been increasing (from 26.8% in 2015 to 49.6% in 2018) as the market became more attractive to institutional investors. The share

[3]This is also the case in countries where investors do not have confidence in the capacity and willingness of their governments to pay debts.

Table 2.2 Treasury bills outstanding shares by maturity

Tenor	2012	2013	2014	2015	2016	2017	2018
4 weeks	34.8	19.2	11.9	17.1	21.4	8.4	8.6
13 weeks	33.2	37.4	32.0	24.2	18.4	18.6	14.6
26 weeks	17.2	32.6	32.3	31.9	23.0	28.5	27.2
52 weeks	14.7	10.9	23.8	26.8	37.3	44.5	49.6
TOTAL	100	100	100	100	100	100	100

Sources NBR, Financial market department

of institutional investment in total outstanding increased from 11.8% in December 2013 to 57.2% in December 2018, while the share of banks reduced from 81.4% to 33.1% in the same period, the remainder being from retail investors.

To encourage banks to invest their liquidity in long-term securities (more than 26 weeks), the NBR's preference has been to issue more CB-bills with 52 weeks maturity. As a result, on average, 78.8% of outstanding investment in central bank bills were of 52 weeks maturity between December 2012 and December 2018.

The Standing Facilities

Standing facilities are central bank operations at the initiative of banks. The lending and deposit standing facilities are the only two facilities available at the NBR since 1 June 2012 in order to enhance liquidity management. The standing deposit facility (SDF) allows commercial banks to place excess reserves with the NBR at CBR minus some percentage points decided by the monetary policy committee. The standing lending facility (SLF) helps banks to borrow from the NBR to fill any liquidity gap that might unexpectedly arise from the daily settlements on money market or other payment operations. To access this facility, banks provide collateral, limited to government securities only, for overnight loan at a predetermined interest rate.

Standing facilities have not been frequently used due to structural short-term excess liquidity in the Rwandan banking sector. The standing deposit facility was more used in October and November 2012, with a total amount of FRW 202, 5 billion transacted at 5.5% (corresponding to KRR of 7.5% −2%). Then, the facility was only used four times in 2013, with a corresponding amount of FRW 7.8 billion at 5.5% and once in 2014 for an amount of FRW 12 billion at 3.67%. Due to excess liquidity in the banking sector in 2014, repo rates were lower than rate on SDF, defined as KRR −2. Thus, to avoid overnight deposit facility to become more attractive than repo operations, the NBR decided to accept overnight deposits at the repo rate − 2%. However, with the improvement in liquidity management and monetary policy operations, the NBR decided in 2019 to remunerate deposits under the deposit facility at KRR −2% and lending facility charged at KRR plus 1%; with the purpose of improving the transmission mechanism between the KRR and money market rates.

Reserve Requirements (RR)

Most central banks require depository institutions to hold minimum reserves against their liabilities, generally in the form of balances at the central bank. While reserve requirements are held for prudential purposes and liquidity management in most cases, the prudential benefits of RR are now covered by supervision and regulation requirements such as capital adequacy, liquidity requirements, deposit insurance, and standing credit facilities by central banks. This explains why currently in most central banks, RR are used to assist monetary authorities in liquidity control, but not as an essential part of monetary policy operating system, because open market operations (OMOs) constitute the pillar of conducting monetary policy. Since the effectiveness of OMOs depends on the development of financial markets, RR are used to supplement other monetary policy instruments in managing liquidity in developing countries with shallow money markets.

The use of RR depends on the country specificities, particularly the financial and macroeconomic environment which should contribute to the decision on the currency to which the RR will be imposed and in which it will be maintained. Stable macroeconomic environment and limited currency substitution may support the maintenance of all RR in local currency. In that case, denominating RR on foreign currency in local currency contributes to controlling domestic liquidity, by increasing the mop up of excess liquidity in the banking sector.

For countries with no exchange controls, the share of foreign currency deposits in total deposits may increase. In that case, central banks will need to take into consideration their monetary policy implications, particularly on banking sector liquidity management. When the share of foreign currency in total deposits is substantial and RR ratios significant, denominating RR on foreign currency deposits in local currency can complicate monetary management, and can lead to financial and monetary instability, capital flight, and financial disintermediation. Under such conditions, it may be advisable to maintain foreign currency denominated RR on foreign currency deposits. This improves monetary control and discourages currency substitution (Ize 1995).

NBR adopted the RR system in August 1990 initially as a measure of protecting depositors but since early 1995, after abandoning direct monetary policy instruments and in the context of absence of open market operations, the RR system is used as a monetary policy instrument aimed at other instruments in regulating the money supply. Banks are required to constitute and maintain reserves in their current accounts opened with NBR, calculated based on their liabilities held both in Rwandan Francs and in foreign currencies.

Directive no. 01/2012 of 22/02/2012 on Reserve Requirement in Rwanda establishes that the following liabilities are subject to the reserve requirement:

1. Current accounts of (i) other financial institutions such as insurance corporations, Development Bank of Rwanda (BRD), and Business Development Fund (BDF); (ii) current accounts of other financial institutions assimilated to banks such as microfinances institutions and saving and credit cooperatives (SACCOs); (iii) current accounts of non-residents such as foreign central banks, foreign

banks, foreign governments, and other non-residents; (iv) current accounts of the government and its entities such as line ministries, projects, public enterprises, social security fund, Rwanda Utilities Regulation Authority (RURA) and Rwanda Development Board (RDB); (v) current accounts of non-financial corporations such as MTN, Brasseries et Limonaderies du Rwanda (BRALIRWA) and all other businesses; and (vi) current accounts of other resident sectors such as households and non-profit institutions.

2. Term liabilities which cover term deposits and borrowings from the same as above, but extend to (i) interbank borrowings, which constitutes a double counting, as these funds have been subjected to the reserve requirement at the initial level (the bank that lent to another bank also reports the liability (deposit or borrowing) relating to this lending and (ii) the borrowing from non-residents mostly made of long-term borrowings from foreign financial institutions in foreign currency, the proceeds of which are often used in FX SWAPS with NBR.
3. Other accounts payable including suspense accounts.
4. Subordinated debts which are unsecured debts whose contracts stipulate that in the event of liquidation, creditors will be paid only after the claims of secured creditors are paid.

The constitution of reserve requirement on deposits in foreign currencies started in 2002, as shares of those deposits were becoming significant in total deposits. Deposits in foreign currency were recorded in 1994 for the first time in Rwanda, representing 10% of total deposits in the banking system. This share increased overtime to average 22% of total deposits between 2010 and 2018 but remained stable, fluctuating between 18.9% and 27.2% with a standard deviation of 2.7. In June 2002, the NBR adjusted the reserve requirement base, by including deposits in foreign currencies to be held in USD.

To accommodate the prevailing banking liquidity conditions, and contribute to the development of the interbank market, many amendments were introduced, including changes in compliance periods, the eligibility of liabilities, and the currency of RR denomination. After the genocide against the Tutsi, there was shortage of goods and services, leading to a significant increase in prices with an inflation rate peaking to 64% in 1994. As a policy response, the NBR raised the reserve requirement ratio twice in 1995, to 12.5% and 14% of all deposits in April and August, respectively. This measure coupled with others, such as the reorganization of the productive system by the government of Rwanda, and the improvement in exchange rate policy, contributed to the reduction of inflation to a monthly average of 10.4% in 1996, and 5% in 1998.

After the establishment of the money market in 1997, and the progressive use of OMOs in a more stable macroeconomic environment characterized by stable exchange rate and low inflation, the NBR reduced progressively the RR ratio, from 12% in 1997 to 10% in 1998, and to 8% in 2000. It remained the same until it was reduced to 5% in the first quarter of 2009, as a policy response to the liquidity crisis experienced by the country at that period. The reserve requirement ratio remained unchanged at 5% up to 1 April 2020 when the rate was reduced to 4% as one of the NBR's policy responses to the economic impact of COVID-19. The NBR maintained a lower reserve requirement ratio as it relies more on OMOs as an efficient way of implementing monetary policy and developing the money market. In general, banks will try to hold more reserves on days they expect the market interest rate to be lower and fewer reserves on days when they expect the rate to be higher.

Owing to the flexibility offered by reserve averaging system, commercial banks' demand for reserve balances becomes more interest-rate-sensitive and the interbank market rate is less sensitive to shocks to demand for and supply of reserves. As pointed out, the reserve averaging system not only contributed to the development of interbank market, it has also helped to reduce the tension between the day-to-day liquidity operations to stabilize short-term rates and liquidity operations to meet the targets on reserve money (Bartolini et al. 2006; Maino and Buzeneca 2007).

Moreover, for better management of liquidity by commercial banks, instruction no 06/2001 of September 2001 fixed the reserve maintenance period to one month. However, in order to eliminate distortions created by a long maintenance period of one month, and due to structural short-term excess liquidity in the Rwandan banking sector, NBR reduced the maintenance period from one month to two weeks in March 2005, to one week in 2007, and adopted an averaging system. During the maintenance period, banks are allowed to be in shortage, but must comply on average at the end of the maintenance period. Penalty fees equivalent to the discount rate plus 5% are imposed to commercial banks failing to comply with the RR. The adoption of RR averaging system aimed at supporting commercial banks to manage their short-term liquidity was one of the strategies adopted by the NBR to promote the interbank market development. Trading on the interbank market between banks with liquidity shortages and those with excess liquidity during the maintenance period helps these institutions to balance their supply and demand of liquidity. This contributed to progressively reduce volatility on overnight market rates and to the stability of the money market rates.

Owing to the high demand of foreign currency by the private sector to finance increasing import bills and the effort of the NBR to manage short-term liquidity in domestic currency, the constitution of RR in foreign currency was abandoned in May 2012 (see the NBR directive no 01/2012 of 22/05/2012). In addition, uniform reserve requirement ratio for both domestic and foreign currency deposit liabilities was adopted that enables NBR to act in a neutral manner, with respect to the currency in which the banks' deposits are denominated. This increases the role of the RR in the NBR's liquidity management in the banking system, regardless of the source of liquidity. The stability of the FRW facilitates the use of the same RR ratio on all kind of reserves, contrary to countries with high depreciation of domestic currencies where banks are forced to increase their reserve balances at the central bank, even if deposits in foreign currency have not increased, thus reducing liquidity in domestic currency.

Foreign Exchange Market Operations

By the decree-law of 3 March 1995 on the organization and management of the foreign exchange market, Rwanda adopted a market-based exchange rate regime, the exchange rate being progressively determined by the fundamentals of the economy.

According to this regulation, licensed banks are free to conserve and manage their foreign currencies, determine the exchange rates in agreement with their customers, and decide the character of transferability of all current transactions. Thus, the import or export licenses which were granted prior by the NBR were replaced by simple import or export bank statements, validated only by the licensed banks. In addition, exporters were allowed to keep all the proceeds of their exports in their foreign currency accounts in commercial banks.

The intervention of the NBR on the foreign currency market, by selling US dollars to commercial banks, is aimed at supporting banks to meet the market demand and essentially finance imports, but mostly to reduce the exchange rate volatility. However, sales of foreign currency (USD) is also a way of moping liquidity in domestic currency from the banking system, by the amount equivalent to USD sold at the prevailing market exchange rate. To protect the country against external shocks, NBR intervention on the forex market has been guided also by the objective of keeping the country's foreign reserves at a level covering at least 4 months of imports.

Between March 1995 and February 2001, the NBR's reference exchange rate was determined as the average of previous day market rates of commercial banks and NBR's operations with clients. After introducing the auction system on 6 February 2001, NBR changed its calculation of the reference rate. Different ways of averaging exchange rates were used from simple average of FX interbank exchange rates to weighted average rates from forex auction to commercial banks, and to the moving average rates of commercial banks and NBR's operations with clients. The objective was to take into consideration the market conditions, and progressively introduce more flexibility in the exchange rate.

With effect from 25 June 2007, the forex auction to commercial banks was abandoned, and replaced by a new arrangement, whereby the NBR sells foreign exchange to commercial banks in unlimited amounts at the day's average reference rate quoted by the NBR. In this new system, the reference rate was a simple average of the rate from sales to banks by the NBR, and the moving average rate of commercial banks and NBR's operations with clients. In the case where the calculated reference rate was higher than the reference rate of the last working day, the reference rate was calculated as the rate of the last working day adjusted by −0.01%. The adjustment on the reference rate was modified over time. In 2014, the NBR's official rate was obtained by considering the average from the previous day's foreign exchange, interbank market, and rate of NBR's interventions. In case there were no interbank transactions or NBR interventions, the previous transacted market rate was maintained as the official rate.

Currently, the NBR's official rate is determined by considering the average from the previous day's foreign exchange, interbank market, and NBR's intervention transactions. In case there is neither interbank transactions nor NBR FX interventions, NBR's reference rate is calculated by applying the change in the commercial banks' forex market to the previous NBR reference rate. Change in commercial banks' forex market is obtained by computing a percentage change between the weighted average of US dollar selling transactions of all banks from the previous day, with the weighted average of the day T-2 (day before the previous day). This is to make NBR official rate reflect the market conditions on the forex market.

As a result of NBR monetary and exchange rate policies, as well as good performance in the Rwandan external sector, the FRW exchange rate against USD, which is the most used in external trade by Rwandans, remains stable. The average depreciation of the FRW against the USD was 5.03% between 2011 and 2018, and 3.80% in the same period excluding 2015 and 2016, where the depreciation was very high (7.6–9.7%) due to external shocks.

2.3.2 Outcomes of NBR Monetary Policy After 1994

As pointed out earlier, Rwanda recorded low economic performance since the 1980s, with the economic growth declining from 4.4% on average in 1975–1980 to 2.5% in 1980–1985, and 2.4% in 1985–1990. In addition, the use of direct monetary policy instruments during that period led to disintermediation, and limited the development of financial sector. Growth in broad money was 8.1% on average while the growth of credit to private sector was 8.5% on average between 1980 and 1993, far below than 17.5 and 18.8% recorded between 2000 and 2019, respectively. After the 1994 genocide against the Tutsi, Rwanda has achieved high and sustainable inclusive economic growth attributable to effective leadership supported by substantial foreign aid. In the wake of the genocide, the Rwandan leadership succeeded to both choose and implement the right policies and create the political conditions necessary for them to work. These conditions include building a social consensus between Rwandans, and between the society and the government, resulting in confidence and trust of the population in their leaders' honesty and integrity.

This is very crucial in balancing short-term sacrifices needed for long-term growth. The leaders of the country created rigorous systems for accountability and governance as well as proper mechanisms to monitor results using appropriate performance indicators and review policies were necessary to allow for feedback as to whether policies were correctly crafted and well implemented. This is important because sustained growth is often the result of persistent fine-tuning of policies. Indeed, policy review is crucial as it helps to determine (a) whether the defined policies have worked in the local context, (b) whether and how implementation and formulation could be improved, or more fundamentally, and (c) whether one should rethink the original policies considering possible changes in the operating environment.

Academic research and country experiences have shown a strong link between effective leadership and economic growth (for more details, see, e.g. Commission of Growth and Development of World Bank 2010). Specifically, strong institutions and capable leaders can arrive at the right set of pro-growth policies and adapt such policies to changing circumstances. Institutions that a country creates are important for development as they are key in policy implementation and because mature markets rely on deep institutional underpinnings, institutions that define property rights, enforce contracts, convey prices, and bridge informational gaps between buyers and sellers, among other things.

It is in this conducive macroeconomic and political environment that NBRs implement monetary policy in coordination with other economic policies. As a result, NBRs contributed to maintain price stability in the country; it is the main mandate. This provided favourable conditions for sustainable economic growth and stable macroeconomic environment, particularly from 2000. The annual average headline inflation in Rwanda was 8.7% between 2005 and 2011, and 3.8% between 2012 and 2018. In the period under review, average core inflation was 7.6% and 3.2%, respectively. In the East African Community (EAC), Rwanda recorded the lowest average headline inflation (4.7%), followed by Uganda (7.2%), Kenya (7.6%), Tanzania (8.2%), and Burundi (8.4%). Apart from recording the lowest inflation, Rwanda's inflation was the most stable, with a standard deviation of 2.7%, followed by Kenya (3%), Tanzania (4.2%), Uganda (4.5%), and Burundi (5.8%) (Table 2.3).

Progressive development of the money market, particularly the interbank market as well as improvement in liquidity forecasting and management helped commercial banks to better manage their liquidity, and reduce excess liquidity for precautionary purpose. The accommodative monetary policy implemented by NBR in that environment contributed to supporting the financing of the economy by the banking system, in line with the government's objective of achieving high and inclusive economic growth. The outstanding bank loan to the private sector increased to FRW 1.8 trillion in 2019 from 70.9 billion in 2000 (Fig. 2.7).

Table 2.3 Inflation developments (annual average)

Year	Domestic	Imported	Headline	Core
2005	10.0	7.6	9.2	5.5
2006	11.2	2.8	8.8	4.5
2007	11.8	2.1	9.1	9.7
2008	14.4	18.5	15.4	17.5
2009	11.2	7.4	10.7	9.0
2010	2.7	0.8	2.3	1.5
2011	5.2	7.4	5.7	5.7
2012	7.0	3.5	6.3	4.0
2013	4.6	2.6	4.2	4.0
2014	1.9	1.5	1.8	2.7
2015	3.0	1.1	2.5	2.1
2016	6.0	4.7	5.7	4.1
2017	4.5	6.0	4.9	3.9
2018	0.5	4.4	1.4	1.6
2019	2.1	3.5	2.4	2.3

Source National Institute of Statistic of Rwanda

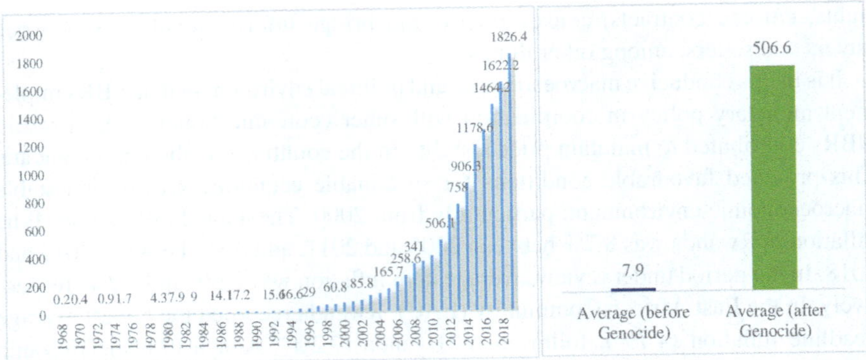

Fig. 2.7 Credit to private sector in FRW billion. *Source* NBR, statistics department

The NBR's monetary and exchange rate policy has contributed to mitigating the effects of different economic shocks on the real economy. For example, between 2008 and 2009, the banking system in Rwanda experienced a liquidity problem due to different factors, including the global financial crisis and liquidity crunch resulting from the decision of Rwanda Social Security Board (RSSB), one of the biggest institutional depositors in the banking system, to diversify its investment, including outside of Rwanda. As a policy response, the NBR decided to reduce the required reserve ratio from 8% to 5% to leave more liquidity in the banking sector, and in collaboration with MINECOFIN, it was decided to not roll over short-term T-bills maturing in 2009. The NBR also introduced a short-term refinancing facility to provided loans to the banking system for 3–12 months. Together with MINECOFIN, a long-term (5 years) facility was established, to enhance long-term liquidity and boost banks that lend to the public.

Furthermore, the NBR decided to ease monetary conditions in the economy by reducing its policy rate progressively. As a result, liquidity in the banking system was rebuilt gradually, supporting credit to private sector and economic growth, while underlying inflationary pressures were well anchored. The net total borrowing by the NBR from commercial banks to absorb short-term excess liquidity increased from zero at end March 2009 to RWF 60.0 billion by end 2009, and the new authorized loans increased by 26.4% between September and December 2009.

In 2012, Rwanda experienced shortage of foreign inflows due to cuts and delays in budget support. To limit the impact of the exchange rate depreciation to the domestic prices, the NBR deliberately increased its sales of foreign exchange to commercial banks, thanks to a comfortable level of official reserves accumulated in the previous periods (Figs. 2.8 and 2.9).

These measures, together with rapid fiscal adjustments, contributed to limiting the negative impact of the shortfalls in foreign exchange inflows on the economy. Following the resumption of donor aid, the successful Euro bond issuance end April 2013 and positive inflation outlook, the NBR cut the central bank rate to 7.0% from 7.5% and to 6.5% in June 2015, to stimulate credit to the private. All these factors

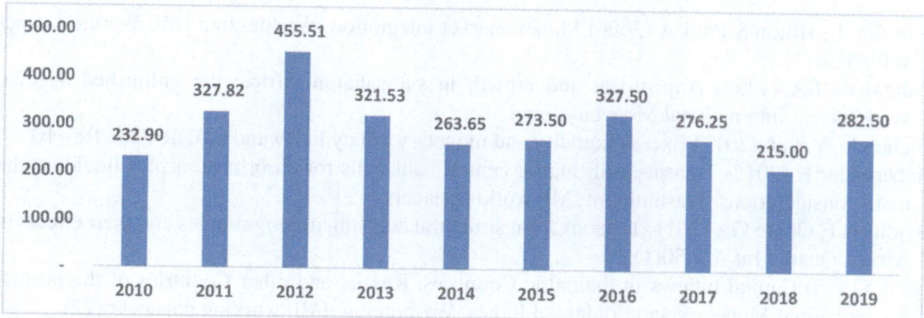

Fig. 2.8 Sales to banks development in FRW billion. *Source* NBR, financial markets department

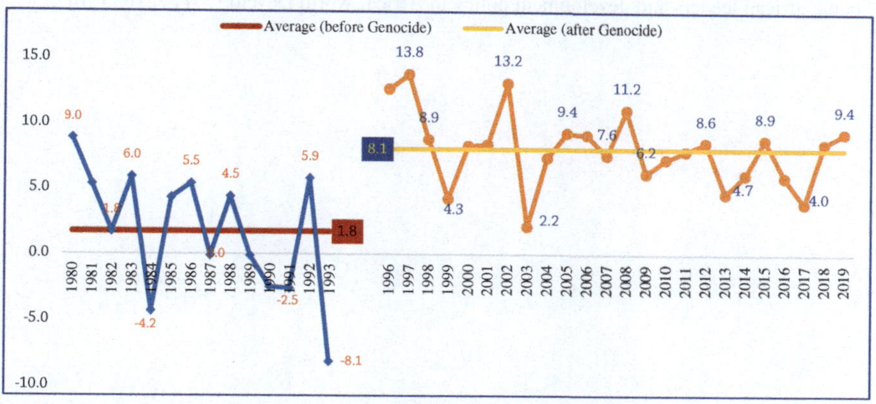

Fig. 2.9 Real GDP growth before and after the genocide against Tutsi. *Source* national institute of statistics of Rwanda

supported the government development agenda. Against this backdrop, Rwanda has enjoyed high economic growth of 8.1% on average between 1996 and 2018, far above the average growth of 1.8% recorded between 1980 and 1993, the period of controlled economy.

References

Agénor P-R, Aizenman J, Hoffmaister A (2004) The credit crunch in east asia: what can bank excess liquid assets tell us? J Int Money Finan 23:27–49

Ansoms A (2005) Resurrection after civil war and genocide: growth, poverty and inequality in post-conflict Rwanda. Euro J Developm Res 17(3)

Aryeetey E, Nissanke M (1998) Financial integration and development:liberalization and reform in sub-saharan Africa, 1st edn. London: Routledge

Balino T, Charles E, William A (1995) The adoption of indirect instruments of monetary policy

Bartolini L, Hilton S Prati A (2006) Money market integration. Washington: IMF Working Paper WP/06/207
Calamitsis EA (1999) Adjustment and growth in sub-saharan Africa: the unfinished agenda. Washington: International Monetary Fund
Gichondo A et al. (2017) Excess liquidity and monetary policy in Rwanda. BNR Econ Rev 10
Habermeier K (2012) Treasury bills and/or central bank bills for absorbing surplus liquidity: the main considerations. Washington: IMF working papers
Heidhues F, Obare GA (2011) Lessons from structural adjustment programmes and their effects in Africa. Quart J Int Agr 50(1):10
Ize A (1995) Capital inflows in the baltic Countries, Russia, and other Countries of the Former Soviet Union: Monetary and Prudential Issues, Washington: IMF working papers 96(22)
Maino R, Buzeneca I (2007) Monetary policy implementation: results from a survey. Washington: IMF Working Papers 07(7)
Owusu F (2003) Pragmatism and the gradual shift from dependency to neoliberalism: the world bank, african leaders and development policy in Africa. World Develop 31(10):1655–1672

Chapter 3
Development of the Monetary Policy Framework in Rwanda

Over the past few decades, policymakers in different countries have become increasingly aware of socio-economic costs of inflation leading central banks to adopt price stability as a goal of monetary policy. There is a consensus today that a central bank that maintains price stability significantly contributes to the achievement of broader economic goals such as higher standards of living and high levels of economic activities. Price stability makes it easier for consumers and firms to make better informed consumption and investment decisions, allow the financial system to allocate resources more efficiently and reduce risk premium for creditors. To achieve the price stability, NBR implemented its monetary policy using monetary targeting framework between 1997 and 2018, before moving to a price-based monetary policy adopted since January 2019.

This chapter presents the features of the monetary targeting framework in Rwanda, used for a period of 22 years and how the new framework, price-based monetary policy, is implemented. The reliance on market-based monetary policy instruments is based on the central bank monopoly to create money. As a monopolistic supplier of base money, a central bank can either control its price (short-term interest rate) or its quantity (base money or one of its components). The effectiveness of money market interventions using indirect monetary policy instruments for the conduct of monetary policy highly depends on initial conditions, including: stable macroeconomic environment and sound fiscal policies, sound and competitive financial system, adequate supervisory framework, sufficient degree of institutional autonomy, and operational capacity at the central bank. Though countries' experiences show that many central banks have adopted money market operations before meeting these conditions, however the effectiveness of their monetary policies increases with progress made in meeting those conditions (Kireyev 2015).

Countries where money markets are not yet well developed or a monetary aggregate is used as intermediate target, that is, has a strong and predictable relationship with inflation, have adopted quantitative or monetary targeting framework because monetary policy impulses are transmitted mainly through changes in quantity of money than changes in its prices.

T. K. Rusuhuzwa, *Monetary Policy in Rwanda*, Frontiers in African Business Research, https://doi.org/10.1007/978-981-33-6746-3_3

Monetary policy framework comprises the primary objective of monetary policy, which is price stability in almost all central banks, the monetary policy strategy (the use of intermediate or indictor variables), and policy formulation framework, describing how the central bank formulates the policy stance and sets the level of the operating target; and the operational framework comprises the instruments to steer the operating target. As indicated, operating target can be a price (short-term interest rate) or a quantity (monetary base) variable and not the two together, and both operating targets rely on the central bank's ability to manage its balance sheet. Indeed, by targeting price, the base money is endogenous because to keep interest rate development consistent with its targeted level, a central bank accommodates any temporary shifts in the demand or supply of monetary base. On the other side, when a central bank target quantity, it does not accommodate shifts in base money demand, which is its operating target but can accommodate the resulting interest rate fluctuations as long as development in base money is consistent with the quantity targeted (Maehle 2000a; Aucremanne et al. 2007; Walsh 2003).

One of central banks' problems is that they wish to achieve certain goals, such as price stability as is the case of the majority of central banks but they do not have direct influence on that goals. Strategically, central banks choose a set of variables called intermediate targets, which have strong and predictable relationship with the price level, the final objective. However, another challenge is that even these intermediate targets are not directly affected by the central banks' policy instruments. Therefore, central banks choose another set of variables called operating targets which are more responsive to its policy tools and which have strong link with intermediate targets. Intermediate (operating) targets have to fulfil the following three criteria. They have to be measurable, controllable by the central bank, and have a predictable effect on the goal of monetary policy (intermediate target). For a central bank, to know if its monetary policy is on track, both intermediate and operating variables have to be measurable. In addition, when the monetary policy is off track, any adjustment of one of the two targets to bring back them on track requires that they have to be highly influenced by central banks' actions. Finally, a variable to be useful as an intermediate (operating) target and its impact on the final goal of monetary policy such as price (intermediate target) has to be predictable (Mishkin 1995; Tsangarides 2010).

3.1 Monetary Targeting Framework in Rwanda

To achieve the objective of price stability, NBR implemented its monetary policy under a monetary targeting framework since 1997, using the reserve money (or base money) as operational target and broad money as intermediate target. The success of monetary targeting framework was supported by different reforms such as new NBR law of 2007, making price stability the main goal of NBR as well as the prohibition for the government to directly borrow from NBR. Theoretically, in this framework, the transmission mechanism of monetary policy sets out from the quantity of base

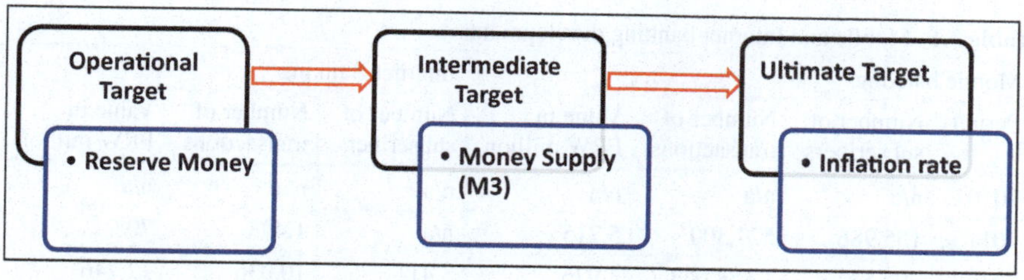

Fig. 3.1 BNR monetary policy framework

money (B) and moves towards inflation through the broad money supply (M3), the intermediate target (Fig. 3.1).

This transmission mechanism is, however, taken with caution. If commercial banks are constrained in their capacity to lend to the private sector, increase in base money mainly attributable to easing monetary policy does not, in itself, necessarily imply an accelerated expansion of credit to the private sector by commercial banks. An example is the use of quantitative easing by central banks in developed countries to respond to the last global financial crisis which has not contributed to high increase in credit to the private sector and in real economic activities as expected.

As monetary liabilities of NBR, the base money which consists of currency in circulation out NBR (currency in the hands of the public and cash held in vault by commercial banks) and reserves of banks at NBR plays an important role in the money supply process. Because everything else being constant, an increase in one or both components of base money will lead to an increase in the money supply. For the last 22 years, NBR interventions on money market were aimed at regulating overall liquidity conditions in the economy by influencing the underlying demand and supply conditions for central bank money, using different monetary policy instruments and accepting money market interest rate fluctuations as long as levels of base money were consistent with the quantity targets.

The broad monetary aggregate M3 used as intermediate target is composed of currency in circulation out the banking system (CIC) representing 15.5% of M3 on average and total deposits in the banking sector representing 84.5% of M3 on average between 1997 and 2019. Currency in circulation increased significantly from FRW 22.6 billion in 1997 to FRW 214.02 billion in 2019 due to increased economic activities as well as government spending through different programmes. However, its share in M3 has been reducing overtime, declining from 25.1% in 1997 to 8.9% in 2019. This down trend is in line with financial sector expansion across the country and the development in payment system, particularly the use of electronic payment. More details on payment system development are given in Appendix 3.1 (Table 3.1).

Deposits in the banking system significantly increased from FRW 67.5 billion in 1997 to FRW 2177.3 billion in 2019 and are dominated by demand deposits representing 41.1% of total deposits followed by term deposits (35.4%) and deposit in foreign currency (23.5%). The ratio of foreign currency deposits to deposits in FRW, describing private sector portfolio management between foreign currency and

Table 3.1 Mobile and Internet banking developments

Mobile banking				Internet Banking		
Period	Number of subscribers	Number of transactions	Value in FRW million	Number of subscribers	Number of transactions	Value in FRW million
2010	n/a	n/a	n/a	n/a	n/a	n/a
2011	155,986	527,300	5,215	n/a	1,493	708
2012	297,537	1,458,063	3,926	3,411	10,036	12,746
2013	412,007	2,538,820	17,459	8,969	89,260	117,147
2014	659,712	4,637,849	41,281	29,840	312,264	332,959
2015	828,799	5,617,368	48,309	36,597	556,152	581,163
2016	980,671	3,906,642	37,164	43,047	460,363	1,014,077
2017	1,158,944	3,082,829	35,849	52,020	339,522	1,418,693
2018	1,845,584	3,206,474	53,287	85,697	769,517	2,027,789
2019	2,065,624	1,999,250	85,462	91,825	1,352,301	2,276,446

Source NBR, Payment systems department

domestic currency in Rwanda, varied between 0.2 and 0.4 in the period under review. As it can be seen in the graph of Fig. 3.2, demand deposits (DD) contributed significantly to the changes in M3 in the period under review, followed by term deposits in FRW (TD).

In formulating its monetary policy, NBR sets M3 growth targets in line with targets on inflation and economic growth and an estimated money demand in the economy. The set target on the supply of money (M3) has to be close to the money demand level in the economy because significant excess or shortfall may lead to significant deviations in outcomes of inflation and economic growth compared to their targets. Thus, a stable money demand is key for effective use of monetary aggregates as intermediate target is in the conduct of monetary policy.

In the monetary targeting framework, it is assumed that there is a stable and predictable long-run relationship between M3 and base money through a stable money multiplier. Thus, the monetary authority could control the overall liquidity

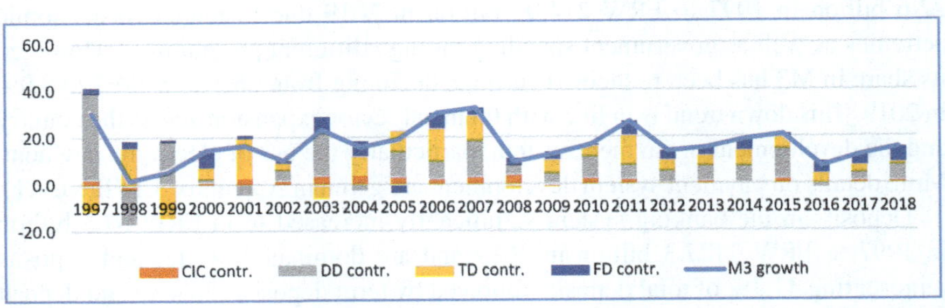

Fig. 3.2 Contribution to M3 growth. *Source* Our compilation using data from NBR, Department of Statistics

condition in the economy so long as the reserve money is kept at a level consistent with desired broad money expansion. In addition, the broad monetary aggregate M3 is expected to have a strong and stable relationship with the final objective (price levels) of the monetary policy.

In practice, deviations of actual money stocks from their target values were frequently observed as NBR used strict monetary targeting regime and this is a common feature in countries using reserve money programme (IMF 2005; Maehle 2020b). These deviations can be explained by different factors such as change in money demand resulting from changes in interest rates as indicated in Eq. (3.18), issues related to liquidity forecasting, as well as forecasting of inflation and economic growth. Theoretically, deviations of M3 and base money from their targets would be fully corrected in subsequent quarters as the actual deviations would be brought back to the predetermined target path. However, in practice, the actual money growth does not tend to move so as to correct deviations from the targets, and new targets have to be set to at least partially accommodate deviations from the previous targets. In an effort of keeping base money as closer as possible to its target, NBR actively intervened on the money market to mop up liquidity.

This resulted in interest rate volatility, with significant variations in the assessment programme periods. To deal with this challenge, on one side, NBR increased its capacity to forecast the liquidity in the economy, focusing both on short-term forecasts of the autonomous liquidity factors, as well as medium-term liquidity forecasting to cover the horizon of base money target. On the other side, NBR adopted two important measures which contributed to introduce more flexibility in the reserve money programme and reduce interest rate volatility through its interventions on the money market. In 2008, NBR introduced repo operations to replace overnight facility and 7-day auctions. In addition, key repo rate (KRR) and an interbank interest rates corridor system were introduced to help commercial banks manage their liquidity. Though KRR was not used to signal the monetary policy stance,[1] NBR decided to use it as reference rate for all its operations on money market since 2012.

To introduce more flexibility, NBR abandoned the pure monetary targeting in 2012 by accepting to miss targets on reserve money as long as it remains in a band of ±2% around a central reserve money target. This significantly contributed to more flexibility in money market rates and to support NBR's effort of developing the interbank market needed for effective use of interest rate as a tool of implementing monetary policy. As shown in Table 3.2, all money market interest rates reduced between 2000–2013 and 2014–2019 and have become more stable in the last period as shown by their standard deviations.

In the two following sub-sections, we describe the behaviour of the main pillars of the monetary targeting regime: stability of money multiplier and money demand in Rwanda as well as assessing the controllability by NBR of base money, the operating target.

[1]For interest rate to signal monetary policy stance it must serve as the de facto operating target.

Table 3.2 Variation of money market rates

	2000–2013		2014–2019	
	Average	Standard deviation	Average	Standard deviation
Repo rates	6	1.1	3.8	0.97
WTB	8.3	1.9	6.5	1.38
TB4	7.5	2	5.2	1.36
TB13	8.1	2	5.8	1.55
TB26	8.4	2.2	6.7	1.46
TB52	8.3	2.2	7.8	1.33
Interbank rate	8	1.5	5.4	0.89

Source Our own calculation based on data from NBR

3.1.1 *Base Money as Operating Target*

As mentioned, one of the conditions to be fulfilled by an operating target is to be well controlled by the central bank. One of the challenges faced by NBR in using reserve money program, as it is the case in many other developing countries, is the big share of currency in circulation in the base money, which cannot be influenced by NBR interventions on money market through open market operations. For example, between 2000 and 2018, cash out banks represented on average 61.0% of the base money on monthly basis and 71.0% when including the cash held by banks in vault to meet currency demand of depositors, at the teller window or in automated teller machines (ATMs). In developing countries where a big part of payments is made by using cash and demand deposits represent important share of total deposits in the banking sector; commercial banks need larger amounts of cash in vault.

The extension of the banking sector across the country and the development of microfinance institutions contributed to reduce currency out banks as percentage of reserve money (CIC out-RM) from an average of 66.4% in the period 2000–2013 to an average of 48.5% in the period 2014–2019 which contributed to the increase in bank reserves as percentage of reserve money (BR-RM). The increase in commercial bank branches across the country has however contributed to increase in cash in vault to FRW 36.1 billion in the period 2014–2019 from FRW FR 9.0 billion in the period 2000–2013. As a result, the share of cash in vault in reserve money (CIV-RM) also increased from an average of 8.1–11.1% in the period under review. The level of cash to be held in vault by banks generally depends on the intraday profile of withdrawals and deposits, as well as the cost associated with shipments and the opportunity costs of holding cash (Fig. 3.3).

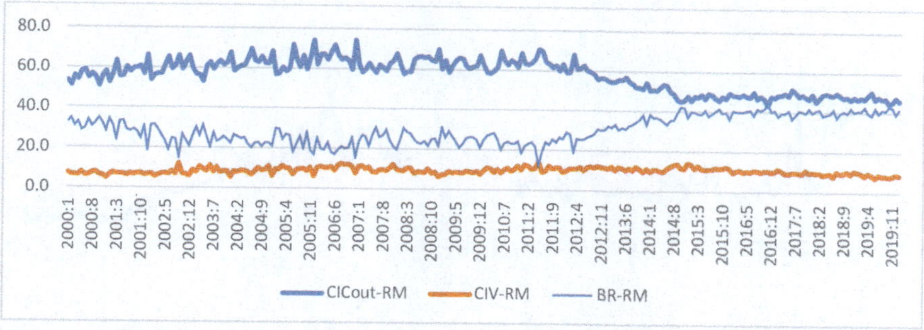

Fig. 3.3 Development of base money components (percentage share of base money)

3.1.2 Money Multiplier

The monetary targeting framework is based on the assumption that the money multiplier is stable to ensure the control of the broad money (intermediate target) by the central bank through changes in base money (the operating target). However, the stability of money multiplier is an empirical issue as it depends on the behaviour of monetary authority, commercial banks, and the public in the process of money creation. Money multiplier can change due to different factors such as change in monetary policy by the central bank or innovations in the financial sector leading to the changes in currency ratio or excess ratio, factors that determine variations in money multiplier. The use of open market operations by NBR to regulate liquidity in the market have impact on day-to-day interest rate movements, which progressively contributed to influence on the portfolio management of banks and households. In addition, the development in financial market has progressively offered to economic agents more substitute for money, such as short-term government securities. Furthermore, innovations in the banking sector by introducing new products to attract term deposits, the extension of the banking sector, high and sustainable economic growth in last decades, and stable macroeconomic environment with low and stable inflation contributed to the increase in both demand and term deposits, but with higher increase in term deposits.

These factors contributed to change in portfolio behaviour of agents. The determinants of money multiplier such as demand to time deposits and bank reserve to total deposits ratios have become more sensitive to the changes in relative rates of returns (Fig. 3.4).

To analyse the behaviour of money multiplier in Rwanda, we develop a money multiplier model for Rwanda. The model will allow to assess changes in determinants of money multiplier in Rwanda, before testing empirically its stability using cointegration framework.

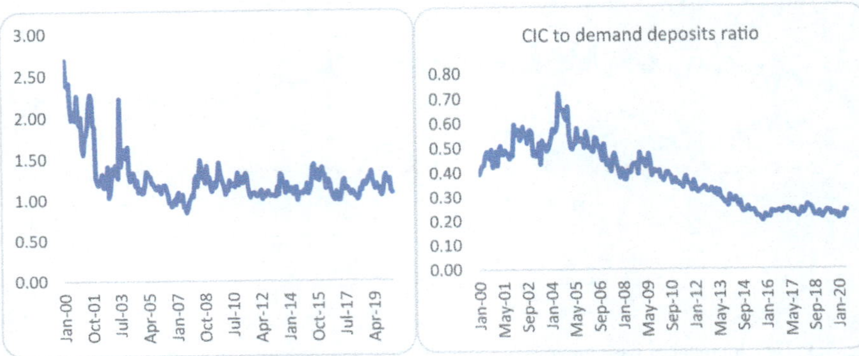

Fig. 3.4 Demand to term deposits ratio and CIC to demand deposits ratio

3.1.3 Money Multiplier Model for Rwanda

The money multiplier, denoted by K, is defined as the ratio of the money supply (M) to base money (B).[2]

$$K = \frac{M}{B} = \frac{D + F + C}{C + R} \tag{3.1}$$

where B is the base money, consisting of currency in circulation out the banking system (C) plus bank reserves with the central bank (R), including cash in vault in banks.

M is the broad money composed of currency in circulation out the banking system (C), deposits in RFW (both demand and time deposits) denoted by D, and foreign currency deposits F expressed in FRW.

R is the total bank reserves which can be divided into required reserves[3] (RR), defined by NBR as a certain fraction, called required reserve ratio, of total deposits held by banks, and the excess reserves (EX) held over this requirement.

The money multiplier becomes:

$$K = \frac{M}{B} = \frac{D + F + C}{C + RR + EX} \tag{3.2}$$

The reserve requirement is also portioned between reserve requirement on deposits in foreign currency and reserve requirement on deposits in domestic currency:

$$RR = r^d D + r^f F \tag{3.3}$$

[2]We use the word reserve money and base money interchangeably.

[3]NBR does not remunerate required reserves.

where r^d and r^f are reserve requirement ratios defined as percentage of D and F, respectively. Because foreign and domestic deposits attract the same reserve requirement ratio in Rwanda, $r^d = r^f = r$ therefore

$$RR = rD + rF = r(D + F) \tag{3.4}$$

The money multiplier becomes:

$$K = \frac{D + F + C}{C + r(D + F) + EX} \tag{3.5}$$

Dividing through by D, the money multiplier can be expressed in terms of four ratios.

$$K = \frac{1 + f + c}{c_r + r(1 + f) + e_r} \tag{3.6}$$

where

$$f = F/D;\ c_r = c/D \text{ and } er{=}EX/D \tag{3.7}$$

The first two ratios, c_r and f, describe private sector portfolio behaviour, between cash and deposits and between foreign and domestic deposits, respectively; r is a policy measure set by NBR, and e_r reflects the banks discretionary portfolio behaviour. A common way of defining the money multiplier is to calculate ratios using total deposits (TD) composed of demand deposits, term deposits, and deposits in foreign currency expressed in FRW: TD = D + F.

Equation (3.5) becomes

$$k = \frac{TD + C}{C + rTD + EX} \tag{3.8}$$

Dividing through by TD, the money multiplier becomes:

$$k = \frac{1 + c_r}{c_r + r + e_r} \tag{3.9}$$

Thus, the money multiplier is a function of three ratios: c_r, currency ratios describing the behaviour of depositors; the excess reserves ratio, e_r reflecting the behaviour of commercial banks, and the reserve requirement ratio, r, set by NBR. Based on Eq. (3.9), changes in the two variables, namely the currency ratio and the excess reserve ratio (given that the reserve requirement ratio does not change regularly), in addition to the base money, can account for all changes in the money supply.

Any bank will hold excess reserve so that an unexpected loss of reserves, for example from a large unexpected cash withdraw, will not leave the bank with total

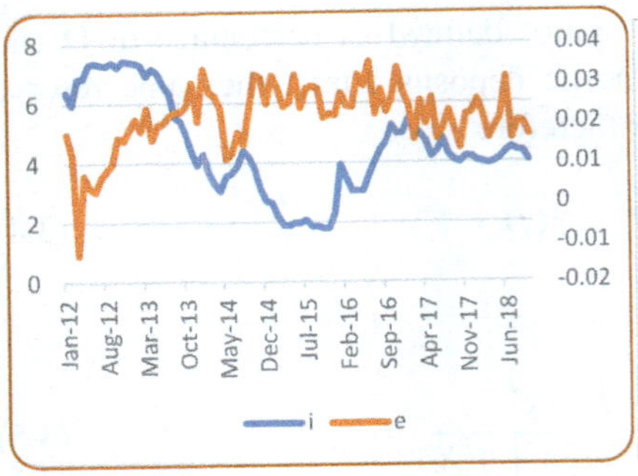

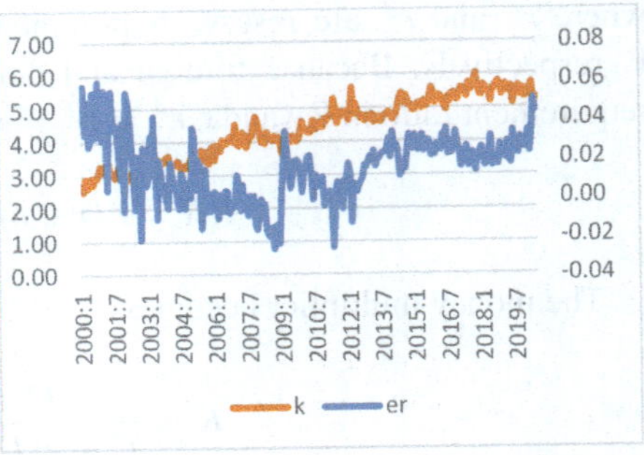

Fig. 3.5 Excess ratio (er) and repo rates (i), money multiplier (k) and excess reserve

reserves below the minimum required reserve. However, each FRW of excess reserve is costly to the bank because excess reserves are not remunerated. The higher the money market rates (i), which is the opportunity cost of holding each FRW of excess reserve, the higher is the cost of each FRW of excess reserves. Therefore, for a bank, holding excess liquidity is associated with opportunity cost, and the interest (i) could be earned on securities or investment in central instruments. Thus, the banking system's excess reserves ratio (er) is negatively related to the market rate (i).

$$e(i) = \frac{ER}{TD} \text{ is such } e^{'}(i) \prec 0 \tag{3.10}$$

As it can be seen in Eq. (3.6), the money multiplier is negatively related to r and (er), for example, any increase in r (or in er) or other factors remaining the same will lead to a decrease in money multiplier. Figure 3.5 shows a negative relationship between (er) and repo rates (i).[4]

Because total reserves (TR) are composed of required reserves (RR) which are proportional to total deposits (TD) and excess reserves (ER), the reserve to deposit ratios (rr) is:

$$rr = \frac{TR}{TD} = \frac{RR + ER}{TD} = \frac{RR}{TD} + \frac{ER}{TD} = r + e_r \prec 1 \tag{3.11}$$

As long as $r + e_r \prec 1$, an increase in c_r ratio in (3.9) will raise the denominator of the money multiplier proportionality by more than it raises the numerator. This will cause the money multiplier to fall. Thus, the money multiplier is negatively related to the currency ratio (c_r). In Rwanda, the currency ratio has been declining, due to various factors such as financial sector development, high and sustainable economic performance, stable inflation, and extension of the banking sector across the country (Fig. 3.6).

---

[4]Money market rates (interbank and treasury bill rates) are highly and positively correlated with repo rates (see, e.g. Kigabo 2019).

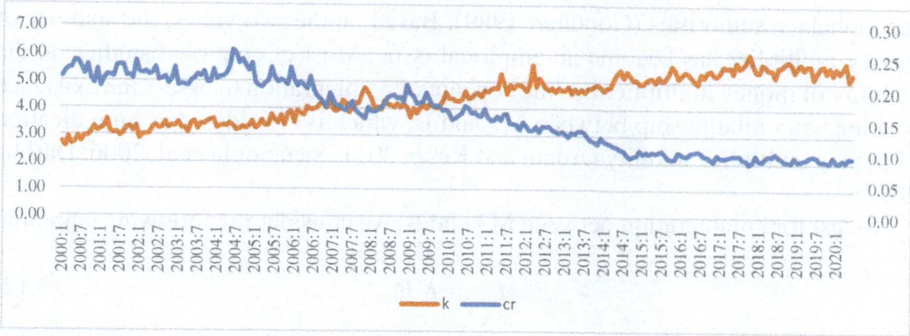

Fig. 3.6 Development in currency ratio (c_r) and money multiplier (k)

3.1.4 *Stability of Money Multiplier*

The analysis of the evolution of M3 and B shows that in short term, variations in money supply and base money were in opposite directions; 44.9% of times between January 2000 and December 2018 (see Fig. 3.7), implying that changes in M3 during those periods were due to change in money multiplier which was not stable in short term. The variations in money multiplier (ΔMM) were higher than those in money stock (ΔM). On monthly basis, ΔM fluctuated between -7.7% and 9.9% with a standard deviation of 2.6, while ΔMM fluctuated between -14.3% and 14.7% with 5.1% as standard deviation and variations in base money (ΔB) fluctuated between -11.4% and 18.5% with 5.2 as standard deviation.

For advocates of money multiplier approach, while in short run the variations in money multiplier may dominate the variations in money stock due to change in public and banks' behaviour, these variations become relatively stable and predictable in long run (Brunner and Metzler 1964). Non-monetarist, however, argues that with the increasing role of market forces in the financial transactions and continuous improvement in asset/liability management, there is very little reason to believe on the stability of money multiplier and the controllability of the monetary base by

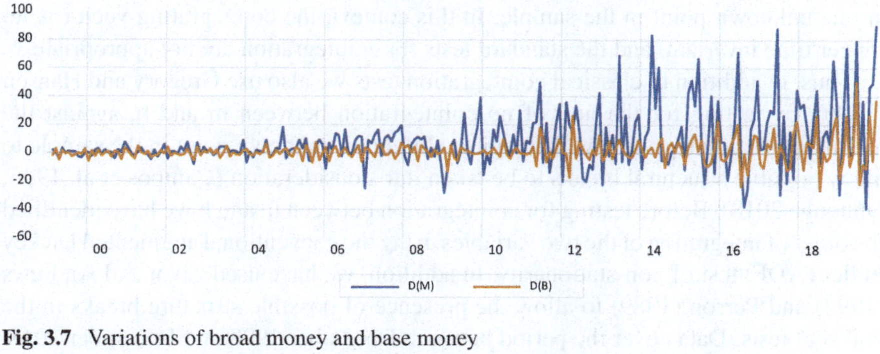

Fig. 3.7 Variations of broad money and base money

the monetary authorities (Goodhart 1989). Based on the two views, the stability of money multiplier has become an empirical issue. Most of empirical studies on the stability of money multiplier use the concept of cointegration to assess the existence of a long-run relationship between M3 and B, which is considered as an indication of money multiplier stability (Adam and Kessy 2011; Saatcioglu et al. 2006; Darbha 2002).

To test for cointegration between M3 and B, we consider the following equation:

$$M_{3t} = K B_t \tag{3.12}$$

This equation indicates that the money stock is in proportion with money base, with K, the proportionality factor called money multiplier. In logarithm form, the money multiplier model can be written as follows:

$$m_t = \beta_0 + \beta_1 b_t + \varepsilon_t \tag{3.13}$$

where m is the logarithm of M3, b the logarithm of B, β_0 is the logarithm of K, and ε the error term.

Most of recent studies have used conventional cointegration tests such as Johansen and Juselius (1990) and the Engle (Engle and Granger 1987) two-step method to test for cointegration between M3 and B (Adam et al. 2011; Baghestania and Mottb 1997). In this approach, if the money multiplier is stable, there must be a long-run relationship (cointegration) between money stock and reserve money and this relation should be time invariant. Assuming a time invariant structural relationship between m and b in Rwanda may be very restrictive, particularly when possible structural changes may have occurred in one or the two variables due to different changes adopted in reserve money programme as well as the development in financial sector. In that case, traditional cointegration tests such as Johansen and Engle Granger tests have low power to not reject the null of no cointegration. Indeed, a linear combination of non-stationary variables may be stationary, but this linear combination may have shifted at one point in the sample. As shown by Gregory and Hansen (1996), two non-stationary series may be cointegrated in the sense of their linear combination, but with the possibility that the cointegrating vector (linear combination) has shifted at one unknown point in the sample. In this context, the cointegrating vector is no longer time invariant, and the standard tests for cointegration are not appropriate.

Thus, in addition to classical cointegration tests we also use Gregory and Hansen (1996), by testing for the null of no cointegration between m and b, against the alternative of cointegration with a regime shift at an unknown point in the sample to allow possible structural breaks to be taken into consideration (Campos et al. 1996; Onuonga 2018). Before testing for cointegration between m and b we have identified the order of integration of the two variables using the conventional augmented Dickey Fuller (ADF) test of non-stationarity. In addition, we have used Zivot and Andrews (1992) and Perron (1989) to allow the presence of possible structure breaks in the unit root tests. Data cover the period between December 1998 and December 2018. The three tests show that the two variables are I (1) (Table 3.3).

Table 3.3 Tests of unit root

Zivot and Andrew (The critical value for Zivot and Andrew test, and Perron test are −4.93 and −5.23, respectively, at 5%)		Perron	Zivot and Andrew	Perron	ADF	ADF
Variables levels			Fist differences levels			Fist differences
M	−4.36	−4.05	−7.59	−17.05	0.26 (0.9)	−16.6 (0.000)
B	−4.36	−4.12	−11.6	−11.7	1.01 (0.99	−10.8 (0.00)

We then test for cointegration using Engle-Granger tests. Results reported in Table 3.4 indicate that the test fails to reject the null hypothesis of absence of cointegration between m and b as the probabilities associated to tau-statistic and z-statistic are less than 5%. This indicates that there exists a long-run relationship between the two variables, which confirms the stability of the money multiplier in Rwanda.

The estimated long-run relationship is:

$$m_t = 0.05 + 1.29b_t \tag{3.14}$$

However, as indicated, Engle-Granger tests assume time variant long-run relationship between the broad money m and the base money b. For detailed information about the estimation method, please see also Arellano and Bond (1991), Favero (2001), Kashyap and Stein (1995), Kashyap and Stein (2000), Charry et al. (2014), Taylor (2000). The following graph on the development of m and b shows a possible structure break in 2010 to be confirmed using more elaborated statistic tests.

The results presented in Table 3.5 show that Chow breakpoint test (break period 2010:10) rejects the null hypothesis that the cointegrating vector is stable overtime. The test statistics are greater than critical value as indicated by the probability of F and Chi-square tests which are less than 5%.

Table 3.4 Engle-Granger cointegration test

Engle-Granger cointegration test		
	Value	Probability
Engle-Granger tau statistic	−3.92	0.011
Engle-Granger Z-statistic	−31.8	0.003

Table 3.5 Chow breakpoint test: 2010M10

Null hypothesis: No breaks at specified breakpoints Varying regressors: All equation variables
Equation sample: 1998M12 2018M12

F-statistic	15.68244	Prob. F(2,237)	0.0000
Log likelihood ratio	29.95326	Prob. Chi-square(2)	0.0000
Wald statistic	31.36487	Prob. Chi-square(2)	0.0000

Table 3.6 Gregory–Hansen cointegration test

Gregory–Hansen cointegration test		
Model break	Z_t—stat	Break
Model with level shift 2010:11	ADF procedure	−5.9*
2010: 10	Phillips procedure	−8.6*
Model with level shift with trend 2010:10	ADF procedure	−5.6*
2010: 10	Phillips procedure	−81*
Model with regime shift 2010:10	ADF procedure	−6.01*
2010:10	Phillips procedure	−8.6*

*Significant at 5%. Critical values for the test at 5% of significance are: −5.5, −4.9, and −4.61 for the three models

This result is confirmed by the Gregory–Hansen test (Table 3.6) which rejects the null of no cointegration against the alternative of cointegration with structural break at 5% level of significance. This test has the advantage compared to Chow test as it allows for an endogenous regime change, where structure break time is not known a priori. We consider three cases: the model with level shift; model with level shift with trend; and model with regime shift. The results of Gregory–Hansen cointegration test indicate that there exist a stable, but time-varying long-run relationship between broad money (m) and reserve money (b) in Rwanda, which has important implication on the use of reserve money programme.

From the above analysis, it appears that the controllability of base money by NBR was very limited, constraining the efficiency of reserve money programme. This was due to the big share of currency in circulation in the base money, which cannot be influenced by NBR monetary policy instruments. About the stability of money multiplier, which is key for the management of the overall liquidity in the economy through changes in base money, the analysis shows that in short term, the money multiplier is not stable weakening the link between M3 and B. In the long run, however, the money multiplier appears to be stable, as the two variables, M3 and B are cointegrated, but the cointegrating vector has shifted towards the end of 2010 complicating the use of reserve money programme.

3.1.5 *The Money Demand*

In the previous section, we have described the process of money creation in the economy, which indicates the factors that influence the quantity of money in the economy, and the role played by the supply of money in explaining the way monetary policy affects the economy. Another essential component of monetary policy using reserve money programme is the stability of money demand. As pointed out, to avoid significant deviations in outcomes of inflation and economic growth compared to their targets, NBR interventions on money market between 1997 and 2018 are aimed at keeping money supply close to its estimated demand level. This requires a good estimation of the money demand in the economy, which is supposed to be stable and predictable.

If the money demand function is unstable and experiences large unpredictable shifts, the velocity of money becomes unpredictable, weakening the link between the quantity of money and aggregate spending (MV = PY). Indeed, explaining nominal income by changes in M suppose that the velocity of money is reasonable constant (Fisher 1911) or grows at some rate overtime (Mishkin 2007). According to Irvin Fisher, as the quantity of money in circulation increases, the price level also increases in direct proportion, and the other things remaining unchanged as it can be seen in the equation of exchange $M\bar{V} = P\bar{Y}$. Considering that the velocity ($\bar{V}$) is constant and the level of transactions ($\bar{Y}$) is given, changes in the quantity of money (M) will lead to proportional changes in the price (P). For Fisher, the velocity of money is considered as stable because its main determinants such as size and habits of population, trade activities, interest rates change vary slowly over time. In addition, the volume of transactions, linked to production is determined independent of the stock of nominal money in the long run, and its key drivers such as capital, labour, and technology also change slowly over time.

However, assuming the velocity of money as a constant number is both unnecessary and incorrect. What is required is that the growth rate of velocity of money be relatively stable so that the relative growth rates of money and prices reflect the relative difference between the growth rates of velocity and real output in the long run. From the equation of exchange, we have $\Delta P = \Delta M + (\Delta V - \Delta Y)$. If ΔV and ΔY, variations of velocity of money and real output, respectively, are approximately equal on average, then the rate of inflation will be approximately equal to the growth rate of money. As indicated in Fig. 3.8, the velocity of money in Rwanda cannot be viewed as constant. There exist large differences in the annual growth rates of the velocity of money between 1998 and 2019 and it was more volatile in recent years. Year on year percentage change in velocity of money fluctuated between −18.8%

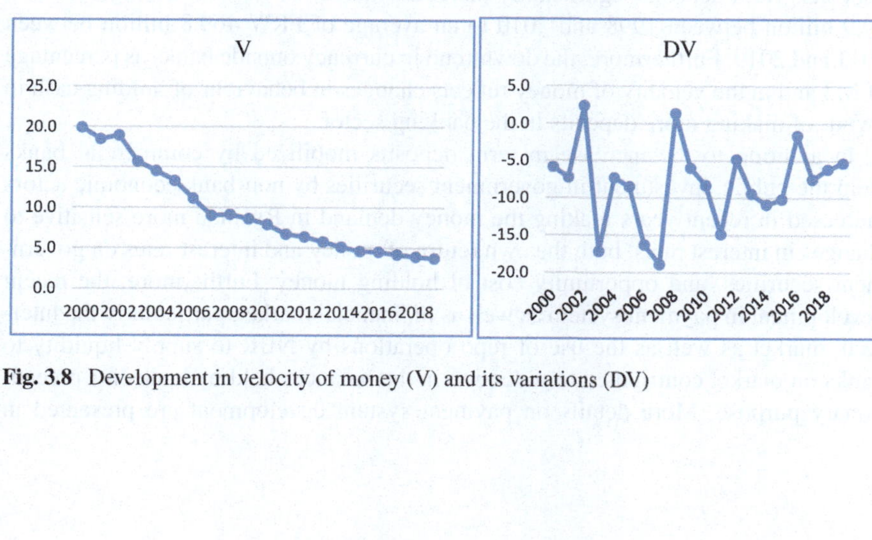

Fig. 3.8 Development in velocity of money (V) and its variations (DV)

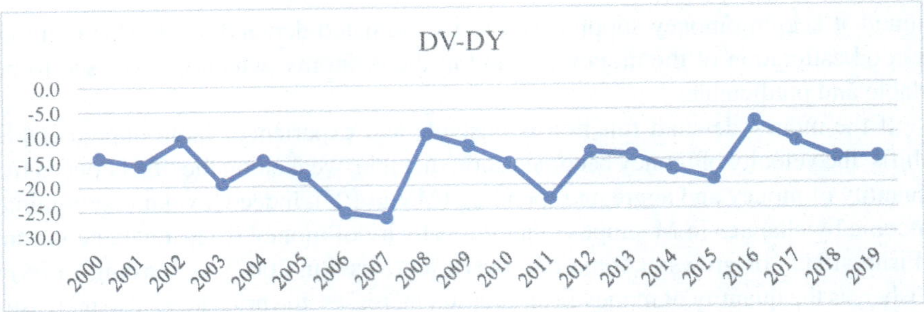

Fig. 3.9 Development in the difference between DV and DY

and 2.5%, in the period under review. In addition, its average percentage change was −4% between 2010 and 2019 against only −0.9% between 1997 and 2009.

Furthermore, as it can be seen in Fig. 3.9, variations of velocity of money and real output (DY) are significantly different. The average growth rates of real GDP and velocity of money were 7.7% and −8.1% between 2000 and 2019 and the variability of velocity of money was much higher than the variability of real GDP; their standard deviations are 6.5 and 2.5, respectively, in the period under review. In this situation, it is not relevant to assume that the rate of inflation will be approximately equal to the growth rate of money. As implication in monetary policy management, setting rigid money supply targets in order to control aggregate spending (PY) in the economy may not be an effective way to conduct monetary policy, and thus the monetary aggregate will no longer provide an adequate signal about the stance of monetary policy.

In addition, the interest sensitivity of M3 has been increasing over time as Rwandans were interested to save their money in the banking sector. This was supported by the development in financial innovation, including the introduction of new financial products such as deposits that combined savings and transactions features, which helped economic actors to reduce the holding of non-interest-bearing demand deposits. Term deposits significantly increase since 2010 from an average of FRW 79.9 billion between 1998 and 2010 to an average of FRW 469.8 billion between 2011 and 2019. Furthermore, the downtrend in currency outside banks as percentage of M3 and in the velocity of money reflects changes in behaviour of holding cash in favour of making more deposits in the banking sector.

In addition to the increase in term deposits mobilized by commercial banks from the public, investment in government securities by non-bank economic actors increased in recent years making the money demand in Rwanda more sensitive to changes in interest rates, both the own return of money and interest rates on government securities, and opportunity cost of holding money. Furthermore, the recent development in payment system as well as in financial market, particularly the interbank market as well as the use of repo operations by NBR to supply liquidity to banks on market contributed to reduction in the balances held by banks for precautionary purpose. More details on payment system development are presented in

Table 3.7 Mobile and internet banking developments

Mobile banking				Internet banking		
Period	Number of subscribers	Number of transactions	Value in FRW million	Number of subscribers	Number of transactions	Value in FRW million
2010	n/a	n/a	n/a	n/a	n/a	n/a
2011	155,986	527,300	5,215	n/a ·	1,493	708
2012	297,537	1,458,063	3,926	3,411	10,036	12,746
2013	412,007	2,538,820	17,459	8,969	89,260	117,147
2014	659,712	4,637,849	41,281	29,840	312,264	332,959
2015	828,799	5,617,368	48,309	36,597	556,152	581,163
2016	980,671	3,906,642	37,164	43,047	460,363	1,014,077
2017	1,158,944	3,082,829	35,849	52,020	339,522	1,418,693
2018	1,845,584	3,206,474	53,287	85,697	769,517	2,027,789
2019	2,065,624	1,999,250	85,462	91,825	1,352,301	2,276,446

Source NBR, Payment system department

Appendix 3.1. All these developments may have contributed to the instability of money demand in Rwanda due to increased focus on changes in interest rates in the portfolio management by economic actors (Table 3.7).

This section formally analyses the behaviour of money demand in Rwanda, focusing on its stability, which is one of the two assumptions of monetary targeting regime. A stable money demand function is the core in conduct of monetary policy as it enables changes in monetary aggregates resulting from central banks' actions to have predictable effects on interest rates, output and ultimately on price. Owing to its importance in the conduct of monetary policy, a steady stream of theoretical and empirical research has been conducted over the past decades in different countries.

3.1.6 Estimation of Money Demand Function in Rwanda

Most of empirical research on money demand used partial adjustment models up to the 1980s. In that analytical framework, demand for money is thought to be function of scale variable and a vector of variables measuring the opportunity costs of holding money. In addition, it was considered that due to adjustment costs, it was necessary to take into consideration the lag necessary for the desired level of holdings to match the actual level. However, in the 1970s money demand function revealed instability due to financial innovation and also the weakness in the way the partial adjustment is modelled.

To deal with the two sources of instability, on one side different scale variables were used to take into consideration the impact of financial innovation in the definition of monetary aggregates. On the other side, to overcome theoretical and econometric problems associated with the partial adjustment models, error correction models were developed and used. The important feature of those models is the possibility of taking into consideration the time series characteristics of data to describe short-term dynamics around the long run equilibrium defined by economic theory (Kigabo 2011; Calza et al. 2001; Sriram 2001).

Generally, empirical analysis of money demand focuses on the transactions and asset theories. The transactions theory considers money functioning as a medium of exchange and is held as a store for transaction purposes. Asset theories consider the demand for money in border senses as part of a problem of allocating wealth among a portfolio of assets which include money, by focusing on liquidity and safety that money implicitly provides in addition to explicit income generated by the portfolio. Taking into consideration the two theories, money demand is generally specified with two main sets of explanatory variables: scale variables and measures of opportunity cost to hold money.

$$(M) = f(y, p, R) \tag{3.15}$$

where M is the demand for nominal money balances; P is the price levels; Y is scale variable and R is a vector of expected rates of return including both the return of money and opportunity cost of holding money.

Many empirical researches assume the price homogeneity in the money demand function and specify the long-run real money demand function. Because our analysis aims at assessing the effectiveness of monetary policy in Rwanda using reserve money programme, we do not assume the price homogeneity, rather we test a long-run unity elasticity of the nominal cash balances with respect to the price level. This is important as it allows deciding if the money demand function will be specified as nominal or real money balances. The latter means that the demand for money is primarily demand for real cash balances which assumes the absence of money illusion[5] and that an increase in the general level of prices will induce a proportionate increase in the nominal demand for money, leaving the level of real balances unchanged.

As money stock, we use the broad money M3 (denoted by M in the equation) which has been used as intermediate target in the reserve money programme. Income, financial wealth, and real GDP are key scale variables used in different theories of money demand. We use real GDP (Y) as scale variable to measure transaction relating to the economic activity, as it is the practice in the majority of empirical studies of money demand due to challenges associated with measurement of income and financial wealth. About the choice of the opportunity cost of holding money, two elements are taken into consideration in the literature: the deposit rate as the own return of money and the rate of return on assets alternative to money. We use short-term rates on government securities (T-bill rates) because these instruments can be considered as closer substitutes for money in Rwanda. Treasury bills have the

[5]Money illusion means that many people have an illusory picture of their wealth and income based on nominal quantity of money, rather than in real terms (in terms of quantity of goods and services which can be bought by the quantity of money at prevailing prices in the market).

Table 3.8 Order of integration of variables

	Level	First differences	Conclusion
LM	−1.32	−3.35*	I(1)
LP	−1.86	−8.36*	I(1)
Lry	−0.81	−8.36*	I(1)
Le	1.4	−3.74*	I(1)
TB-DR	−2.84	−6.32*	I(1)

same maturities than deposits in the banking system: 1, 3, 6, and 12 months. In our analysis, we include both the weighted deposit rate (DR) as own rate of return of money and weighted T-bill rate (TB) as rate of return on assets alternative to money.

The inclusion of the two variables in the money demand function is important because the omission of own rate of money often leads to break down of the estimated money demand function, especially when the economy is experiencing financial innovation. Concretely, we use the spread between TB and DR to measure the sensitivity of the money demand to changes in treasury bill rates compared to deposit rates. We also include the FRW exchange rate vis-à-vis the USD (E) to capture the fact that foreign assets are part of the portfolio as the Rwandan economy is open but also because we are interested with the demand for money M3 which includes deposits in foreign currencies, mainly USD but expressed in Rwandan Franc (FRW). The function f is supposed to increase in both Y and return of money, and decrease in rates of return on alternative assets to hold money. More formally, the long-run money demand function is specified in the following (semi) log linear form:

$$m_t = \alpha_0 + \alpha_1 y_t + \alpha_2 p_t + \alpha_3 e_t + \alpha_4 (TB - DR)_t + \varepsilon_t \tag{3.16}$$

Variables in lower case denote natural logarithms and ε_t is the error term.

We use quarterly data covering the period 2006–2018.

Before testing the existence of long-run relationship between the six variables, we determine their order of integration using augmented Dickey Fuller (ADF) test. The results presented in the Table 3.8 show that all variables are I(1).

We use the Johansen procedure based on a first-order[6] vector autoregression (VAR) based on Eq. (3.16). Both trace and maximum eigenvalue tests have identified one cointegrating relationship. We report here in Table 3.9 the results from trace test which is considered in empirical literature as more robust in the presence of either skewness or excess kurtosis (Cheung and Lai 1993).

The hypothesis of unitary income elasticity is not rejected with $\chi^2(1) = 0.40$ (p = 0.53), indicating that in the period under review, changes in real income have been inducing a proportionate increase in the demand for real broad money on average. As a consequence, we adopt the following money demand function as demand for real money balances:

[6]Information criteria have identified one as lag to be used in the VAR.

Table 3.9 Johansen test for cointegration rank test (Trace)

H0: rank = r	Eigenvalue	Trace statistic	0.05 Critical value	Prob.**
r = 0	0.652234	88.1*	63.9	0.0001
$r \leq 1$	0.304260	36.3	42.99	0.1936
$r \leq 2$	0.205153	18. 6	25.9	0.3064
$r \leq 3$	0.138900	7.3	12.5	0.3116

* Means rejection of null hypothesis at 5% significant level

$$(m - p)_t = \beta_0 + \beta_1 y_t + \beta_2 e_t + \beta_3 (TB - DR)_t + \varepsilon_t \tag{3.17}$$

The estimated long-run money demand shows that money holding in Rwanda results from portfolio management decisions at some extent in addition to transaction motives. All coefficients in the model are statistically significant from zero at 5%.

$$m_t = -10.1 + 1.1 y_t + 0.7 e_t - 0.02(TB - DR)_t \tag{3.18}$$

3.1.7 *Stability of Money Demand in Rwanda*

Using the quantity theory of money which is also the theory of demand for money, we have shown how the nominal value of aggregate income is determined and how much money is held for a given amount of aggregate income. This theory suggests that interest rates have no effect on the demand for money.

The equation $M = \frac{1}{V} PY$ tells us how much money is held for a given amount of aggregate income (PY). When the money market is in equilibrium, the quantity of money M hold is equal to the quantity of money demanded M^d so that $M^d = \frac{1}{V} PY = kPY$ with $k = \frac{1}{V}$ a constant. This shows that the demand for money is purely a function of income, and interest rates have no effect on the demand for money. In his theory of liquidity preference, John Maynard Keynes (1936) identified three motives of holding money: the transactions motive, the precautionary motive, and the speculative motive. Based on the three motives, Keynes main contribution was to show the important role of interest rate in the demand for money. Considering money as a store of wealth, Keynes analyses the factors that influence the decisions regarding how much money to hold as a store of wealth. Decomposing the assets into two categories: money and bonds Keynes showed that people would want to hold money if its expected return was greater than the expected return from holding bonds (i). The liquidity preference function can be presented as follows: $\frac{M^d}{P} = f(i, Y)$ with the demand for money negatively related to the interest rate i, and positively related to real income Y. The liquidity preference equation can be rewritten as $\frac{P}{M^d} = \frac{1}{f(i,Y)}$ or $V = \frac{PY}{M} = \frac{Y}{f(i,Y)}$. The equation shows that the velocity of money cannot be considered as constant because it depends on interest rates which fluctuate substantially over time.

By pursuing the question of why people choose to hold money, Friedman applied the theory of asset demand to money and show that the demand for money should be a function of wealth and the expected returns on other assets relative to the expected return on money. Friedman expressed his formulation of the demand for money as follows:

$$\frac{M^d}{P} = f(Y_p, r_b - r_m, r_e - r_m, \text{inf}^e - r_m), \tag{3.19}$$

M^d/P is the demand for real money balances; Y_p is the permanent income; r_m is the expected return on money; r_b is the expected return on bonds; r_e is the expected return on equity, and inf^e is the expected inflation rate. Friedman's theory suggests that changes in interest rates should have little effect on the demand for money because the differences between returns on other assets relative to the expected return on money as defined in the money demand function are expected to be constant. In this case, the money demand function depends essentially on permanent income so that the velocity of money $V = \frac{Y}{f(Yp)}$ is constant. This analysis clearly shows that the stability of velocity of money is an empirical issue. In our specification of the money demand function, variables (rates of return) other than the real GDP have been used. As shown in Fig. 3.10, the difference between return on treasury bill rates and deposit rates (SP = TB-DR) has significantly changed over time, fluctuating between −4.8% and 3.8% with 1.7 as standard deviation between January 2008 and December 2019. This is a clear indication of the instability of velocity of money in Rwanda.

Furthermore, we test the stability of parameters in the demand function using CUSUM test introduced by Brown et al. (1975) and largely used it in empirical studies on the stability of money demand (Bahmani-Oskooee and Bohl 2000). The CUSUM test is based on the cumulative sum of the recursive residuals based on the first set of n observations, updated recursively and plotted against the break points. A similar procedure is used when carrying out the CUSUMSQ test, which is based on the squared recursive residuals. If the plot of CUSUM or CUSUMQ stays within a

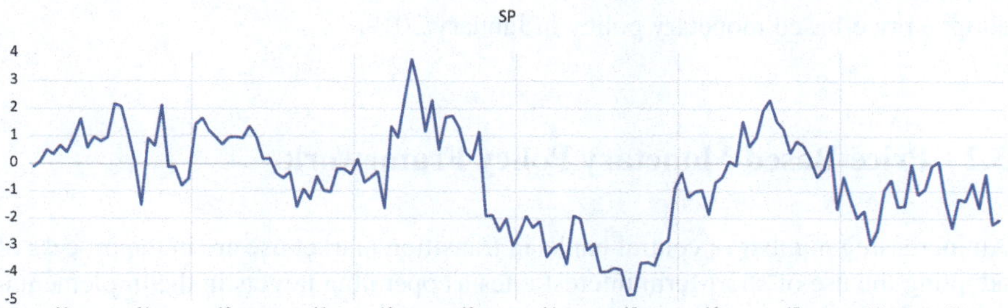

Fig. 3.10 Spread between weighted treasury bill rates and weighted deposit rates

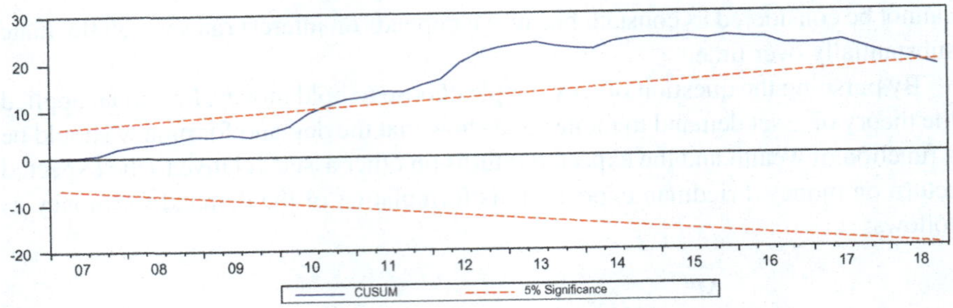

Fig. 3.11 Stability of money demand

5% significance level (as portrayed by two straight lines), then the estimated regression coefficients are generally stable over the sample period. Figure 3.11 presents a graphical representation of the CUSUM tests of the recursive residuals and show that coefficients in money demand in Rwanda are unstable since 2010.

As discussed in this chapter, the money multiplier and money demand in Rwanda became unstable in recent years due to developments in the financial system, limiting the effectiveness of the reserve money programme used by NBR to implement its monetary policy. The instability of the money demand weakens the relationship between monetary aggregates and goal variables, which are inflation and nominal income. This implies that managing liquidity in the banking sector to achieve target on monetary aggregates may not produce the desired outcome for a goal variable such as inflation. Thus, the reserve money programme was no longer an appropriate framework for NBR in designing and implementing monetary policy.

Considering the weakness in the monetary targeting framework, NBR started preparatory works necessary for the adoption of a price-based monetary policy, including the development of money market, particularly interbank market, the development of a clear communication strategy to increase transparency and accountability of the bank, the improvement of the decision-making process by establishing an information inclusive strategy in which many variables and not just monetary aggregates are used in making decisions about monetary policy stance, and internal capacity in modelling and forecasting. Details on forecasting models in NBR are presented in Appendix 3.2. Success achieved in those areas influenced the decision of NBR to adopt a price-based monetary policy in January 2019.

3.2 Price-Based Monetary Policy Framework

An increasing number of central banks in transition market use are in the process of adopting the use of short-term interest rates as operating targets in the implementation of their monetary policies due to the disconnect between monetary aggregates and nominal income. In this framework, central banks target the domestic price of money, which through a broad transmission mechanism influences inflation, the ultimate goal of monetary policy. For central banks, using short-term interest rates as operating target has advantages compared to monetary targets because interest rates are well understood by the public, making easy the communication to the public by central banks. A price-based monetary policy to be successful; central banks have to be independent and committed to only target inflation. In addition to the two conditions, central banks must have established medium-term explicit quantitative targets or benchmarks for inflation; set up a framework for inflation forecasting based on a number of indicators, including information on future inflation; and define a clear forward-looking operating procedure in which monetary policy instruments are adjusted to hit the chosen target. Furthermore, central banks must have minimum technical and institutional capacity to model and forecast inflation, to estimate the appropriate lags in monetary transmission mechanism and to evaluate the relative effectiveness of various instruments of monetary policy at their disposal.

Another important element for the effectiveness of price-based monetary policy is the transparency and predictability of central banks' actions to help economic agents forming their expectations. In particular, consumption and investment decisions depend on private expectations regarding future central banks decisions on interest rates. Thus, the effectiveness of a price-based monetary policy will depend on how change in policy rate will influence market expectations about the future path of both short and long-term interest rates. In short term, financial markets need to correctly anticipate the next monetary policy decision of a central bank. Thus, to ensure the appropriateness of monetary policy decisions towards achieving the price stability objective, financial market and the public at large have to be in a position to predict the broader picture course of monetary policy (Krueger and Kuttner 1996; Poole and Rasche 2000; Kuttner 2001; Blattner et al. 2008).

NBR adopted the price-based monetary policy in January 2019, after a decade of preparation, focusing on money market development, particularly the interbank market; banking sector liquidity forecasting; building capacity of NBR staff in modelling and forecasting; in monetary policy operations, and improvement in monetary policy decision-making process, as well as in monetary policy communication. In the new framework, NBR uses the central bank rate (CBR, previously called KRR) to signal its monetary policy stance and its focus is to align CBR with interbank market rates to anchor short-term interest rates. As implication, the monetary transmission mechanism can be presented as follows: from changes in CBR to changes in money market rates (interbank rates, repo rates, and treasury bill rates), then from changes in money market rates to changes in market rates (deposit rates and lending rates), finally from changes in market rates to inflation, though they impact on aggregate demand in the economy. The new framework adopted by NBR is expected to enhance the role of price (particularly interest rates) signals in the economy, which improves saving mobilization and strengthen their market allocation.

To ensure the transparency and predictability of its monetary policy actions, NBR sets and communicated its medium benchmark of inflation at 5%. However, to take into consideration other factors contributing to price changes in Rwanda than monetary policy, NBR announced that it will adjust the level of CBR to change its monetary policy stance aiming at keeping monetary conditions in the economy consistent with the inflation objective of keeping inflation in ±3 around the 5% headline inflation benchmark band, while allowing it to converge to the medium benchmark of 5% (Figs. 3.12 and 3.13).

In the last five years, important development was observed on the money market. Transactions in interbank market increased significantly amounting FRW 512 billion between 2012 and 2014 and FRW 3.498 trillion between 2015 and 2019, which is an increase of 583%. Similarly, the number of transactions more than tripled to 1,713 from 439 in the period under review. The development is contributing to the financing of short and medium-term positions of banks and facilitates the mitigation of their business liquidity risk, smoothen financial intermediation, and boosts the lending to the economy. By playing its role of return from holding liquidity, the interbank rate influences the bank's portfolio decision for holding short-term liquid and long-term illiquid assets, progressively making the interbank market the first link of liquidity trading in the economy and the transparent price setting mechanism.

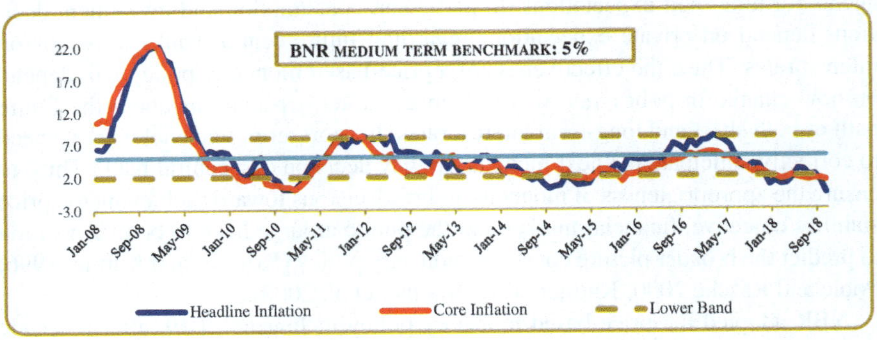

Fig. 3.12 Inflation band: 5% with a band of ± 3%

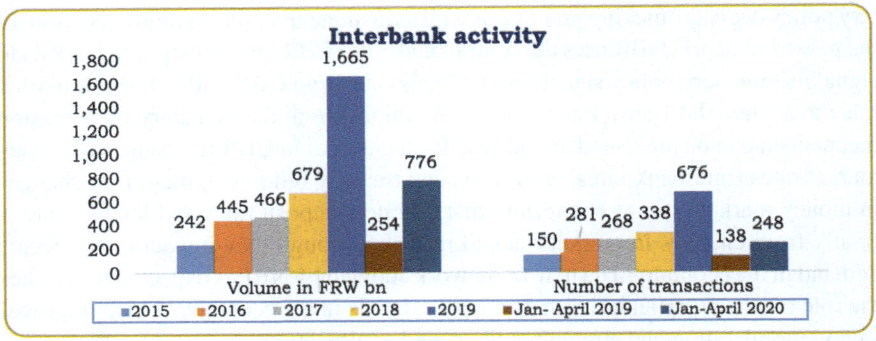

Fig. 3.13 Interbank activities. *Source* Our own compilation using data from NBR, financial market department

Money market is expected to continue playing an important role in signalling the stance of the NBR monetary policy and in transmitting effect of monetary policy decision to financial market in general with implication on private sector' spending and saving decisions and ultimately to the determination of the price level in the economy. It is expected that participants in money market will progressively build their capacity to anticipate future monetary policy decisions and build expectations about the future path of the very short-term interest rates, which will contribute to the formation of longer maturity interest rates and yields that are key for spending and saving decisions. Ultimately, by affecting aggregate demand through the link between short-term and long-term interest rates, the control of inflation by NBR will improve.

For consistency between policy signal and interventions on money market, day-to-day operations target short-term interest rates to ensure that they remain closer to CBR. This contributed to the stability and predictability of short-term interest rates to support commercial banks to place surplus of their liquidity with, and obtain short-term funding from each other or the central bank in a predictable way. Money market rates become less volatile in recent period (2015–2019), compared to the period 2012–2014. Measured by standard deviation, volatility in repo rates reduced significantly by 71.4% from 2.1 between 2012 and 2014 to 0.6 between 2015 and 2018, while it reduced by 80.8% from 2.6 to 0.5 for the interbank rates in the period under review. The same trend was observed in treasury bills rates, for all maturities (Table 3.10).

In addition, the stability and predictability of short-term interest rates and development in money market have been contributing to improve the transmission mechanism of monetary policy impulses, particularly from CBR to interbank rate and to other money market rates as it will be shown in Chap. 4. The day-to-day interventions on money market is facilitated by the improved capacity of the bank staff in liquidity forecasting, contributing to adequately assess the scope, timing and size of interventions on money market. While participants in money market (banks and non-banks investors) independently decide whether or not to exchange cash or short-term financial instruments, central bank can influence their decisions by properly managing liquidity and collaborate with money market participants such as treasurers of commercial banks (Fig. 3.14).

Table 3.10 Money market rates variability: Changes in standard deviation

	Repo rates	Weighted treasury bill rates	4-Week treasury bill rate	13-Week treasury bill rate	26-Week-treasury bill rate	52-Week treasury bill rate	Interbank rate
2012–2014	1.7	2.7	2.9	3.0	2.9	2.5	2.2
2015–2018	1.1	1.6	1.6	1.8	1.7	1.5	1.1
Percentage change	−34.0	−41.0	−45.4	−40.3	−41.7	−38.4	−50.8

Source NBR, Financial market department

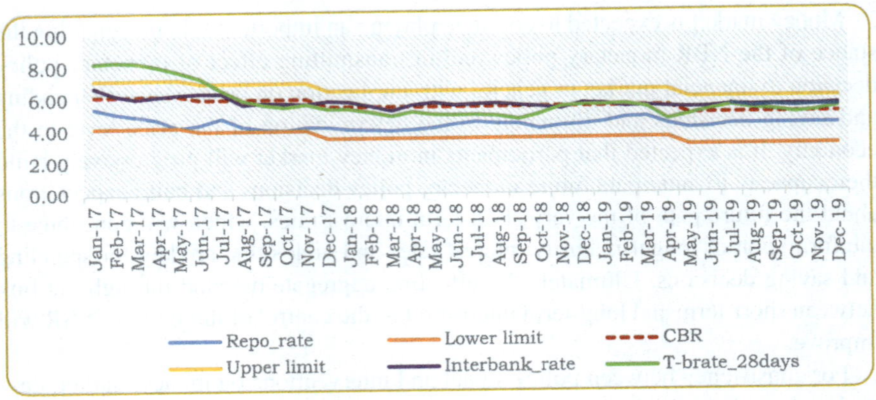

Fig. 3.14 Money market rates development

To ensure appropriate interventions on money market, the Financial Market Operation Committee (FMOC) was formed in 2018 and members of the committee meet every working day from 9 am to 10 am to intervene on money market guided by their daily liquidity forecasting. An excel sheet presented in Appendix 3.3 was developed to capture all factors contributing to changes in liquidity such as transactions in foreign currencies, government domestic operations through Ordinateur Tresorier du Rwanda (OTR) and line ministries, commercial banks operations with NBR and change in currency in circulation. Furthermore, the collaboration between NBR and the Ministry of Finances and Economic Planning was strengthened to ensure good treasury management and exchange of information, including information on government cash flow.

The improvement in liquidity forecasting and management, the development of interbank market, and the use of reverse repo by NBR helped commercial banks to reduce significantly their holding of precautionary excess liquidity. Commercial banks are ensured that they can borrow money from NBR through reverse repo operations in case a bank fails to mobilize the needed liquidity through interbank market. Since July 2019, NBR has regularly used reverse repo instrument to provide liquidity to commercial banks. As indicated in Table 3.11, between July 2019 and April 2020, NBR injected FRW 552,618 billion in the banking system using 7-day reverse repo instrument at an average rate of 5.4%. This development contributed to progressive improvement in the interest rate pass-through by making CBR cost of fund for commercial banks and strengthen the convergence between CBR and interbank rates.

Furthermore, CBR becomes progressively a credible and relevant signal of NBR actions as its spread with interbank rates reduced significantly over time, from 112 basis points in 2014 to only 15 basis point in 2018. For further development of interbank market, NBR interventions on money market ensure that interbank rates remain in a symmetrical band defined by standing lending rate and standing deposit rate defined as CBR ± 1%. Given that monetary policy in the new framework has to be

Table 3.11 Monthly reverse repos

Date	Amount in FRW billion	Interest rate in percentage
Jul-19	39,358	5.530
Aug-19	55,400	5.352
Sep-19	68,400	5.429
Oct-19	117,000	5.356
Nov-19	20,000	5.416
Dec-19	55,000	5.404
Jan-20	60,850	5.452
Feb-20	67,360	5.455
Mar-20	45,000	5.435
Apr-20	24,250	5.478

Source NBR, Financial market department

forward-looking, because central banks cannot influence current inflation and output given substantial and variable lags in the monetary policy transmission mechanism, NBR developed the capacity of its staff in modelling and forecasting as well as in economic analysis to support MPC in its decision process about monetary policy stance.

Progressively, forecasts of inflation, output, and other macroeconomic variables become an essential input in the NBR monetary policy decision-making process. Thus, NBR monetary policy committee members base their decisions on a broad spectrum of information provided by the economic analysis and the monetary analysis. The monetary analysis assesses medium to long-term developments in inflation originating from development in monetary sector, while the economic analysis identifies short to medium-term risks to price stability from non-monetary economic and financial variables, such as developments in overall output in Rwanda and development in global and regional economic conditions.

To support the Monetary Policy Committee (MPC) members decision about NBR monetary policy stance, the bank reviewed its monetary policy decision-making process since 2019, by establishing a calendar of meetings to discuss economic development and outlook before deciding about monetary policy stance. To achieve that objective, the forecasting team (FT) was appointed by Governor in 2019 to produce working documents for MPC members.

According to the law N°48/2017 of 23/09/2017 governing the NBR (hereafter referred to as Central Bank Law), the MPC, the main monetary policy decision-making body comprises nine members, including the Governor (Chairperson), the Deputy Governor (Vice-Chairperson), two senior officers (one involved in monetary policy analysis and another from monetary policy implementation), and other NBR officers and/or external members (appointed by the Board of Director). According to the law, the Board of Directors may appoint other persons who are not staff of NBR basing on their knowledge, experience and expertise in the concerned Committee's responsibilities and determines their benefits. Their term of office is three years (3) renewable once.

In addition to Governor and Deputy Governor, currently the MPC is formed of one external member who also is a board member, the bank Chief economist and executive director, monetary policy and research directorate; the executive director financial stability directorate, the executive director, operations directorate, and the director of monetary policy who serve as rapporteur of committee. The law assigns to the MPC an ultimate responsibility of formulating a monetary policy that is consistent with development and outlook of domestic and global economic conditions to ensure price stability. As the central bank law provides, the Governor convenes the MPC once a quarter and whenever necessary. The minimum quorum required to hold an MPC meeting is two-thirds of the MPC memberships.

Appointed by the Governor, FT is composed of a forecast coordinator, who coordinates the process of the forecasting and policy analysis system (FPAS) at NBR; a technical coordinator responsible for coordinating the technical team, including sectoral experts and model operators; a model operator who runs the quarterly projection model (QPM) during the forecasting round; sectoral experts; and a database administrator. The mandate of the forecasting team (FT) is to regularly inform the MPC on the trends, developments, and outlook of the domestic and global economy, and advise on the appropriate course of action towards achieving the ultimate objective of monetary policy (i.e. price stability). To ensure the full support of FT to MPC in its monetary policy decision-making, two pre-MPC meetings are organized before the main MPC meeting where the NBR monetary policy stance is taken. During the first pre-MPC meeting, initial economic conditions are discussed based on the staff assessment on key macroeconomic trends and developments.

During this meeting, sectoral experts present developments and trends in the global economic conditions, domestic economy (real sector), external sector (balance of payments), inflation, monetary, and financial sectors. The presentations also feature model-based assessment of initial conditions, the starting point of medium-term projections, including current inflation and cost pressures, business cycle developments and demand drivers, and current monetary policy conditions. Feedback from MPC members during the first pre-MPC meeting will constitute an input into further macroeconomic analysis and forecasting.

During the second pre-MPC meeting, staff projections are discussed. The forecasting coordinator presents the first version of the baseline forecasts (i.e. the most likely courses of key macroeconomic variables over the medium term) and their assumptions, and answers technical questions arising from MPC members. Based on the presentation, MPC members express their views about plausible risks to the baseline forecasts, and propose alternative scenarios that the FT must assess between the second and the final MPC meeting.

The final MPC meeting consists of three main parts. During the first stage of the meeting, the forecast coordinator makes a final "staff" presentation on model-based macroeconomic analysis, medium-term baseline projections, and their assumptions and alternative scenarios. The forecast coordinator also presents staff policy recommendation based on the baseline scenario. The presentation is followed by a brief questions and answers session, whereby the forecast coordinator answers "technical" questions directly to the MPC members. In the second stage, the meeting proceeds to a round-table discussion on individual MPC member's views on the most appropriate course of CBR, without any intervention of the forecast coordinator (except for the purpose of collecting feedback for future policy rounds). Finally, the chairperson calls for a round-table voting session, based on which a final policy decision is made and announced. In principle, given the data release and forecast schedule, the main MPC meeting takes place six weeks after the commencement of the policy cycle. A full monetary policy report is published on NBR website one week after the MPC meeting.

Going forward, the new monetary policy framework needs to be strengthened in different dimensions. NBR needs to reinforce its economic analytical capacity to support the decision-making process by MPC on monetary policy stance. The efficiency of that process will heavily rely on the capacity of its members to interpret current data on the economy (both global and domestic) and financial market with the objective of anticipating future inflationary forces and to countering them by taking actions in advance. This requires not only to have a set of economic indicators used by the bank in its regular assessment of the monetary policy stance but also these indicators have to be well understood by MPC members to help them designing systematic response of monetary policy to changing economic developments. This is also supported by good understanding of MPC members about how monetary policy affects the economy, that is the transmission mechanism of monetary policy.

It will be also important for NBR to progressively increase the predictability of its monetary policy, the ability of financial markets, and the public in general to correctly anticipate the next monetary policy decision of a central bank (Poole and Rasche 2000; Kuttner 2001). This is crucial for the effectiveness of monetary policy, because for a central bank to maintain price stability in the medium term, the general has to predict the broader future course of monetary policy to guide price and wage-setting behaviour consistent with the objective of the central bank. The predictability of interest rate decisions by central banks is considered as an important ingredient in effective conduct of monetary policy (King 2000; Woodford 2003; Bernanke 2004b; Issing 2005). This is because central banks can only influence very short-term interest rates directly, through their monetary policy actions.

However, what matters for consumption and investment decisions of households and firms are long-term interest rates, which largely depend on private expectations regarding future central bank decisions (Blattner et al. 2008). Thus, the effectiveness of the use of interest rate as operating objective by NBR is fundamentally dependent upon the impact of changes in CBR on market expectations about the future path of short-term interest rates. In addition, given the lags in the transmission of monetary policy, predictability of long-term interest rates is also desirable to have immediate monetary policy decisions incorporated into economic actors' investment and consumption decisions. To achieve the objective of having monetary policy which is predictable, NBR will need to continue increasing its transparency by improving its communication with the public and to financial markets in particular.

Another important element to be mentioned here is the need for NBR to strengthen its operational and liquidity management frameworks. On one side, the management of excess reserves and the conditions in the interbank money market through interventions on money market using different monetary policy instruments have to contribute to the achievement of the operating target. Thus, NBR interventions on money market will need to consistently ensure the consistency between policy signals and that money market rates are stable, predictable, and close to CBR. This will help commercial banks to place surplus liquidity with, and obtain short-term funding from, each other or the central banks in a predictable way. As pointed out in this paragraph, short-term market rates have to be close to CBR to ensure that the CBR is a credible and relevant signal of NBR actions. Stability of money market rates is needed to provide a reliable basis for longer-term decisions, such as the pricing of loans and securities, and can improve financial market development.

References

Adam C, Kessy P (2011) Assessing the stability and predictability of the money multiplier in the EAC: the case of Tanzania. IGC working paper, reference no. S-40021-TZA-1

Arellano M, Bond S (1991) Some tests of specification for panel data: monte Carlo evidence and an application to employment equations. Rev Econ Stud 58(2):277–297

Aucremanne L, Boeckx J, Vergote O (2007) Interest rate policy or monetary base policy: implications for a central bank's balance sheet. Econ Rev 3:17–26

Baghestania H, Mottb T (1997) A Cointegration Analysis of the U.S. money supply process. J Macroecon 19(2), 269–283

Bahmani-Oskooee M, Bohl MT (2000) German monetary unification and the stability of the German M3 money demand function. Econo Lett 66(2):203–208

Bernanke BS (2004) Central bank talk and monetary policy, remarks at japan society corporate luncheon, board of governors of the federal reserve system

Blattner T, Catenaro M, Ehrmann M, Strauch R, Turunen J (2008) The predictability of monetary policy. European Central Bank, Occasional Paper Series, No. 83, March 2008

Brown RL, Durbin J, Evans JM (1975) Techniques for testing the constancy of regression relationships over time. J Royal Statist Soc. Series B (Methodological), 37(2):149–192

Brunner K, Metzler AH (1964) Some Further investigations of demand and supply of money. J Finance 19:240–283

Calza A et al (2001) Euro area money demand: measuring the opportunity costs appropriately. IMF working paper, WP/01/179

Campos J et al (1996) Cointegration tests in the presence of structural breaks. J Econ

Cem S et al (2006) Stability of money multipliers: evidence from turkey. J Bus Econ Res

Charry L, Gupta P, Thakoor V (2014) Introducing a semi-structural macroeconomic model for Rwanda. IMF Woking Paper Series, WP No. 14/159

Cheung Y-W, Lai KS (1993) A fractional cointegration analysis of purchasing power parity. J Bus Econ Statist 11(1):103–112

Darbha G (2002) Testing for long-run stability—an application to money multiplier in India. Appl Econ Lett 9:33–37

ECB monthly bulletin, May 2020

Engle R, Granger C (1987) Co-integration and error correction representation: estimation and testing. Econometrica 55:251–276

Favero CA (2001) Applied macroeconometrics. University Press, Oxford

Fisher I (1911) The purchasing power of money. Publicat Amer Stat Assoc 12(96):818–829
Goodhart C (1989) The conduct of monetary policy. Econ J 99:293–346
Gregory A, Hansen B (1996) Residual-based tests for cointegration in models with regime shifts. J Econ 70(1):99–126
IMF (2005) Monetary and fiscal policy issues in low-income countries. International Monetary Fund, Washington
Issing O (2005) Communication, transparency, accountability: monetary policy in the twenty first century. Federal Reserve Bank of St. Louis Review, pp 65–83
Johansen S, Juselius K (1990) Maximum likelihood estimation and inference on cointegration-with applications to the demand for money. Oxford Bull Econ Stat 52:169–210
Kashyap A, Stein J (1995) The impact of monetary policy on bank balance sheets. In: Carnegie rochester conference series on public policy, pp 151–195
Kashyap A, Stein J (2000) What do a million observations say about the transmission mechanism of monetary policy. Am Econ Rev 90(3):407–428
Keynes JM (1936) The general theory of employment, interest and money. London: Macmillan
Kigabo TR (2011) Estimation d'une function de demande de monnaie au Rwanda et Burundi. Editions universitaires européennes
Kigabo TR (2019) Moving from Monetary Targeting Framework to Price-Based Monetary Policy: the experience of the National Bank of Rwanda. NBR economic Review, vol 14
King M (2000) Monetary policy: theory in practice, address to the joint luncheon of the american economic association and the american finance association, Boston, 7 January 2000
Kireyev A (2015) How to improve the effectiveness of monetary policy in the West African Economic and Monetary Union, Washington: IMF working papers
Krueger & Kuttner (1996) The Fed funds futures rates as a predictor of fed reserve policy. J Futures Markets 16(8):865-79
Kuttner KN (2001) Monetary policy surprises and interest rates: evidence from the Fed funds futures market. J Monetary Econ 47:523–544
Luisa C, Pranav G, Vimal T (2014) Introducing a Semi-Structural Macroeconomic Model for Rwanda. IMF working paper. WP/14/159
Maehle N (2000a) Monetary policy implementation: operational issues for countries with evolving monetary policy frameworks, Washington: IMF WP/20/26
Maehle N (2020b) Monetary policy implementation: operational issues for countries with evolving monetary policy frameworks, Washington: IMF working papers 20(26)
Mishkin FS (1995) Monetary transmission mechanism. J Econ Perspect 9(4):49–72
Mishkin FS (2007) Comment on "Monetary Rules in Emerging Economies with Financial Market Imperfections", NBER Chapters, in: International Dimensions of Monetary Policy, pages 311–317, National Bureau of Economic Research, Inc
Onuonga, Susan, moraa (2018) Assessing the stability of money multipliers: evidence from Kenya. IOSR J Econ Financ (IOSR-JEF)
Perron P (1989) The great crash, the oil price shock and the unit root hypothesis. Econometrica 57:1361–1401
Poole & Rasche (2000) Perfecting market's knowledge of monetary policy. J Financ Serv Res 18(2/3):255-298
Sriram SS (2001) A survey of recent empirical money demand studies. IMF Staff Papers Vol 47, No 3/2001
Taylor J (2000) Low inflation, pass-through and the pricing power of firms. Europ Econ Rev 44:139–140
Tsangarides C (2010) Monetary policy transmission in mauritius using a VAR Analysis, Washington: IMF Working Paper No. 10/36
Walsh CE (2003) Monetary theory and policy. MIT press, s.l
Woodford M (2003) Interest and prices. Princeton University Press
Zivot E, Andrews D (1992) Further evidence on the great crash, the oil-price shock, and the unit-root hypothesis. J Bus Econ Stat 10(3):251–270

Chapter 4
Monetary Transmission Mechanism in Rwanda

4.1 Introduction

Monetary policy plays a fundamental role in price stability, which is a precondition for sustainable output growth and employment over the long run and is also a powerful tool in influencing economic activity in short term through several transmission channels. By influencing the investment and consumption decisions of firms, households, and financial intermediaries, central bank actions, at least in theory, steer the economy in the desired direction. Monetary policy actions can influence the real cost of borrowing and the aggregate demand by setting nominal short-term interest rates considering the nominal price rigidities. It can also affect the economic activities in short and medium term due to wealth, income, and liquidity effects and by its impact on inflationary expectations. Understanding how monetary transmission channels work by describing their relative dominance, importance, and spread of propagating effects (time-lag) is key for central banks in designing and implementing their monetary policies.

The literature distinguishes the following main channels through which monetary policy impulses are transmitted to the real economy: interest rates, bank lending, and firm balance sheets, exchange rates, equity, and real estate prices (Mishkin 1995). This chapter assesses channels through which monetary impulses are transmitted in Rwanda, focusing on interest rate channel, bank lending channel, and exchange rate channel which are found to be working at some extent in emerging and developing countries (Mishra and Montiel 2012; Al-Mashat and Billmeier 2007; Tsangarides 2010).

The interest rate channel works through the effect of real interest rate developments on aggregate demand. By influencing the real cost of borrowing through changes in nominal short-term interest rates and considering price rigidities, monetary policy actions have an impact on business, households, and firm's investment and consumer spending. The interest rate channel has two main blocks: the interest rate

T. K. Rusuhuzwa, *Monetary Policy in Rwanda*, Frontiers in African Business Research, https://doi.org/10.1007/978-981-33-6746-3_4

pass-through, which describes the transmission from the policy rate to the deposit rates and lending rates; and the transmission of changes in bank interest rates on aggregate demand.

The bank lending channel operates through the impact of monetary policy on the supply of bank loans, that is the quantity of credit rather than its price. An expansionary monetary policy leads to an increase in bank reserves and therefore the supply of loanable funds with possibly an increase in investment by bank-dependent borrowers and in consumer spending. If the banking sector is competitive, the increase in loanable funds would be expected to reduce bank lending rates and increase credit to the economy with impact on aggregate demand (Brooks 2007; Kourelis 1994; Mishra et al. 2016). Linked to that, the expansionary monetary policy may cause an increase in financial and physical asset prices, the net worth of firms, and hence the value of collateral, company cash flow, and firms' creditworthiness. In addition, an increase in asset prices increases the ratio of liquid financial assets to household debt, reduces the probability of financial distress, and therefore increases consumption and housing investment (Mishkin 2001). This channel is referred to as balance sheet channel, which is based on the notion of asymmetric information in credit markets, emphasizing the role of collateral in reducing moral hazards.

The exchange rate channel works either through changes in interest rates, via the risk-adjusted uncovered interest rate parity or through central bank intervention on the foreign exchange market by selling or buying forex, or through its influence on inflationary expectations. Changes in exchange rates as a result of monetary policy actions affect aggregate demand and the price level through their influence on the cost of imported goods and the resulting cost of production and investment as well as international competitiveness and net exports.

4.2 Determinants of Monetary Transmission Mechanism

Determinants of monetary transmission channels have been identified by different studies and help to explain why transmission channels are different in countries and to identify policies to strengthen channels where they are weak. Those determinants include institutional environment offering protection for loan contracts; the size of formal financial sector; functioning of the financial system including competitive banking sector, and functioning of financial market; degree of international capital mobility; exchange rate regime; independence of central banks; and macroeconomic environment of the country (Creel and Levasseur 2005; Mishra and Montiel 2010; Tieman 2004; Gigineishvili 2011, Dabla-Norris and Floerkemeier 2006).

As explained in Chapter one, well-functioning financial system needs protection of property right and enforcement of contracts as crucial for financial transactions and investment. For example, weak regulations and institutional environment can weigh on the interest-rate transmission by creating asymmetric information and contract enforcement problem, which raise the cost of financial intermediation. This reduces the elasticity of the demand for loans and makes bank rates less sensitive to changes in the policy rate. A better institutional and regulatory environment can also help to develop capital markets, thus strengthening the monetary transmission mechanism. Institutional characteristics which are linked to the effectiveness of monetary policy cover government effectiveness, regulatory quality, the rule of law, and control of corruption (Montiel et al. 2010).

The structure and development of financial system is another key determinant of monetary transmission mechanism. The depth and structure of the financial system facilitate the link between monetary policy instruments such as short-term interest rates and base money, and variables that affect the condition in the non-financial sector such as lending rates, deposit rates, exchange rate, and asset prices. For example, in a country with undeveloped financial market (money market and capital market), economic agents will not have more opportunities to save their money and borrow to finance their investment in addition to financial services offered by commercial banks. As a result, the demand for deposits and loans will be less sensitive to changes in deposits and lending rates resulting from central bank actions. The same will happen if the banking sector is less competitive. In a non-competitive banking sector, an increase of supply of loanable resources resulting from easing monetary policy will not necessarily lead to reduction of cost of finance for non-bank sector and increase in credit to private sector.

In less competitive banking sector, banks may use their market power and just increase their profit from a reduction in the policy rate by maintaining lending rates fixed (De Bondt 2002; Dabla-Norris and Floerkermeier 2006). In addition, how a bank changes its interest rates as response to change in policy rate depends on the elasticity of demand for bank loans, that is how borrowers react when commercial banks change the lending rates. This behaviour of borrowers is influenced by their possibility of having alternative source of capital, which depends on the structure and the level of development of the financial market. The healthy financial system is also key for the effectiveness of the monetary transmission mechanisms. Banks which are financially weak may build up liquidity or increase margins in order to raise capital positions and increase provisioning as response to central bank liquidity injection or lower policy interest rates, rather than extending credit. In addition, banks holding bad loans on their balance sheet may reduce the approval of new loans and limit the impact of the reduction of interest rates by central banks.

Central bank independence which includes the autonomy to set the policy rate without government interference (i.e. instrument independence); the autonomy of the central bank board in taking their decisions; limiting or banning central bank lending to the government and the financial autonomy of the central bank play important role to strengthen the monetary transmission. Central bank independence gives autonomy to the central bank to undertake monetary policy actions and enhances its signalling function to market (Cukierman et al. 1992). Direct central bank lending to the government undermines the balance sheet of the central bank and constrains its ability to clearly signal the changes in the monetary policy stance and in performing open market operations. Similarly, eliminating fiscal dominance enhances transmission of monetary policy as it does not subordinate monetary policy, to the objectives of fiscal policy and strengthens central bank independence (Samiei and Martijn 1999;

Bernanke and Gertler 2000; Bernanke and Mishkin 1997). High fiscal deficits can also raise interest rates by increasing the risk premium, thus interfering with the pass-through of the policy rate to market interest rates. Exchange rate regime is another important determinant of monetary transmission mechanism. In a country with flexible exchange rate, the policy rate of the central bank becomes clearly the primary monetary policy tool, sending clearer policy signals to market participants, and boosting monetary policy independence.

As in many empirical researches on monetary transmission mechanisms, we use vector auto regressive (VAR) models to identify the extent to which channels of monetary transmission work in Rwanda. However, to capture the possible impact of recent developments in monetary and financial sectors in Rwanda, we first analyse some particular aspects of monetary transmission such as interest rate pass-through and exchange rate pass-through to domestic prices. In addition, if the bank-lending channel is identified as working, we will go further and analyse if banks in Rwanda react differently to monetary policy actions depending on their own characteristics.

4.3 Interest Rate Pass-Through

In this section, we analyse the interest rate pass-through, that is, how bank lending and deposit rates react to policy rate changes. The second step describing the impact of bank interest rates on aggregate demand will be analysed later using VAR model. To assess the interest rate pass-through in Rwanda in a more formal way, we use a marginal pricing model which considers that a bank sets an interest rate equal to the marginal cost of funding approximated by a market interest rate and a constant mark-up (see, e.g. Tieman 2004; De Bondt 2002; Borio 1997; Hofmann and Mizen 2004).

$$i_t^m = \alpha + \beta i_t^p + \varepsilon_t \tag{4.1}$$

where β is the pass-through parameter. It highly depends on the level of the demand for deposits and loans elasticities to the deposit and lending rates, respectively. That elasticity depends on the possibility of substitution for economic agents between bank deposits and other investment facilities with the same maturity like T-bills; and between bank lending and other types of external finance like equity or bond markets on the other hand as well as the level of banking sector competition.

Equation (4.1) describes a long-term relationship between the two variables because it does not take into consideration the adjustment process of market rates to changes in policy rate. To model short-term dynamics adjustment, an error correction model (ECM) linked to cointegration concept may be specified as follows (see, e.g. Engle and Granger 1987):

$$\Delta i_t^m = \gamma_1 + \gamma_2 \Delta i_t^r + \gamma_3 (i_{t-1}^m - \beta i_{t-1}^p - \alpha) + \nu_t \tag{4.2}$$

Table 4.1 Augmented Dickey-Fuller unit root tests

	Levels		First differences	
	t-statistics	Probability	t-statistics	Probability
CBR	−2.28	0.44	−11.04	0.00
RR	−2.43	0.36	−9.3	0.00
INTER	−2.05	0.57	−12.2	0.00
TB4	−3.26	0.08	−5.74	0.00
TB13	−2.2	0.5	−7.7	0.00
TB26	−2.7	0.4	−9.3	0.00
TB52	−2.4	0.4	−8.6	0.00
WTB	−2.7	0.2	−8.5	0.00

In such an ECM, the coefficient γ_3 indicates the speed of adjustment of the short-run dynamics to the long-run equilibrium relationship. The higher is this coefficient, the faster is the market response to the policy rate change. To assess the interest rate pass-through in Rwanda, we estimate the pass-through from money market rates (repo rates, interbank rates, and treasury bill rates with different maturities: 4, 13, 26, and 52 weeks denoted as tb4, tb13, tb26, and tb52) to deposit and lending rates. Using the standard augmented Dickey-Fuller test, we find that all those variables are integrated of order one, I(1) (Table 4.1).

In the new monetary policy framework adopted since January 2019, NBR interventions on money market aim at aligning interbank market rates to CBR, to anchor short-term interest rates. Thus, we first assess the pass-through from CBR to interbank rate in the full sample covering the period from January 2008 to May 2020 and in the sub-sample from January 2016 to May 2020 to assess if recent development in money market achieved during the last five years has contributed to improvement in the pass-through. This assessment is important because in more developed money and interbank markets, the pass-through from the policy rate to bank deposit and lending rates improves when the first step in transmission from the policy rate to the interbank rates improves (Yang et al. 2011).

In the recent period, interbank rates have been converging towards the central bank rate. For example, the spread between the two rates reduced significantly by 87.5% from 0.16 between January 2008 and December 2015 to only 0.02 between January 2016 and May 2020 and was less volatile with a standard deviation reducing by more than 72.2% from 1.8 between 2008 and 2016 to 0.5 between 2016 and 2019 (Fig. 4.1).

While there is no evidence of long-run relationship between interbank rates and CBR in the full sample, Engle-Granger tests identify both long and short-term relationships between the two variables in the sub-sample considered (2016–2019). The results of tests indicate that the two variables are cointegrated as the probability corresponding to tau-statistic is less than 5% as indicated in Table 4.2.

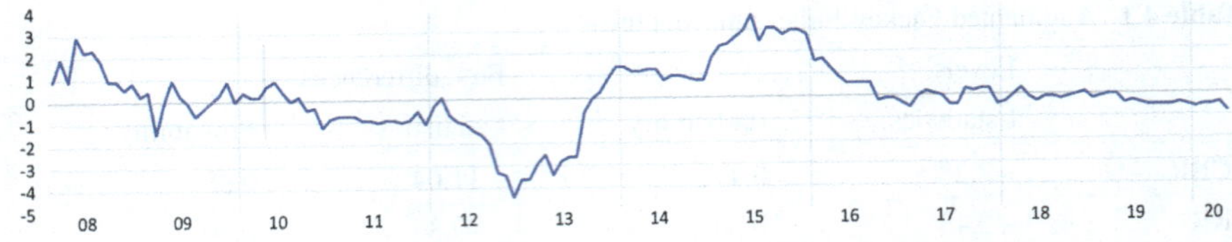

Fig. 4.1 Development in the spread between interbank and central bank rates

Table 4.2 Cointegration test—Engle-granger

Specification: INTER CBR C		
Cointegrating equation deterministic: C		
Null hypothesis: Series are not cointegrated		
Automatic lag specification (lag = 0 based on Schwarz Info Criterion, maxlag = 10)		
	Value	Prob.[a]
Engle-Granger tau-statistic	−3.545891	0.0408
Engle-Granger z-statistic	−14.13446	0.1385

[a]MacKinnon (1996) p-values

We have then estimated the long-run relationship between the interbank rates and the central bank rate as well as the corresponding ECM. Results of estimation show the existence of pass-through, though incomplete with long-run parameter statistically significant (0.4). In addition, the coefficient of adjustment is negative and statistically significant (−0.28).

The improvement in pass-through between interest rates and central bank rate in Rwanda in recent period is the result of development in interbank market; improved liquidity forecasting and management; improvement in operational capacity of NBR staff; and the communication with commercial banks' treasurers. As a result, the interbank rate becomes progressively an important element for banks in their portfolio management helping to make proper decision about holding short-term liquid assets and long-term illiquid assets and determine the terms at which banks can borrow liquid assets in response to idiosyncratic shocks. Clearly, the interbank market has been progressively acting as an effective channel for liquidity management in the banking sector and allow for more efficient financial intermediation (Table 4.3).

We then analyse the pass-through from repo rates considered as proxy of CBR[1] to interbank rates and treasury bill rates with different maturities. The objective is to assess how money market rates react to changes in NBR actions reflected in changes in repo rates. Engle-Granger cointegration tests on pair of series show that there exists complete pass-through from repo rates to only money market rates with very short maturity such as interbank rates (intr), tb4, tb13, and tb26 but not with weighted treasury bill rate and tb56.[2] The coefficient γ_3 in the error correction model which

[1]CBR does not change every month.

[2]We only present results on pair of series which are cointegrated.

Table 4.3 Long and short-run relationship between interbank rates and CBR

Dependent Variable: INTER				
Cointegrating equation deterministic: C				
Long-run covariance estimate (Bartlett kernel, Newey-West fixed bandwidth = 4.0000)				
Variable	Coefficient	Std. Error	t-Statistic	Prob.
CBR	0.411089	0.145364	2.827999	0.0067
C	3.354919	0.834846	4.018609	0.0002
Dependent Variable: D(INTER)				
Variable	Coefficient	Std. error	t-Statistic	Prob.
D(CBR)	−0.033057	0.229495	−0.144043	0.8861
E(-1)	−0.278603	0.074918	−3.718796	0.0005
C	0.014010	0.029910	0.468413	0.6416

measures the speed of the adjustment to long-run equilibrium relationship is negative in all equations as indicated in Table 4.4 and varies between −0.17 (interbank rate) and −0.32 (treasury bill with 4-month maturity).

To further understand the link between money market rates, we have estimated the pass-through from interbank rates to treasury bill rates of different maturities. Contrary to repo rates, all treasury bill rates react to changes in interbank rates but with different magnitude. The results in Table 4.5 indicate complete pass-through

Table 4.4 Long-term equation and short-term equation (money market rates as function of repo rates)

	Long-run equation			Short-term equation		
	α	β	R-square	γ_1	γ_2	γ_3
Intr	1.33	1.09[a]	0.69	−0.006	0.40[a]	−0.17[a]
tb4	0.53	1.18[a]	0.62	0.00	0.21	−0.32[a]
tb13	1.28	1.16[a]	0.53	0.002	0.28[a]	−0.07[a]
tb26	2.60	1.01[a]	0.41	0.01	0.13	−0.26[a]

[a]Significant at 5%

Table 4.5 Pass-through between interbank rates and T-bills rates

	Long-run equation			Short-term equation		
	α	β	R-square	γ_1	γ_2	γ_3
WTB	1.3	0.9[a]	0.74	0.008	0.4[a]	−0.14[a]
Tb4	−0.52	1.03[a]	0.75	0.00	0.50[a]	−0.43[a]
Tb13	−0.34	1.09[a]	0.80	00	0.47[a]	−0.12[a]
Tb26	1.28	0.94[a]	0.63	0.01	0.32[a]	−0.41[a]

[a]Significant at 5%

Table 4.6 Pass-through to deposit rates and lending rates from TB rates

	Long-run equation			Short-term equation		
	α	β	R-square	γ_1	γ_2	γ_3
WDR-WTB	5.7	0.29*	0.19	0.01	0.05	−0.30*
DR1-TB26	3.1	0.16*	0.05	−0.01	0.09	−0.48*
WLR-WDR	15.5	0.18*	0.12	0.00	0.03	−0.57*
WLR-DR3	16.2	0.11*	0.06	0.00	0.005	−0.53*
WLR-DR6	16.1	0.18*	0.08	0.003	0.006	−0.54*
LRS-DR6	16.6	0.1*	0.03	0.01	0.05	−0.63*
LRL-DR6	14	0.18*	0.07	0.04	0.1	−0.58*
LRL-WDR	12.4	0.37*	0.12	−0.003	0.17	−0.63*
WLR-TB52	16.5	0.05*	0.04	0.000	0.04	−0.49

*Significant at 5%

to short-term treasury bill rates (TB4 and TB13) and incomplete pass-through to weighted treasury bill rate (WTB) and TB26. In addition, the speed of adjustment to long-run relationship is higher for TB4 and TB26. As indicated in Table 4.5, 86% and 82% of deviations from long-run relationship between TB4, and interbank rates, and between TB26 and interbank rates, respectively, are corrected within two months following a shock.

Finally, we assess the pass-through from money market rates to banking rates (deposit rates and lending rates) as well as the link between deposit rates and lending rates. In Table 4.6 we report pairs of cointegrated variables, meaning pairs of variables for which long-run relationships were found. Our estimations show that deposit rates generally react more to changes in money market rates than do loan rates. This might be due to several factors, including the fact that market for deposits in Rwanda is more competitive on contrary to loan market; and the existence of important non-interest determinants of lending rates.

The weighted deposit rates (WDR) react to weighted treasury bill rate (WTB) and one-month deposit rate (DR1) reacts to changes in 26-week treasury bill rates (TB26), though long-run pass-through coefficients are low at 0.29 and 0.16, respectively. The speed of DR1 adjustment to changes in TB26 is bigger than between the one of WDR to changes in WTB. 96% and 60% of deviations from the long-run relationship between DR1 and TB26 and between WDR and WTB, respectively, are corrected within two months following the shocks. Weak deposit rates elasticities to TB rates as shown by smaller long-run coefficients may be due to different factors, including the monopoly of few institutional investors as big depositors in the banking sector. Between 2015 and 2019, Rwanda Social Security Board (RSSB) accounted for 31.1% of term deposits in the banking sector while other financial corporations (OFC) such as insurance companies, microfinancial institutions, and SACCOs accounted for 14.3% on average. Thus, commercial banks have to pay high deposit rates to maintain these term deposits.

In addition, the imperfect substitution between bank deposits and investment in T-bill by non-bank financial institutions and households reduce the sensitivity of deposit rates to change in T-bill rates. As indicated, short-term government securities market is highly dominated by commercial banks, with institutional investors accounting for only 16.7% of outstanding investment in T-bills on average between 2013 and 2019. However, the recent development in capital market shows an increasing participation of non-bank financial institutions and retail investments in treasury bonds. This trend supported by intensive financial education across the country focusing on usage of existing financial products including investing in debt securities is expected to improve the interest rate pass-through to deposit rates.

The pass-through to lending rate is only established from 56 treasury bill rates maturity. While the long-term pass-through coefficient is very low (0.05), the speed of short-term adjustment is high, as 98% of deviations are corrected within two months following a given shock. As expected, the lending rates react more on deposit rates as cost of fund. There is pass-through to weighted average lending rate (WLR) from weighted deposit rate (WDR), as well as from deposit rates with 3 and 6-month maturities. Long-run coefficients are low, between 0.11 and 0.18, reflecting the impacts of other factors on lending rates such as operating costs, credit risks, and market power of banks. In the short run, the adjustment mechanism is very faster with the adjustment coefficient ranging from 0.53 to 0.57. The pass-through to lending rates charged on long-term maturity loans from weighted deposit rates and 6-month deposit rates (DR6) is also incomplete but with higher adjustment coefficients ranging from 0.58 to 0.63. The same trend is observed between interest rates on short-term loans (LRS) and DR6.

In recent period, we have observed a clear declining trend in lending rates for both corporates and individuals in line with NBR accommodative monetary policy implemented since 2013. The decline in overall lending rate was mainly observed since 2016, following several consecutive cuts of central bank rate, from 7.5% in March 2013 to 4.5% in September 2020. Different factors have contributed to the adjustment of lending rates to reduction of CBR. As a result of NBR communication about its accommodative monetary policy, journalists and the public in general put some pressures to commercial banks to reduce lending rates as NBR has been regularly cutting its CBR. Supported by a stable macroeconomic environment characterized by high and sustainable economic growth with stable and low inflation, commercial banks improved their business and pricing models which led to a reduction in overhead costs to income from 52.2% on average between 2010 and 2015 to 45% between 2016 and 2019 on average (Fig. 4.2).

4.4 Exchange Rate Pass-Through

There exists considerable literature on exchange rate pass-through (ERPT) to domestic prices mainly in advanced and emerging countries. Initially, ERPT was defined as percentage change in import prices expressed in domestic currency, in

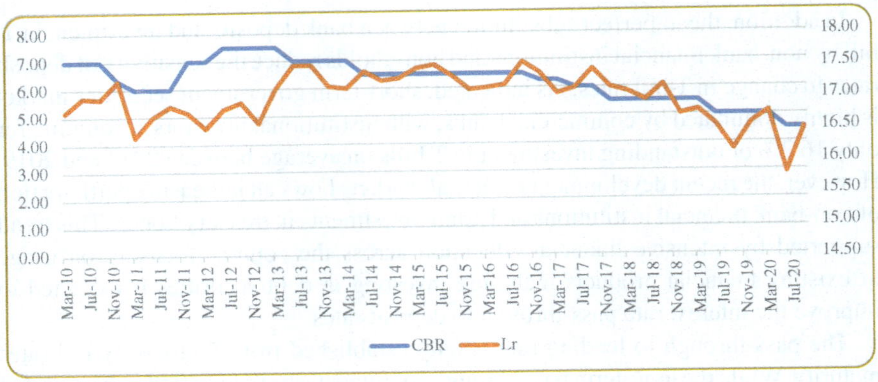

Fig. 4.2 Lending rate and CBR development

response to a 1% change in the exchange rate. The literature on the pass-through of a country's exchange rate fluctuations to its import prices have been surveyed comprehensively by Goldberg and Knetter (1997).

However, the definition of ERPT has been extended to address the effect of exchange rate movements on producer or consumer prices. Indeed, a large price increase of imported goods as a result of exchange rate depreciation would spill over to the other sectors of the economy, raise the overall domestic production costs, and might lead to an inflationary spiral. In addition, the increase in production costs would raise the price of export products in local currency, which might lead to unchanged or even weakening international price competitiveness (Woo 1984; Feinberg 1989; Popper 1998).

Understanding the process and magnitude of the adjustment of domestic prices as response to changes in the exchange rate is crucial for the formulation of different macroeconomic policies. In a country with low exchange rate pass-through, monetary authority has more room to implement countercyclical monetary policy during downward phases of the business cycle and tight monetary policy to contain inflation in the period when the economy is facing strong demand pressures. Thus, the extent to which exchange rates and import prices influence domestic inflation is a major concern for monetary policy. For example, in the bank of England's inflation report, exchange rates and import prices are among the major considerations for the inflation forecasts underlying the deliberations of the monetary policy committee. In addition, the European central bank has cited the possible inflationary effects of the weak euro as one factor behind its tightening of monetary policy in 2000 (ECB monthly bulletin May 2020). Furthermore, appropriate estimates of the exchange rate pass-through provide insights to define the appropriate degree of exchange rate flexibility by taking into consideration country economic characteristics as well as the design of the country's trade policy. If, for example, the degree of pass-through is high, the exchange rate changes will impact the relative prices of tradables and non-tradables so that the adjustment in trade balance will be relatively prompt (Frankel et al. 2012; McCarthy 2007).

Indeed, if the pass-through is higher, the imported goods will become expensive leading to their substitution by domestically produced goods where possible and the external balances will be corrected after a period, say several months. If the degree of pass-through is low, the exchange rate does not have much impact on trade balance. However, if there is a complete pass-through from nominal exchange rate depreciation to domestic prices, export competitiveness from nominal depreciation would be cancelled out.

A large number of theoretical models were developed to analyse the link between exchange rate and inflation, considering the interaction between micro and macro factors. On the micro side, models analyse how producers adjust sales prices to changes in exchange rate. When the structure of domestic economy is close to a monopoly or imperfect competition, producers may maximize profits by fully transmitting the changes in the exchange rate into sales prices, the so-called "producer currency pricing" by Obstfeld and Rogoff (1995). However, when markets are more competitive, producers may need to bear a part of the exchange rate changes by reducing mark-ups to keep market share behaviour, referred to as a "pricing to market" by Krugman (1987).

On the macro side, studies generally utilize the framework of new open macroeconomics or new Keynesian models to analyse the effects of exchange rate changes on inflation (Choi and Cook 2008) and have concluded to declining pass-through since the late 1990s in developing countries mainly due to low inflationary environment achieved since that period (Choudhri and Hakura 2001; Taylor 2000; Takhtamanova 2008). Choudhri and Hakura (2001) studies a sample of 71 countries, including emerging markets and developing economies, and confirm a strong correlation between the exchange rate pass-through and an inflationary environment. In developing countries, Frankel et al. (2005) concluded to a rapid downward trending pass-through since the 1990s, more so than did high-income countries and attributed the development to different factors, including income, trade openness, inflation environment, and exchange rate variability. The same development in exchange rate pass-through was observed in emerging economies that could reach and maintain macroeconomic stability. However, the degree of pass-through was found much larger in emerging economies with severe macroeconomic instability (See Ca'Zorzi 2007; Mishra and Montiel 2010).

A number of studies on exchange rate pass-through have used VAR system in order to better address endogeneity between exchange rate and domestic prices and capture short-run dynamic impact, which are likely to characterize the pass-through. VAR analysis allows to take into consideration interactions between exchange rate and other domestic macroeconomic variables in investigating the exchange rate pass-through to inflation. It also helps to examine the impact of other shocks on key macroeconomic variables, such as monetary policy stance and economic activities on inflation. In this work, we use the same methodology in order to measure the extent and speed of exchange rate pass-through to various domestic prices. Three models are considered to analyse the exchange rate pass-through to domestic prices by considering core CPI, local goods CPI, and headline inflation CPI.

The VAR model estimated is of the following form:

$$AY_t = C(L)Y_t + Bu_t \tag{4.3}$$

where Y_t is a vector of endogenous variables (nominal effective exchange rate, output, broad money M3, imported goods CPI, local goods CPI, core CPI, and headline CPI); L is the lag operator; A, B, and C are matrices of coefficients; and u_t is a vector of normally distributed errors (u_t ~ N (0, I)). By multiplying Eq. (4.3) by A^{-1}, the inverse of matrix A, we obtain:

$$Y_t = A^{-1}C(L)Y_t + A^{-1}Bu \tag{4.4}$$

By denoting $A^{-1}Bu_t = e_t$ the residuals from unrestricted model, we have $Bu_t = Ae_t$.

To identify the VAR, we used Cholesky decomposition by imposing zero restrictions on upper triangle of the matrix A and considering that structural shocks are uncorrelated. We estimate three different VAR price models and variables ordered as follows: nominal effective exchange rate, output gap, broad money, imported goods CPI, and headline CPI in model 1. In alternative models, local goods CPI (model 2) and core CPI (model 3) replace headline CPI.

As Rwanda is a small open economy, each model also includes global oil prices as exogenous variable. Data are on quarterly basis from 2006 to 2019 and are transformed by calculating quarter on quarter annualized changes to address stationarity issues. Before using estimated models to analyse the exchange rate pass-through, we have analysed the quality of VAR. All models are stable as inverted roots lie into the unit circle; results from LM autocorrelation test suggest that all three VARs have no issue of autocorrelation, and normality tests confirm that residuals are multivariate normal. Tables 4.7 and 4.8 show the tests on the quality of model 3, and the impulse response functions for the three models are given in Appendix A.

Model 1 evaluates transmission of exchange rate changes to headline inflation, while models 2 and 3 investigate transmission to local goods inflation and core inflation, respectively. All three models include imported goods inflation as the first stage of transmission. Impulse response functions show that the pass-through from change in exchange rate to prices of imported goods, core inflation, and headline inflation is almost immediate as the impact appears in the next quarter with maximum effect in the third quarter. The link between changes in imported goods prices and headline inflation as well as core inflation is explained by the fact that a country with high import share in GDP and in CPI basket, exchange rate, and import price

Table 4.7 VAR residual serial correlation LM tests

Null hypothesis: No serial correlation at lag h

Lag	LRE* stat	Df	Prob.	Rao F-stat	Df	Prob.
1	67.84996	25	0.0000	3.256861	(25, 116.7)	0.0000
2	30.64304	25	0.2011	1.260419	(25, 116.7)	0.2047
3	27.97425	25	0.3090	1.138276	(25, 116.7)	0.3132

Table 4.8 VAR residual normality tests

Orthogonalization: residual correlation (Doornik-Hansen)				
Null hypothesis: residuals are multivariate normal				
Component	Skewness	Chi-square	df	Prob.
1	−0.275770	0.793918	1	0.3729
2	−0.159585	0.270319	1	0.6031
3	0.500989	2.484404	1	0.1150
4	0.191122	0.386292	1	0.5343
5	0.816719	5.933246	1	0.0149
Joint		9.868179	5	0.0791
Component	Kurtosis	Chi-square	df	Prob.
1	2.242164	1.672805	1	0.1959
2	3.171428	0.904701	1	0.3415
3	3.162973	0.001186	1	0.9725
4	3.418636	1.788428	1	0.1811
5	4.429238	0.536320	1	0.4640
Joint		4.903440	5	0.4278
Component	Jarque-Bera	df	Prob.	
1	2.466724	2	0.2913	
2	1.175020	2	0.5557	
3	2.485590	2	0.2886	
4	2.174720	2	0.3371	
5	6.469566	2	0.0394	
Joint	14.77162	10	0.1406	

*Note*Approximate p-values do not account for coefficient estimation

fluctuations are expected to have greater pass-through to domestic prices. In Rwanda, imported goods represent 22.7% in headline CPI basket and 20.2% in core CPI basket.

Furthermore, high and sustainable GDP growth in Rwanda achieved during the last two decades was supported by increased import of goods. Between 2015 and 2019, total import value CIF (including cost, insurance and freight) represented around 25.6% of GDP on average. Considering the accumulated impulse responses, the results of VAR (Fig. 4.3) show that a depreciation of 1% will lead to an increase of around 0.7% in imported goods prices; 0.6% in headline CPI, 0.57 in local goods CPI, and 0.52 in core CPI. Results of estimation also show that the second-round effect on domestic materializes after the change in exchange rates, with the maximum effect in the third quarter.

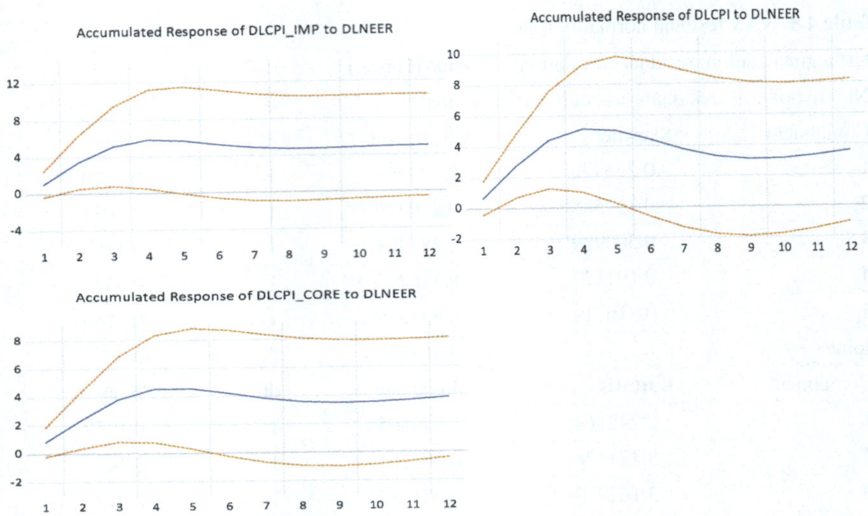

Fig. 4.3 Impulse responses (response to one S.D. innovations ±2 S.E)

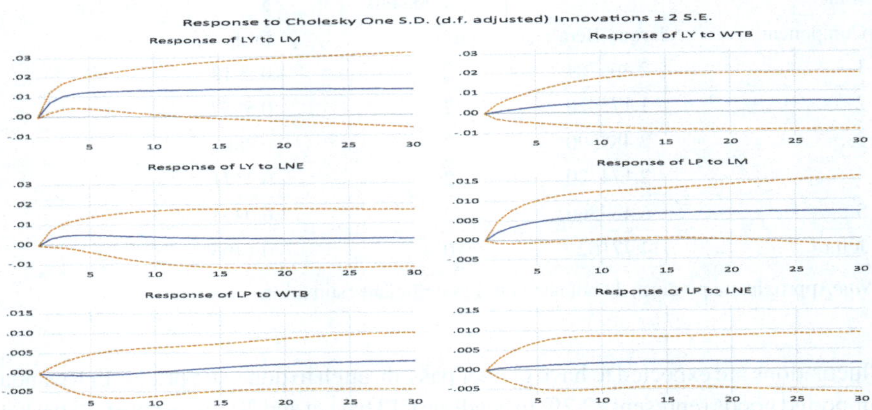

Fig. 4.4 Impulse responses to 1 SD innovations ±2 S.E

4.5 Monetary Transmission Mechanism Assessment: A Vector Autoregressive Framework

We start the analysis by specifying the following VAR model describing the Rwandan economy:

$$H(L)Y_t = K(L)X_t + \varepsilon_t \tag{4.5}$$

The corresponding reduced form is

$$Y_t = A(L)Y_{t-1} + B(L)Z_t + \mu_t \tag{4.6}$$

where Y_t is a vector of endogenous variables and Z_t is a vector of exogenous variables. Y_t consists of constant GDP (y), price 2001, consumer price (p) index CPI, nominal effective exchange rate (e), monetary aggregates (m), or total credit to the private sector (CPS), and short-term interest rates such as T-bills rate (i). A(L) corresponds to matrices of coefficients to be estimated, with lag lengths determined by standard information criteria. The vector Z_t consists of exogenous variables used to control for changes in global economy. In this work, we use international oil price because the Rwandan economy does not have an impact on its determination. All data are expressed in natural logs, with exception of interest rate and data used are quarterly data covering the period from 2000 to 2019. All data are from NBR except data on GDP which are produced by the National Institute of Statistics of Rwanda (NISR) and data on oil prices are from international statistics produced by IMF.

We adopt the following order of endogenous variables:

$$Y_t^{'} = [y_t, p_t, m_t/cps, i_t, e_t] \tag{4.7}$$

To characterize relationships between output, prices, and policy-related variables, we use augmented Dickey-Fuller (ADF) to identify the level of integration of those variables. As in most VAR models of the monetary transmission mechanism, we do not perform an explicit analysis of the economy's long-run behaviour because monetary transmission mechanism is a short-run phenomenon (Favero 2001). The results of ADF tests suggest that all series are integrated of order one, that is, they are I(1) as indicated in Table 4.1, Appendix B.

Using the estimated VAR model, we can analyse short-term dynamics based on impulse responses over the short to medium term. By estimating the VAR in levels, we implicitly allow cointegration relationships in the data. Based on the estimated VAR model we examine the effect on both output and price, of a one standard deviation shock to the interest rates, monetary aggregates (M3 or CPS), and exchange rate. We estimate the reduced form by computing the Cholesky factorization of the reduced form VAR covariance matrix. In this framework, it is assumed that in ordering variables in VAR model as given by (4.7) a variable has no immediate effects on the preceding one. The relation between the reduced form errors (μ) and the structural disturbance (ε) can be presented as follows:

$$\begin{bmatrix} \varepsilon_t^y \\ \varepsilon_t^p \\ \varepsilon_t^m \\ \varepsilon_t^i \\ \varepsilon_t^e \end{bmatrix} = \begin{bmatrix} 1 & 0 & 0 & 0 & 0 \\ e_{21} & 1 & 0 & 0 & 0 \\ e_{31} & e_{32} & 1 & 0 & 0 \\ e_{41} & e_{42} & e_{43} & 1 & 0 \\ e_{51} & e_{52} & e_{53} & e_{54} & 1 \end{bmatrix} \begin{bmatrix} \mu_t^y \\ \mu_t^p \\ \mu_t^m \\ \mu_t^i \\ \mu_t^e \end{bmatrix} \tag{4.8}$$

Lag length criteria indicate the use of one lag (Table 4.2, Appendix B), the VAR is stable (Table 4.3 in Appendix B), and residual diagnostic tests suggest well-behaved residuals (Tables 4.4 and 4.5 in Appendix B). Impulse response functions show the impact of policy-related variables on output and prices, with the dotted lines representing 95% confidence intervals. The analysis shows that one standard deviation shock on the treasury bill rates is associated with a drop in output and inflation. While the shape of the response function is consistent with the findings in different studies, the effect of that shock in Rwanda is not statistically significant. This is consistent with the findings on interest rates pass-through, showing weak pass-through from market rates to lending rates.

In addition, results indicate that the exchange rate channel is not important in the entire period considered in this analysis. This may be explained by very stable FRW nominal exchange vis-à-vis USD, the most used foreign currency in Rwanda. Between 2006 and 2015, quarterly average change in exchange rates was only 0.2% before increasing to 1.3% in recent period (between 2016 and 2019) due to high depreciation of FRW against USD recorded between 2015 and 2016. On annual basis, FRW depreciated by 3.6% between 2008 and 2014 and by 6.1% on average between 2015 and 2019.

Because in almost the entire sample, NBR used monetary targeting framework, with the broad money M3 as intermediate target, we assess how changes in M3 resulting from NBR actions were transmitted to output and inflation. Impulse response functions show that a shock to M3 have a very rapid and significant impact on output with maximum effects after around three quarters. This is consistent with the real effects of monetary aggregates found in different studies, both in emerging and developing economies. In the case of Rwanda, the result may be a reflection of the increasing monetization of the economy that has taken place over the period under review. In addition, a monetary shock results in a modest impact of prices appearing after a big lag (almost two years) (Fig. 4.4).

As pointed out in Chapter two, the FRW depreciated significantly since 2015 with possible increase of exchange rate pass-through to domestic prices. In addition, significant changes were introduced in the reserve money programme in Rwanda since 2012. Furthermore, taking into consideration the extension of the financial sector across the country which contributed to more access to bank loans by the private sector, the introduction of digital financial services since 2010 such as mobile payments, mobile banking, and internet banking which contributed to expend financial services in the country, we have estimated the impulse response function in the sub-sample starting by 2012 first quarter to analyse if those changes have affected monetary transmission mechanism in Rwanda, using the outstanding credit to the private sector and not the broad monetary aggregate M3.

Figure 4.5 shows that accommodative monetary policy implemented by NBR contributed to a decline in weighted treasury bill rates, reducing incentives for commercial banks to invest in government securities, which lead to an increase in the credit to the private sector. This exerted inflationary pressures through the impact of credit to private sector on aggregate demand as well as the impact of FRW depreciation due to high demand for imports. Impulse response functions show that the effect of a shock to T-bill rates on the credit to the private sector appears almost immediate but not lasting for long. The increase in the credit to the private sector

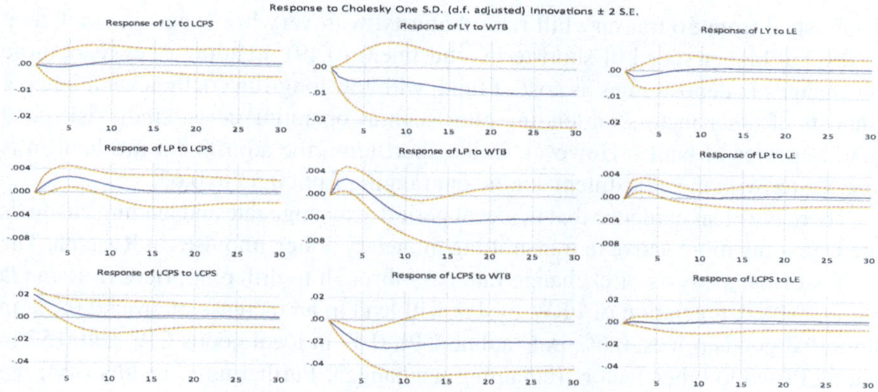

Fig. 4.5 Impulse responses using of credit to the private sector (LCPS) and weighted treasury interest rates (WTB)

leads to FRW exchange rate depreciation because of more demand for USD to pay import bills. As a result, the effect of increase in prices of imported goods in FRW on domestic prices appears immediately picking after two quarters and last up to quarter six. Furthermore, the impact of an increase in credit to the private sector to inflation appears after two quarters through its impact on the aggregate demand, and picks after around one quarter. Similar results are obtained using interbank rate in the model instead of T-bill rates as presented in Fig. 4.4 in Appendix B.

The impact of monetary policy actions on the GDP remains limited due to different factors such as still low financial deepening and monetization. Though credit, M3, and deposit ratios to GDP have been increasing over time, their levels are still low compared to those in developed and emerging economies as discussed in Chapter one. This is an indication of small size of the formal financial sector, which limits the impact of monetary policy on aggregate demand and prices. In addition, limited competition in the banking sector may weaken the link between NBR policy rate and the aggregate demand.

In summary, our analysis has shown that interest rate pass-through in Rwanda remains weak but improving progressively. Good developments noted comprise the significant link between CBR and interbank rates in recent period making NBR policy rate more relevant as a tool of signalling monetary policy stance; complete pass-through from interbank rates to short-term maturity T-bonds (TB4 and TB13) and high speed of short-term adjustment to long-run relationship between interbank rates with TB13 as well as with TB26. In addition, results of our analysis show that deposit rate generally reacts more to changes in money market rates than do loan rates. The weighted deposit rates (WDR) react to changes in weighted treasury bill rate (WTB), and one-month deposit rate (DR1) reacts to changes in 26-week treasury bill rates (TB26). Though the pass-through is incomplete with small but statistically significant long-run pass-through coefficients, the speed of short-term adjustment is high, equal to 0.30 and 0.48, respectively. The pass-through to lending rate is only established from 56 treasury bill rates maturity, with very low long-run coefficient (0.05) but higher speed of short-term adjustment (0.49). Lending rates react more on changes in deposit rates as cost of fund, with low long-run coefficients reflecting impacts of other factors on lending rates such as operating costs, credit risks, and market power of banks. However, in the short term, the adjustment mechanism is very faster with the adjustment coefficient ranging from 0.53 to 0.63.

There is a clear evidence that in recent period, exchange rate and lending channels are becoming more active in transmitting monetary policy impulses in Rwanda. The results of the analysis of exchange rate pass-through to different prices in Rwanda show that a depreciation of FRW by 1% will lead to an increase of around 0.7% in imported goods prices, 0.6% in headline CPI, 0.57 in local goods CPI, and 0.52 in core CPI while other factors remaining unchanged. Furthermore, results from the estimation of VAR model show that in recent period, NBR accommodative monetary policy lead to a decline in money market rates, an increase in the credit to the private sector, and FRW depreciation against USD. This exerted inflationary pressures through the impact of credit to private sector on aggregate demand as well as the impact of FRW depreciation due to high demand for imports. Given the importance of lending channel in Rwanda, we analyse in detail the characteristics of that channel, which is linked to the crucial role of banks in financing the economy in Rwanda as in other developing countries where financial markets are not well developed.

As pointed out, this channel works through the impact of monetary policy actions on the ability of banks to provide new loans and affect the capacity of borrowers that are more dependent on bank's financing. The existing literature show that the response of banks to monetary policy actions in terms of ability to provide new loans crucially depends on their balance sheets structure. This makes bank characteristics a source of banks' asymmetric reaction to monetary policy changes (Kashyap and Stein 1995, 2000; Chileshe 2017).

To better understand how banks in Rwanda respond differently to monetary policy, depending on their characteristics, we use the generalized method of moments (GMM) dynamic panel estimator proposed by Arellano and Bond (1991) and employed in different studies on lending channel of monetary transmission. This analytical framework helps in controlling for potential biases induced by endogeneity, resulting from possible significant correlation between the error term and lagged dependent variables used as regressors in the model.

The model specification is as follows:

$$\begin{aligned}\Delta \log(L_{i,t}) = \lambda_i + \sum_{j=1}^{p} \delta_j \Delta \log(L_{i,t-j}) + \sum_{j=1}^{p} \gamma_j \Delta \log(y_{t-j}) \\ + \sum_{j=0}^{p} \omega_j \pi_{t-j} + \sum_{j=1}^{p} \mu_j \Delta \log(NPL_{i,t-j}) + \sum_{j=1}^{p} \alpha_j \Delta r_{t-j} \\ + \sum_{j=1}^{p} \beta \Delta Xi, t-j + \varphi own + \sum_{j=1}^{p} \tau_j (\Delta X_{i,t-1} * \Delta r_{t-j}) + \varepsilon_{it} \quad (4.8)\end{aligned}$$

Δ and log indicate first difference and natural logarithm of the variables, respectively. λ_i captures bank-specific fixed effects (i = 1, 2, …, N; N is the number of banks) while ε_{it} is the white noise error term, t indicates the time observation for each variable, and p is the number of lags. The variable L_{it} is the amount of loans by bank i at time t; y is the real GDP, while π and NPL stand for the inflation rate and non-performing loans, respectively.

r is the repo rate used as tool to signal monetary policy stance. As tighter monetary policy stance should result in slower credit growth, the coefficient of r is expected to be negative. Because the effect of monetary policy materialized after a certain period (lag), we use lagged repo rate in the equation. For example, banks may not adjust their lending behaviour immediately after changes in repo rates as some loan agreements may have been signed before. X_{it} stands for the following variables representing bank characteristics: bank size, liquidity, capitalization, and market power. Liquidity and bank capitalization are defined as the ratio of liquid assets (cash, interbank lending, and securities) to total assets and the ratio of bank equity capital plus reserves to total risky weighted assets, respectively.

4.6 Exchange Rate Pass-Through

For bank i at time t, the size (S), liquidity (LQ), and capitalization (CA) indicators are therefore computed as:

$$S_{it} = Log A_{it} - \frac{1}{N}\sum_{i}^{N} Log A_{it} \tag{4.9}$$

$$LQ_{it} = \frac{LA_{it}}{A_{it}} - \frac{1}{T}\sum_{t=1}^{T}\left[\frac{1}{N}\sum_{i=1}^{N}\frac{LA_{it}}{A_{it}}\right] \tag{4.10}$$

$$CA_{it} = \frac{C_{it}}{TRWA_{it}} - \frac{1}{T}\sum_{t=1}^{T}\left[\frac{1}{N}\sum_{i=1}^{N}\frac{C_{it}}{TRWA_{it}}\right] \tag{4.11}$$

$\Delta X_{it-1} * \Delta r_{t-j}$ measures the interaction between the monetary policy and the bank characteristics. Its coefficient is expected to be positive because a small, less liquid or less capitalized bank is expected to react more strongly to the monetary policy change (Kashyap and Stein 1995). "own" is the dummy variable to capture the ownership structure of banks, which takes the value of one, if bank is domestic and zero if bank is foreign. Because foreign-owned banks enjoy the benefit of connection with their larger mother banks from abroad that enable them to finance at cheaper rate, domestic banks are the one expected to react more on monetary actions.

A, LA, C, and TRW represent assets, liquid assets, core capital, and total risky weighted assets, respectively. The market power of a bank is measured by its share in total loans of the banking system and banks with high market power are expected to be less sensitive to monetary policy actions. In the analysis, the demand in the economy is proxied by two variables: real GDP (Y) and inflation rate (π). While real GDP is expected to have a positive effect on the amount of loans, the impact of the inflation rate (π) is ambiguous. On the one side, higher inflation increases credit risk while on the other hand, it increases spending due to the phenomenon of money illusion. The non-performing loans (NPLs) account for the cost implications on commercial banks when they need to make loan loss provisions and its coefficient is expected to be negative. Data on bank-specific variables and non-performing loans are obtained from the quarterly balance sheets of 10 commercial banks operating in Rwanda and for which data are available in the period under review. Data on financial variables such as interest rates are from the National Bank of Rwanda database while GDP and inflation rate are obtained from the National Institute of Statistics of Rwanda.

Table 4.9 shows that the lending behaviour of the banks in Rwanda is persistent as indicated by high and significant coefficient (0.89) of lagged loan supply. In addition, the level of economic activities and non-performing loans (NPL) are determinants

Table 4.9 GMM-in difference estimates of loan supply function for Rwanda; one-step results

Variable	Parameter	Coefficient	Standard error	P value
Constant/intercept	Λ	0.50	0.23	0.03
$\log(L_{i,t-1})$	δ	0.89	0.02	0.00
Macroeconomic variables				
$\log(y_{t-1})$	Γ	0.25	0.065	0.00
π_{t-1}	Ω	0.001	0.001	0.29
$\log(NPL_{i,t-1})$	μ	−0.03	0.003	0.000
r_{t-1}	A	−0.004	0.002	0.077
Bank characteristics				
$Size_{i,t-1}$	B	0.124	0.02	0.000
$Liquidity_{i,t-1}$	B	0.041	0.037	0.26
$Capital_{i,t-1}$	B	0.184	0.05	0.00
$Market\_Power_{i,t-1}$	B	0.13	0.09	0.16
Ownership	Φ	0.003	0.012	0.76
Interaction terms				
$(Size^*\Delta r_{t-1})$	T	0.002	0.001	0.09
$(Liquidity^*\Delta r_{t-1})$	T	−0.036	0.007	0.00
$(Capital^*\Delta r_{t-1})$	T	−0.032	0.013	0.01
Number of observations: 260 Number of banks: 10 Estimation procedure: One step				

Source Author's computations

of loan supply by banks. One percent increase in GDP leads to 0.25% increase in loan supplied by banks and 1% increase in NPL results in 0.03% reduction in loan supply, while other factors remain the same.

As expected, the lagged monetary policy variable (repo rate) is negatively and statistically significant, although the effect is small. One percentage point increase in the repo rate leads to a contemporaneously decrease in the bank's loan supply by 0.004 percentage point. The smaller size of the coefficient can be explained by the indirect relationship between the monetary policy variable and credit growth in the sense that tight or loose monetary policy would first affect the short-term rates, which in turn affects market lending rates and subsequently growth in credit. As shown before, the interest rate pass-through (the link between short-term interest rate and lending rates) in Rwanda is weak.

Looking at bank-specific characteristics, the results of our estimation show that bank size and capitalization have significant effects on bank loan supply with an increase in bank size by 1% leading to 0.12% increase in loan supply while an increase by 1% in bank's capital leads to 0.18% increase in loan supply. While the coefficient of liquidity variable has the expected sign, it is not statistically significant. On the asymmetrical effects of monetary policy on loan supply, the size turned out to be an important bank characteristic that affects the way Rwandan banks react to monetary policy changes. The positive interaction coefficient of bank size and monetary policy variable implies that larger banks are likely to respond less to monetary policy shocks compared to smaller banks. The responses of the banks to monetary policy change are significantly affected by capitalization and liquidity, however, in a rather unexpected manner. The negative coefficients suggest that, compared to less capitalized or less liquid banks, well-capitalized and more liquid banks respond strongly to monetary policy. Regarding bank capital Chileshe (2017) had found the same response in Zambia with well-capitalized banks responding more to monetary policy.

To avoid over-parameterization and unmask possible heterogeneities, the data set was split into two groups to assess whether monetary policy transmission is uniform in small banks and large banks, less and more liquid banks, less and well-capitalized banks. The findings in Table 4.10 confirm the impact of policy rate change to loans supply of banks by category. The reaction of relatively less liquid and less capitalized banks is negative and statistically significant as expected, while being not statistically significant for more liquid and more capitalized banks. These findings support the role of bank characteristics in monetary policy transmission mechanism in Rwanda and a potentially working bank lending channel.

Regarding small banks versus large banks, the effect of change in liquidity is more evident in small banks than in large banks, while the impact from change in capital is more pronounced in large banks than in small banks. For small banks, the increase in liquidity leads to more lending whereas the effect from change in capitalization is not statistically significant. For larger banks, it is rather capitalization, which positively influences the loan supply while effect from change in liquidity is not statistically significant.

Table 4.10 Distributional effect of monetary policy on loan supply by group banks

	Small banks	Large banks	Less liquid	More liquid	Less capitalized	More capitalized
Constant/intercept	−0.073	0.50**	0.28	0.35	0.52*	−1.93
$\Delta \log(L_{i,t-1})$	0.61***	0.89***	1.05***	1.03***	1.03***	1.05***
Macroeconomic variables						
$\Delta \log(y_{t-1})$	0.990***	0.25***	−0.05	−0.051	−0.11	0.236**
π_{t-1}	0.002	0.001	0.003	0.02*	0.00003	−0.005
$\Delta \log(NPL_{i,t-1})$	−0.048***	−0.037***	−0.057***	−0.043***	−0.025***	−0.055***
Δr_{t-1}	−0.009**	−0.004*	−0.003*	−0.0039	−0.007***	0.008
Bank characteristics						
$\Delta Size_{i,t-1}$	0.208***	0.124***	0.02*	0.001**	0.007	0.02
$\Delta Liquidity_{i,t-1}$	0.10*	0.041	0.26***	0.137***	0.13*	0.015
$\Delta Capital_{i,t-1}$	0.04	0.18***	0.18***	0.31*	0.66***	0.132*
Interaction terms						
$(Size^*\Delta r_{t-1})$	0.0058***	0.0029***	−0.005*	−0.004	−0.023	−0.0012
$(Liquidity^*\Delta r_{t-1})$	−0.04***	−0.036***	0.037***	−0.019**	0.0051	−0.024
$(Capital^*\Delta r_{t-1})$	−0.03*	−0.032**	−0.21	−0.012*	−0.096***	−0.002

Number of observations: 260
Number of banks: 10
Estimation procedure: One step
*, **, ***On coefficients indicate the level of significance at 1%, 5%, and 10%, respectively, while *elsewhere stands for multiplication sign

Source Author's computations

About less liquid versus more liquid banks, there is no big differences as a change in both capital and size positively affects the volume of loans for both less and more liquid banks although the impact from capital is larger when the bank is liquid. On less capitalized banks versus more capitalized banks, lending from the former category of banks is influenced by change in liquidity, while lending from the latter is not sensitive to both liquidity and size. As indicated by the interaction terms between the policy variable and bank characteristics, the effects of monetary policy changes are likely to be higher in small banks than larger banks, which may mean that larger banks possess a buffer in their balance sheets that enables them to mitigate the effects of monetary policy on their lending. The findings on liquidity and capitalization somehow confirm the insight from the full model as more capitalized banks and more liquid banks respond more to monetary policy change than less capitalized and less liquid banks except in two sub-categories, namely less liquid and less capitalized banks.

References

Al-Mashat RA, Billmeier A (2007) The monetary transmission mechanism in Egypt, Washington, IMF working paper no. 07/285
Arellano M, Bond S (1991) Some tests of specification for panel data: Monte Carlo evidence and an application to employment equations. Rev Econ. Stud. 58(2):277–297
Bernanke B, Mishkin F (1997) Inflation targeting: a new framework for monetary policy? J Econ Perspect 11(2):97–116
Borio CEV (1997) The implementation of monetary policy in industrial countries: a survey, BIS economic papers 47. Bank for International Settlements, Basel
Bernanke B, Gertler M (2000) Monetary policy and asset price volatility. NBR Working Paper Series, 7559 http://www.nber.org/papers/w75597559
Brooks PK (2007) The bank lending channel of monetary transmission: does it work in Turkey? Washington, IMF working paper, WP/07/272
Ca'Zorzi (2007) Exchange rate pass-through in emerging markets. European central bank working paper series no 739
Chileshe PM (2017) Banking structure and the bank lending channel of monetary policy transmission: evidence from panel data methods. Bank of Zambia Working Paper, Lusaka
Choi and Cook (2008) New Keynesian exchange rate pass-through. IMF working paper no. 08/213
Choudhri and Hakura (2001) Exchange rate pass through to domestic prices. Do the inflationary environment matters? IMF working paper, WP 01/194
Creel J, Levasseur S (2005) Monetary policy transmission mechanisms in the CEECs: how important are the differences with the euro area? Documents de Travail de l'OFCE 2005-02, Observatoire Francais des Conjonctures Economiques (OFCE)
Cukierman A, Webb SB, Neyapti B (1992) Measuring the independence of central banks and its effect on policy outcomes. World Bank Econ Rev 6(3):353–398
Dabla-Norris E, Floerkemeier H (2006) Transmission mechanisms of monetary policy in Armenia: evidence from VAR analysis. IMF working paper no. 06/248, Washington
De Bondt G (2002) Retail Bank interest rate pass-through: new evidence at the Euro Area Level. ECB Working Paper 136, European Central Bank, Frankfurt
Engle R, Granger C (1987) Co-integration and error correction representation: estimation and testing. Econometrica 55:251–276
Favero CA (2001) Applied macroeconometrics. Econ. Notes. 31(3):559–563
Feinberg RM (1989) The effects of foreign exchange movements on U.S. domestic prices. Rev Econ Stat 71:505–11
Frankel J et al. (2005) Slow pass-through around the world: a new import for developing countries? Working paper no. 11199, National Bureau of Economic Research
Frankel J, Parsley D, Wei S-J (2012) Slow pass-through around the world: a new import for developing countries? Open Econ Rev 23(2):213–251
Gigineishvili, N., (2011). Determinants of Interest Rate Pass-Through: Do Macroeconomic Conditions and Financial Market Structure Matter? Washington: IMF working paper, WP/11/176
Goldberg PK, Knetter MM (1997) Goods prices and exchange rates: what have we learned? J Econ Literat 35(3):1243–1272
Hofmann B, Mizen P (2004) Interest rate pass-through and monetary transmission: evidence from individual financial institutions' retail rates. Economica 71(281):99–123 New Series
Kashyap AK, Stein JC (1995) The impact of monetary policy on bank balance sheets. Carnegie-Rochester Conference Series on Public Policy, 42 (June), 151–195
Kashyap AK, Stein JC (2000) What do a million observations on banks say about the transmission of monetary policy? Am. Econ. Rev. 90(3):407–428
Kourelis CCaA (1994) Financial structure, bank lending rates, and the transmission mechanism of Monetary Policy, Washington, IMF working paper, WP/94/39
Krugman P (1987) Pricing to market when the exchange rate changes. MIT Press, Cambridge, MA

MacKinnon JG (1996) Numerical distribution functions for unit root and cointegration tests. J of App Econ 11(6):601–618

McCarthy J (2007) Pass-through of exchange rates and import prices to domestic inflation in some industrialized economies. Eastern Econ J 33(4):511–537

Mishkin FS (1995) Monetary transmission mechanism. J Econ Perspect 9(4):49–72

Mishkin F (2001) The transmission mechanism and the role of asset prices in Monetary Policy, National Bureau Economic Research working paper no. 8617

Mishra P, Montiel PJ (2010) How effective is Monetary transmission in low-income countries? A survey of the empirical evidence, Washington DC, IMF working paper no. 12/143

Mishra P, Montiel PJ (2012) How effective is monetary transmission in low-income countries? A survey of the empirical evidence, Washington, IMF working paper no. 12/143

Mishra P, Montiel PJ, Sengupta R (2016) Monetary transmission in developing countries: evidence from India, Washington, Working paper no. 16/167

Montiel PJ, Spilimbergo A, Mishra P (2010) Monetary transmission in low income countries, Washington, IMF working paper no. 10/223

Obstfeld M, Rogoff BK (1995) Exchange rate dynamics redux. J Polit Econ 103(31)

Popper DP aH (1998) Exchange rates, domestic prices and Central Bank actions: recent US experience. Southern Econ J 64(4):957–972

Samiei H, Martijn JK (1999) Central Bank independence and the conduct of Monetary Policy in the United Kingdom, Washington DC, IMF working paper no. 99/170

Takhtamanova (2008) Understanding changes in exchange rate pass-through federal Reserve Bank of San Francisco working paper series

Taylor J (2000) Low inflation, pass-through, and the pricing power of firms. Eur. Econ. Rev. 44(7):1389–1408

Tieman A (2004) Interest rate pass through in Romania And other central European economies, Washington, IMF working paper no. WP/04/211

Tsangarides C (2010) Monetary policy transmission in Mauritius using a VAR analysis, Washington, IMF working paper no. 10/36

Woo WT (1984) Exchange rates and the prices of non-food, non-fuel products. Brookings Papers Econ Activity 2:511–30

Yang Y, Davies M, Wang S, Dunn J, Wu Y (2011). Monetary policy transmission mechanisms in Pacific Island countries. IMF working paper, WP/11/96

Chapter 5
Monetary Policy Communication at the National Bank of Rwanda

5.1 Introduction

Central banks' communication journey has evolved from an era of mystery to an era of transparency, openness, and accountability, leading monetary policy communication to become a distinct tool for monetary policy implementation. Prior to the 1990s, central banks were hesitant or shared little about their policies, living actions speaking for themselves. At the time, central bankers guarded this mystery as essential to their success (Woodford 2005), with the conviction that monetary policy was effective by surprising and not informing the market. This was explained by different factors including the absence of clear monetary policy frameworks; the desire for central banks to maximize power and prestige and avoid accountability (Mishkin 2004); the desire to ensure maximum policy discretion by trying to be free of constraint, including constraints that might arise from prior statements by central banks (Cecchetti 1999; Cecchetti and Schoenholtz 2019); and a way of limiting pressure for excessively accommodative monetary by politicians leading to time inconstancy problem (Kydland and Prescott 1977; Calvo 1978). Time horizons for politicians are shorter due to their objectives of implementing short-term popular policies than the optimum time horizon needed for monetary policy focusing on achieving long-term stability.

Different factors have contributed to the push for more transparency and accountability for central banks, including the role of expectations in economic behaviour that gained widespread attention in the thinking of economists since 1970s and the development of more democratic systems pushing different institutions to be more open and transparent. As pointed out, expectations played an important role in the behaviour of economic agents, by taking into account all possible unknown future economic events while making their decisions (Kryvtsov and Petersen 2013). For example, expectations about future income, interest rate, and inflation rate influence the households' decisions about consumption and saving and firms' decision about making investment and production.

T. K. Rusuhuzwa, *Monetary Policy in Rwanda*, Frontiers in African Business Research, https://doi.org/10.1007/978-981-33-6746-3_5

The important role of expectations in monetary policy transmission mechanism emerged over time and according to Blinder (1998), performance of monetary policy results from effective management of expectations rather than influencing overnight interest rates. Indeed, changes in central bank rate affect only the short-term liquidity that commercial banks obtain from the central bank. The objective of central banks was to have those changes in central bank rate transmitted to other interest rates that affect the economy as a whole. This generally occurs through market expectations about future monetary policy and crucially depends on the extent to which public understands current policies and future ones. This explains why monetary policy becomes gradually the art of managing expectations through communication (Haan et al. 2004). A good illustration is the role played by central banks' communication in advanced countries, during the global financial crisis where the effects of unconventional monetary policy were transmitted mostly through expectation channel.

In exceptional circumstances such as global financial crisis and Covid-19, central banks act in order to eliminate panic from the financial markets and sectors by providing liquidity to ensure functionality of the credit markets and prevent the collapse of systemic financial institutions. This is generally achieved by reducing central bank rates. However, when interest rates hit their zero lower band, communication becomes a policy tool used by central banks to manage public expectations by maintaining confidence of the financial markets participants and central banks' credibility, and thus contributing to stimulate the economy (Tsuji 2016; Nier 2009). Central bank communication is defined as the provision of information that the central banks make available to the general public on the objectives of monetary policy, the monetary policy strategy, the economic outlook, and the future policy decisions (De Haan and Jansen 2007; Blinder 2008). However, due to the interest for central banks to work with, rather than against markets, central bank communication becomes progressively a two-way process, involving genuine listening and engagement with different audiences, rather than simply one-way broadcasting of central bank announcements (Haldane and McMahon 2018; Powell 2019).

The increasing need for more transparency and accountability pushed central banks to seek clearer policy frameworks and led to the development of new monetary policy strategy in many countries, focusing on single goal of controlling inflation using a single instrument, either the quantity of central bank money such as base money, for countries with less developed financial market or the value of central bank money (policy rate). In many advanced economies, inflation targeting (IT) with floating exchange rates emerged as the new monetary policy framework of choice with the Reserve Bank of New Zealand (RBNZ) becoming the first central bank to adopt IT in 1990 and this move marked the start of a more open central banks.

Key characteristics of IT framework are the public announcement by central banks of medium-term numerical targets for inflation; firm commitment to price stability as the primary, long-run goal of monetary policy and to achieve the inflation goal; the existence of an information inclusive strategy in which many variables and not just monetary aggregates are used in making decisions about monetary policy; transparency of the monetary policy strategy through communication with the public and the markets about the plans and objectives of monetary policymakers; and increased accountability of the central bank for attaining its inflation objectives (Mishkin 2000). As it can be understood, under IT framework, communication becomes crucial in bringing the expectations of economic actors closer to goals announced by central banks by helping the public understanding of central banks' reaction function.

For central bank, anchoring public expectations around the objective of monetary policy is crucial to ensure that reactions of economic agents to the macroeconomic shocks remain in line with the path of adjustment that the central bank wants the economy to follow. Indeed, by determining the long-term interest rates, expectations of inflation and of the future path of short-term (real) interest rates influence investment and consumption decisions and, ultimately, medium and long-term price developments. Thus, the understanding of expectations about future central banks behaviour by the public provides the essential link between short-term rates and long-term rates, which is key for central banks to influence the aggregate demand in the immediate future, given the forward-looking nature of economic agents (Blinder 1998). Communication plays an important role to help the public understand that central banks' policy actions are not a response to current conditions rather to medium-term trends of objective, because the impacts of monetary policy on the economy and on inflation occur with a lag. In other words, the decision today by central bank about its monetary policy stance is not to deal with current inflationary pressures rather to keep the inflation rate closer to its target after a certain period.

To help the public to anticipate the direction of monetary policy, central banks communicate not only its policy stance but also its assessment of the current economic condition as well as its most likely evolution in the future using its assessment of future economic trends and how monetary policy relates to these trends. Thus, the more the central banks use effective communication to provide a useful and clear path of the future trajectory of interest rates to market participants, the more would be the impact on long-term interest rates (Issing 2005).

The existing literature on monetary policy communication focuses mainly on advanced and emerging countries with more developed financial markets. However, there is increasing interest in improving communication strategies in developing countries' central banks with the aim to improve monetary transmission channels by trying to anchor public expectations around monetary policy objectives. This is due to different factors including the development in financial systems and their link with the real economy, the breakdown of the links between monetary aggregates and prices leading to the adoption of more market-based monetary policy instruments and the increasing pressures on central banks to be transparent in their operations and be accountable to the public and governments. Due to the expected impact of central bank policy actions on the economy through its influence on aggregate demand, the need for central banks to provide an explanation on their decisions and the rationale underlying these decisions contributed to the increased importance of communicating with different economic agents such as financial sector players, other economic policymakers, the business community, households, researchers, and journalists.

A good example is the case of the East African Community (EAC). The harmonization and strengthening of monetary policy communication across partner states' central banks is one of the priorities in enhancing monetary policy transmission mechanism as they transit to a price-based monetary policy framework. EAC central banks adopted a harmonized monetary policy communication framework in 2010 and the respective central banks' governors recommended that partner states' central banks develop harmonized tools for assessing the effectiveness of monetary policy in November 2014.

There is great commonality on how monetary policy decisions are taken and communicated in Rwanda, Kenya, Uganda, and Tanzania. In the four countries, the monetary policy making organ is the monetary policy committee (MPC) whose mandates are clearly articulated in the bank act of those countries. Governors chair monetary policy committees in the four countries while the composition of MPC varies, with the National Bank of Rwanda, Bank of Tanzania, and Central Bank of Kenya having both internal and external members in their committees but the Bank of Uganda having only internal members. Press conferences are the primary mode of communicating MPC decisions. Other channels are also used including bi-annual monetary policy statements in all EAC central banks, except the Bank of the Republic of Burundi, and meetings with different economic actors as well as different publications by central banks on their website.

The 20th ordinary monetary affairs committee meeting of Governors in July 2016 decided that partner states' central banks should expedite the assessment of the effectiveness of monetary policy communication in their countries and in 2018, it was decided to: (i) convene a communication symposium to exchange ideas on how to develop a regional communication policy framework by bringing together different teams from central banks and expertise from other central banks and institutions, and (ii) to continue sharing experiences on the status of implementation of their policy communication frameworks. The Central Bank of Kenya hosted a symposium in March 2019 to exchange ideas on how to develop policy communication frameworks and hence, a policy communication framework for the region is under development. Different tools are used by EAC central banks to assess the impact of their communications on their main target groups including market intelligence (e.g. informal discussions with market participants); formal surveys of market participants; and empirical studies in some banks that try to quantify the impact of various monetary policy communication efforts on managing expectations.

The adoption by central banks of more clear monetary policy strategies brought two additional important dimensions to the monetary policy communication. Not only central banks announce and explain their monetary policy decisions when they are taken but also they communicate about their assessment of the current economic situation and its most likely evolution in the future. This is because good financial decisions of households and firms which are key for the efficiency of monetary policy highly depend on information about the central bank's assessment of the economy. Furthermore, the importance of working with the markets was progressively recognized as crucial in ensuring the effectiveness of monetary policy. To have the monetary transmission mechanism working smoothly, the public (households, businesses and financial market participants) has to better understand the objective pursued by central bank in conducting monetary policy; the tools that are used to achieve that objective, and the central bank's view of the economy that support its actions.

One of the current debated issues about how to help the public understand the future behaviour of central banks is whether to what extent and how the central bank should signal its future policy intentions. Academics have emphasized that it may be important for central bank to provide market participants with precise quantitative indications about the likely future path of policy interest rates and to help align market expectations more closely with those of the central bank. However, the feasibility and desirability of announcing a specific likely future path of policy rates poses serious concerns for central banks. In a world of uncertainty surrounding the future evolution of a large number of exogenous variables that may affect the economic outlook and the risks to the attainment of the policy objectives, it is difficult to support the idea of providing markets with a likely future path of policy rates, particularly beyond the short-term horizon. Doing so may undermine the initial intention to support the public in making informed economic decisions by reducing the uncertainty about the future course of economic activities and inflation.

In a particular case of monetary policy, this type of uncertainty increases with the length of the forecast horizon, making it difficult to determine the explicit path of interest rates in a reliable manner. Finally, because there is high probability of future policy rates often deviating from the subsequent actual path of interest rates, this may undermine the central bank's credibility. This explains why many central banks around the world have refined the way they communicate decisions related to the stance of monetary policy as well as their assessment of economic conditions supporting those decisions.

In general, central banks communicate about at least four different aspects of monetary policy: their overall objectives and strategy, the motives behind a particular policy decision, the economic outlook, and future monetary policy decisions (Blinder 2008). Because the laws establishing central banks clearly indicate their objectives and mandates, the most important communication of central banks with the public is about their monetary policy decisions.

The channel through which central banks communication is passed on through the public is either via qualitative communication instruments (e.g. press releases, public speeches, publications, statements and minutes), or quantitative communication instruments, such forecast on inflation and other macro variables. For central banks mainly those implementing price-based monetary policy or those called inflation targeters press releases to announce the policy rate decision, and a monetary policy report or an inflation report are currently considered as standard communication vehicles. In addition, most of those central banks hold press conferences to explain their policy decision.

In addition, in an effort to promote transparency in some countries, parliamentary hearings, and an open letter in the event that inflation misses the target by a prespecified amount, serve as accountability mechanisms to ensure that central banks are holding their missions. Furthermore, central banks organize other communication events with the public, via speeches, interviews, and meetings with the private sector businesses, as well as outreach programmes with colleges and universities, community groups, local associations, and so on to further explain their decision and what it was based on.

Central banks' websites have also become a major communication vehicle, where big amounts of information for general and specialized audiences are posted such as research-based publications, press releases, speeches related to monetary policy, as well as statistical information. In some advanced central banks, short, direct backgrounders, and animated and interactive presentations are also available explaining various aspects of monetary policy and other central bank functions. Central banks with currency museums have also developed materials and products for students of different ages. With these communication efforts, more emphasis has also been placed on straight talk and plain language to facilitate access to monetary policy messages to a broad public audience as possible.

About the assessment of the impact of communication, studies in developed countries show that communication by central banks has contributed to reduce volatility of financial markets by increasing transparency and reducing uncertainty (Knutter et al. 2011). Different studies on the impact of central bank communication tools on financial markets and asset prices show that the most effective in terms of influencing markets are the statements and press conferences that follow rate decisions. The two tools contribute to form expectations for market players for the course of short- and long-term interest rates, increase predictability particularly at times of uncertainty, and have a general positive impact on asset prices. The record of votes is third, followed by the meeting minutes, the tapes, press conferences, and research papers (Knutter et al. 2011; Born et al. 2013).

5.2 Monetary Communication in National Bank of Rwanda

NBR communication journey started in 2005 when the Governor presented the first monetary policy and financial stability statement to the public. The next step was the improvement of the way monetary policy decisions are taken, moving progressively from the Governor as single decision maker to the establishment of the Monetary Policy Committee (MPC) in 2008 composed of more members in addition to the Governor. Changes in NBR's decision-making process and improvement in communication were in line with the effort of the bank to increase its transparency, credibility, and accountability, as well as making the monetary policy more predictable. The predictability of monetary policy is the ability of financial markets and the general public to correctly anticipate the next monetary policy decision of a central bank and predict the broader future course of monetary policy. Thus, more focus has been to increase the transparency about how monetary policy decisions are taken, implemented, and communicated, particularly after the adoption of a price-based monetary policy since January 2019, from the use of a monetary targeting framework that was exercised since 1997.

The improvement in NBR institutional framework reinforcing its independence and related accountability has contributed to this change. For instance, in article 4 of the Law no. 48/2017 of 23 September 2017 governing the National Bank of Rwanda that provides special legal status to NBR, it is stated that the bank has legal personality as well as administrative and financial autonomy. It is clearly indicated that NBR is not subject to any directive from any person or institution in the exercising of its powers or in performance of its mission. It is important to note that this independence brought an obligation for the NBR to be more accountable to ensure that delegated responsibilities by the government to the bank are properly executed. It is in the same vain that the article 68 of the law governing the National Bank of Rwanda states that within four months after the closing of each financial year, the governor submits to the President of the Republic and to the Parliament, both chambers, the NBR's annual activity report.

To improve the monetary transmission mechanism, NBR has also invested more effort in engaging a wider audience, to improve its understanding about monetary policy tools used to manage the liquidity in the banking sector, the bank actions, as well as its assessment of the economy that support those actions. In the bank's communication strategy, NBR has to take into consideration that the public it targets is composed of groups with different levels of education and knowledge about the use of financial systems, contrary to advanced countries where big percentage of people work with banks and financial markets.

Based on FINSCOP (2020) survey, 93% representing about 7 million adults in Rwanda are financially included, using both formal and informal financial products and services. Banked population growth has increased by 1.1 million since 2016 and the bank uptake and usage are driven by transactional products, as more people are receiving their income through banking accounts. For example, about only 25% of banked adults use digital payments; this is up from 6% in 2016. The survey indicates that key barriers to the uptake of mobile money relate to lack of product knowledge and lack of interest in the product. The same survey reveals that only 9% of adult population in Rwanda have knowledge about credit reference bureau, 4% about bank cards, 12% about deposit guarantee funds, and 32% about agriculture insurance. As financial products and services are always in constant evolution, it is imperative to offer financial education among adults because the knowledge level of adults regarding financial products significantly influences their decisions.

Therefore, financial education is an important part of NBR communication strategy aiming at accelerating financial inclusion which is the access and usage of financial products by all population. In addition, the information to be communicated to the public in an effort to increase the proportion of the Rwandan population that follows the NBR's communique has to be clear, simplified, and adapted to the audience. Thus, the identification of target groups is crucial to help NBR designing channels and tools of communication depending on what is being communicated and the targeted audience. Currently NBR targets the following groups when communicating with the public: the financial system, business community, households, think tanks, media, youths, academia, NBR staff, parliament, and other stakeholders including public authorities and international organizations.

Table 5.1 Key NBR communication documents and frequency of release

Key communication documents	Frequency
MPC press release	Quarterly
Financial stability committee press release	Bi-annual
MPC working document	Quarterly
Financial stability report	Bi-annual
Monetary policy and financial stability statement	Bi-annual
Quarterly inflation report	Quarterly
Daily economic update	Daily
NBR annual report	Annual
NBR economic review	Bi-annual
News and data on NBR website	Regular
The banker	Bi-annual

Source NBR, communication division

5.2.1 NBR Communication Strategy

After the adoption of the price-based monetary policy framework, the NBR board of directors adopted the bank's communication strategy in September 2020 aiming at creating awareness about the bank's policies and how they relate to the public; enhancing the bank's engagement with policymakers, sector players, and the general public; protecting the bank's image and institutional reputation; and ensuring the availability of a broad range of financial education initiatives that promote financial literacy, financial inclusion, and consumer protection.

As mentioned before, in developing countries like Rwanda a big part of the population does not work with the formal financial system and does not have information about the importance and the ways of accessing formal financial products. This therefore emphasizes why communication at NBR shall not just be a matter of openness and transparency, but also of education, guidance, dialogue, listening, and learning. While communication to target groups will be regular and consistent through the identified communication channels, a clear agenda of major policy decisions and communication is as presented in Table 5.1.

5.2.2 Monetary Communication Tools

A variety of tools used by NBR to communicate its monetary policy were adopted progressively as a response to the need of improving the communication with the public, which has been further enabled by technology advancement and penetration in Rwanda. These tools include MPC press releases; press conferences by the Governor; central bank publications; the use of social media such as, Twitter, YouTube, Instagram, Facebook, Email, WhatsApp Group with Journalists and Slido App; and a semi-annual Monetary Policy and Financial Stability Statement held every February and August.

In addition, NBR also organizes regular meetings with stakeholders in the financial sector to discuss key issues relevant to the central bank missions of achieving price stability, sustaining the financial sector stability, and supporting government development programmes. NBR also uses its website to publish plenty of information accessible by many stakeholders and users, and also use it as a platform to ensure the bank's transparency by familiarizing the public with the work of NBR. The information published on the website includes NBR's economic reviews, the Rwandan banker, Governor's monetary policy and financial stability statements, NBR's annual reports, press releases, and different statistics.

NBR relies heavily on the media to get their key messages out to the public, be it through newspapers or magazines, television and radio, or the wire services. The media acts as a filter, deciding which central bank statements they will feature. It also interprets the banks' policy decisions, comments on how they see the central bank fulfilling its mandate. Therefore, the way the media interprets the bank's information is key to avoid misunderstanding of the central bank's communication. Hence, the need for the media to be well informed about monetary policy and its complexities and conditional nature. For this reason, NBR devotes considerable resources to media relations including training journalists.

Communicating MPC Decision on Monetary Policy Stance

MPC meets on a quarterly basis: February, May, August, and November. A day after the MPC, a press conference is organized to allow the media an opportunity to ask questions during the press conference. During the press conference, a press release is shared to journalists and posted on NBR's website for the public. In the press release, the NBR indicates the decision by MPC on monetary policy stance as well as economic development and forecasts supporting the MPC decisions. Figure 5.1 illustrates the National Bank of Rwanda (NBR) communication model, which is derived

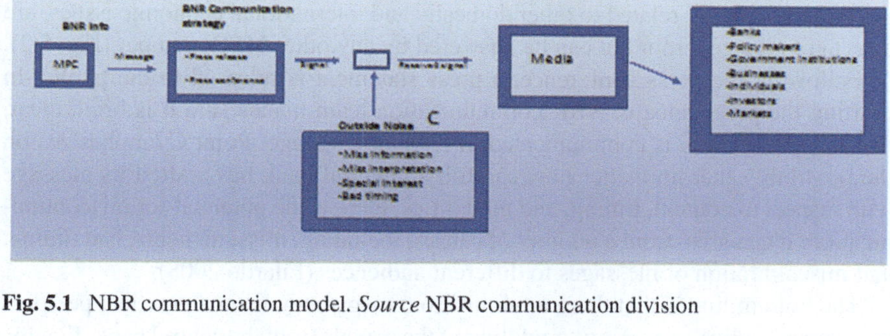

Fig. 5.1 NBR communication model. *Source* NBR communication division

from the original simple Shannon's 1948 telecommunication model. In telecommunication, transmission is easier since it is mostly a telephone call from one party to another, therefore there is no much room for anything to be lost in transmission.

However, for central banks, considerable resources are devoted to sending the right signals in a timely manner and to various constituencies, such as other policymakers, government officials, financial markets, and the general public (Filardo 2008). With the development of new technologies allowing for new ways of interaction, a deep understanding of the entire communication process from central bank at the sending end, the intermediation, and interpretation of messages sent by the central banks via markets, media, analysts, politicians, to the perception thereof by the recipients become crucial for policy decisions.

While admittedly simple and pedagogical, the Shannon model sheds light on various aspects of the communication channel of monetary policy. In a nutshell, the central bank starts by taking stock of information about monetary policy that it wants to share with the public (left-hand side of Fig. 5.1, point A). This includes information about the policy framework, the decision-making process, the policy decision, assessments of the economy, future predictions, and so on (Filardo 2008).

In line with NBR's policy decision-making, at point A, NBR's team from the Monetary Policy and Research Directorate (MPRD) conducts preliminary analyses to support MPC decision-making process. These analyses include current economic trends and projections and their implications on the domestic economy as a whole and on inflation in particular. The economic analysis covers development in global economy as well as in domestic economy (real sector, external sector, and monetary sector).

Given the enormous and the intensity of the information at point A, NBR carefully chooses its communication strategy at point B. Following the technical meetings, the monetary policy committee chaired by the Governor is held to decide on monetary policy stance reflected in the review of the central bank rate. After the decision on the central bank rate, several steps are taken to inform the public about the monetary policy stance. Following the MPC decision, the main channel used at NBR is a press conference, not only to provide detailed information on monetary policy stance but also offer the media an opportunity to ask different questions in a direct and open manner. Questions by different media generally in line with information provided in the press release, or related to other domestic and international economic issues, are directed to the governor but can be answered by any other MPC member (Fig. 5.2).

Following the press conference, a press statement is released to the public. In drafting the press release, NBR communication team makes sure it is brief, clear, and the information is communicated in layman language. Point C emphasizes on the possibility that no matter how carefully a central bank has crafted its message with respect to content, timing, and modalities, there is the potential for miscommunication. It can arise from a number of causes, including, misstatements, bad timing, and miscalibration of messages to different audiences (Filardo 2008).

The bottom line is that there are limits to transparency from a practical perspective, hence leading to a serious muddling of the signals from the central bank. Finally, misinterpretation of the signals by the intended recipients (points D&E) is always

Fig. 5.2 MPC members briefing the media a day after the MPC meeting. *Source* NBR, communication division

possible, especially when different groups of recipients are seeking different types of information. Moreover, differences in their abilities to absorb and interpret information and different levels of interest in the details of the conduct of monetary policy reduce the effectiveness of a one-size-fits-all communication strategy. Furthermore, the recipients of the messages are not all passive consumers and transmitters of information; some, such as the press, may have their own agenda when passing on the information to various audiences.

The current intense activity to communicate monetary policy stance by NBR is a reflection of the increasing demand for an open and frank exchange of views between the bank and representatives of the media on one side but also NBR's effort to make the public understanding its actions. During the press conference that is held in English, NBR governor makes a summary of key decision in Kinyarwanda, the national language spoken by all Rwandans. Communicating in Kinyarwanda overcomes potential cultural, linguistic, or other national barriers of communication experienced in countries with various languages and bringing NBR policy closer to the people.

In addition to the press conference with journalists, a meeting is organized between the Governor and other senior staff of NBR with managing directors of commercial banks and non-banks financial institutions in the evening of that day to discuss the monetary policy stance along with the bank economic analysis and forecasting. On the second day after MPC meeting, the chief economist and other staff from monetary policy and research directorate meet all NBR staff to share MPC decisions. Different

Fig. 5.3 MPC decisions communicated to BNR staff. *Source* NBR, communication division

social media are also used to communicate MPC decision during the press conference. They include twitter; YouTube; Instagram; Facebook; email; and WhatsApp Group with journalists (Fig. 5.3).

The press release shared with media and published on NBR website serves local and regional media to publish their own news, comments with views of different analysts, or institutions on the MPC decision or related economic analysis and forecasting. From August 2019 MPC meeting to February 2020 MPC meeting, we recorded 413 engagements using all media channels talking about MPC decisions and other related bank activities. In addition, 12 media houses reported about the bank's work 314 times, including MPC and Financial Stability Committee (FSC) decisions, cashless campaign and other bank' activities, and 17 interviews were conducted by Governor or in same occasions by Deputy Governor or senior staff with different media houses on MPC decisions and other NBR activities. Details on media coverage of bank activities are presented in Appendix 5.1. The monetary policy report which provides national economic status, global economic developments, the bank's projections, and the major risks that could affect the inflation outlook is published on NBR website, one week after the MPC meeting.

Monetary Policy and Financial Stability Statement (MPFSS)

The first NBR Governor's Monetary Policy and Financial Stability Statement was done in March 2005 in Kigali to a big audience composed of cabinet members, representative of business community, chief executive officers of financial institutions, representatives of international institutions in Rwanda, academicians, and NBR staff. To reach more people, the statement is extended to other provinces and universities out of Kigali since 2010. For a given year, MPFSS made in February gives the policy orientation of the year after reviewing the achievements and challenges of the previous one, while the second made in August is a mid-term review of the performance over the first half of the year and sets out the perspectives for the remaining period of the year. Fifteen years after, tremendous improvement has been realized in terms of organization, number of participants and institutions represented, and the quality of the statement which covers development in global economy, in domestic economy (real and external sectors), monetary sector (monetary policy formation and implementation and outcome, financial market development), development in inflation and outlook, financial sector stability, and payment system development.

The statement is published as booklet, distributed to all participants, and posted on NBR website. As shown in this paragraph, information shared during the MPFSS is key for different policymakers in the country and international partners in their decision-making process. To allow for a big participation to MPFSS, including people in the region and other countries who not only can follow the presentation and discussion by participants in the meeting room but can also send questions to panellists (Governor, Deputy Governor, Chief economist and Executive Director of financial stability directorate), different channels have been used. Those channels include YouTube, Twitter, and Facebook and slido application. As shown in the table in Appendix 5.1, from August 2019 MPFSS to February 2020 MPFSS, 226 viewers were recorded using YouTube; 1875 engagements via twitter; 259 people followed the Governor's presentation on Facebook; and 207 joined the conversion, including asking questions using slido application, which was introduced in February 2020; 44 questions were asked and 129 liked using the app. During the MPSS, two other important publications of the bank are distributed to the participants: NBR economic review and the Rwandan banker (Fig. 5.4).

Periodic Economic Reports

As for many central banks, the most important reporting vehicles in NBR include regular central bank publications on the bank website. They include monetary policy report which is published one week after each monetary policy committee meeting and contains detailed economic analysis that underlies the MPC's decisions and

Fig. 5.4 Monetary policy and financial stability statement presentation in August 2020. *Source* NBR, communication division

presents the Bank's assessment of the prospects for inflation over the monetary horizon period. As previously indicated NBR economic review is published twice year on the bank website and contains research papers published by NBR staff and covering different topics in applied economics.

Those researches provide key input in NBR decision-making process, not only in the area of monetary policy but also in other domains linked to the mandates of NBR such as financial stability, financial sector development, payment system, and financial inclusion. The bi-annual publication also avail information on various topics to the public, including academicians and research community. The Rwandan Banker Magazine is a bi-annual magazine published by NBR as one of the tools to communicate to the public. This publication aims to bring into context what NBR Staff do on a daily basis, in a bid to raise awareness about the work of the bank and ensure the public understands what the bank does.

Engagement with Stakeholders

The NBR also conducts outreach programmes dubbed NBR Engage to provide different platforms for the bank to engage with the public on issues related to the economy, in an effort to create a better understanding of what the bank does. Financial literacy occupies a centre stage in the quest to achieve an overall strategy of financial inclusion, which has a strong bearing on financial stability, economic growth, and development. For this to happen, it is essential for the public to understand and develop the ability to evaluate financial products and services and also transact in the financial markets.

It was noted that individuals are increasingly faced with a number of financial decisions as a result of changes in the market and economy which requires sound knowledge and efficient use of financial services. The public needs to know about fees, charges/commissions, interest rates, regulations, payment services, and other contractual terms associated with financial transactions to enable them make right decisions. The number of policies, regulatory arrangements, institutional provisions, channels, and delivery methodologies/technology have been on the increase. Services such as remittances, mobile payments, pension and insurance, savings, and credits are gaining increasing diversity and complexity and this requires consumers to be appropriately informed about their rights to take adequate advantage of the opportunities that they offer.

The NBR communication team in collaboration with other departments of the bank has put in place different initiatives targeting different stakeholders ranging from students in secondary schools, university students, to the public. Through these initiatives, NBR staff educates the public on different economic concepts through hosting and leading the discussions with public. NBR engage programmes include: NBR economic clubs, NBR quiz challenges, NBR visit day, NBR with media, NBR in conversation, NBR debates, NBR monetary policy challenge, and NBR youth dialogue.

The economic clubs are channels through which economic and financial matters are shared with the students to help the young generation gain skills that will help them make informed financial decisions in future. In these clubs, NBR staff discusses in details the core functions of the central bank especially on monitoring the economy, formulation and implementation of monetary policy, and ensuring a sound and inclusive financial sector. It is through the NBR economic clubs that the bank team follows up with the economic clubs and discuss the topics that are issued by the NBR and the Government in regards to the economy and financial sector at large.

The NBR also organizes a competition that brings together economic clubs from different schools. The objective of this competition is to educate secondary school students and test their knowledge on the economy in general. Prior to the competition, the NBR team coaches the students on how to take part in the competition and facilitate them with different reading materials in preparation for the competition. There is a specific programme for university students called monetary policy challenge. Universities participating in the challenge are given the chance to step into the shoes of the Monetary Policy Committee, analyse economic data and make a recommendation on what the central bank rate should be. Furthermore, there is a platform for the youth generation to have discussions with NBR management, including Governor and Deputy Governor on different economic and financial topics (Fig. 5.5).

In addition, the NBR has a visit day which is an open day for the public to visit NBR premises and interact with the staff of the bank. Different groups of people are received during the bank visit day. On this day, the public gets a chance to interact with the bank staff on main concerns related to core missions of the bank and have presentations on the bank's common roles; for instance, monetary policy, regulatory roles, financial markets operations, payment systems, currency and so on. Furthermore, every year, NBR organizes a four-day training for journalists, communication staff, marketing, and public relations staff from different financial institutions and stakeholders. The main objective of the training is to provide skills

Fig. 5.5 BNR Quiz challenge to secondary school students. *Source* NBR, communication division

that will assist in improving their professionalism while reporting on economic and financial matters. NBR also has a session called NBR in conversation, where the bank staff meet with the public to give clarity to what might be a burning issue regarding new developments within the economy.

5.3 Monitoring the Impact of Monetary Policy Communication

The international experience shows that central banks have not only developed their strategies to communicate with markets but they have also invested in receiving feedback from the industry, economic sectors, the market and the public about the impact of monetary policy communication. Feedback from the market contributes to improving internal deliberations about monetary policy and promoting the formulation of more effective policies. The assessment of the impact of central banks' communication is mainly achieved using surveys and econometric modelling. However, with the development of technology, text mining, web scraping, and machine learning techniques are used in some banks with adequate skills.

NBR uses informal discussions with market participants (market intelligence) and formal surveys to assess the impact of its communication on their main target groups. NBR staff have also conducted few empirical studies that try to quantify the impact of various monetary policy communication efforts on managing expectations. The financial market operation committee (FMOC) which meets every working day collects information through bilateral phone calls with treasures of commercial banks. These discussions with external contacts provide additional insights beyond analysis of data alone. They help to ensure that the NBR's policy decisions are made and implemented with a detailed understanding of the financial market context in which the bank operates. The market intelligence not only contributes to feeding into internal analysis on policy relevant issues, decision-making, policy implementation, and communication, it also collects feedbacks from treasurers about how they view NBR's interventions on the money market.

Regarding formal surveys, their purpose is to capture market views on the work done by NBR. The main survey conducted by NBR as a tool of assessing the impact of its communication is the survey done during the MPFSS. All participants respond to a questionnaire (see Appendix 5.2) distributed in the meeting room and results from the survey are discussed in an internal meeting. The results from this survey have contributed a lot to improving the quality of the MPFSS. Findings from the surveys covering 11 MPFSSs show that on average 90.2% of participants were satisfied with the time allocated for the governor's presentation, 90.6% of participants were very satisfied (excellent and very good raking) with the content of MPFSS (Fig. 5.6).

In the questionnaire used to assess the views of participants in MPFSS, two important questions are asked to assess the extent to which policymakers use the MPFSS in their decision-making process. The findings of the survey show that on average,

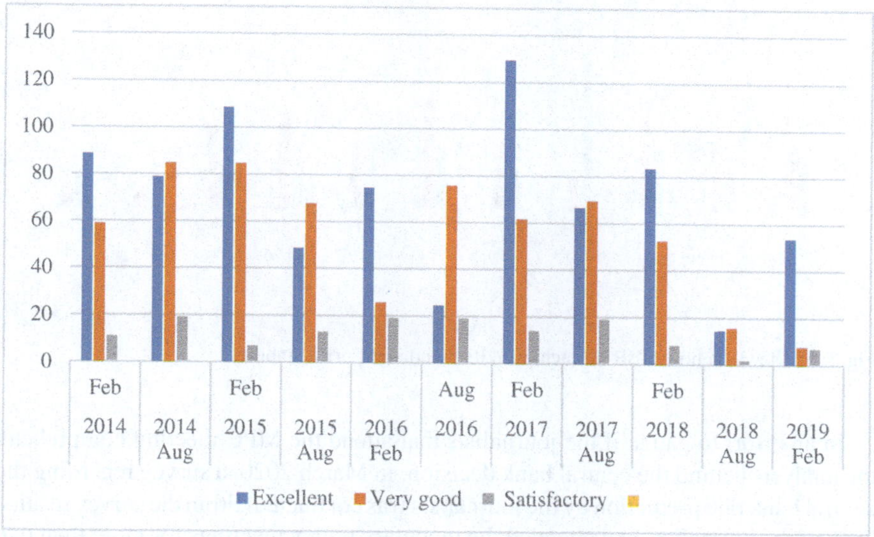

Fig. 5.6 Views about the content of MPFSS

80.1% of participants confirm that they use MPFSS as key source of information in their regular works and 90.9% of participants on average are satisfied with the content provided as pointed out (Fig. 5.7).

As indicated, communication is a key instrument in ensuring monetary policies are contributing to anchoring expectations around the policy objective. While NBR is not committed to a single inflation target, it has clearly considered and communicated for the last 10 years that its medium inflation benchmark is 5%. NBR also communicated to the public its strategy to maintain price stability and the way the bank monetary policy responds to shocks, aiming at keeping inflation around the benchmark. The results from the survey showed that on average, 96.8% of participants in 11 MPFSSs are satisfied by the way NBR has been achieving its objective of price stability (Fig. 5.8).

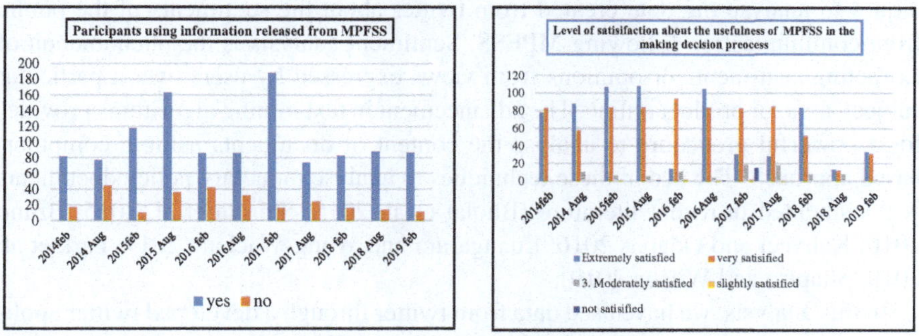

Fig. 5.7 Views about how participants use MPFSS

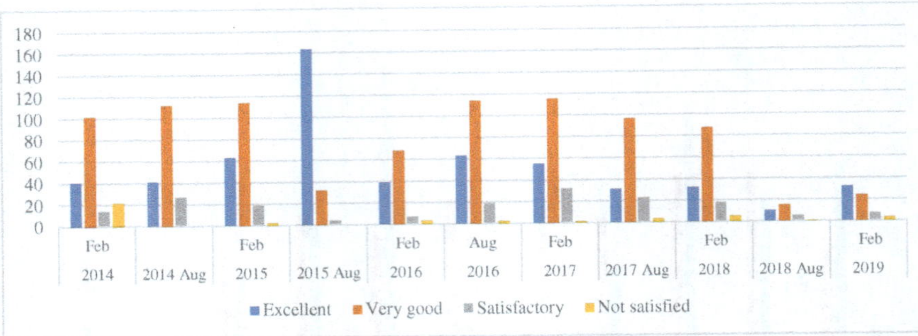

Fig. 5.8 Views on how NBR has achieved its mandate of price stability

In an effort to gauge if the journalists that attend the MPC meeting comprehend the analysis behind the central bank decision, in March 2020, a survey regarding the central bank rate prediction by the journalists was conducted. From the survey results, 70% of the journalists had attended the monetary policy meetings for more than two times. 60% of all the journalists that attended the meeting attempted to predict what the CBR would be prior to the meeting. From the journalists who attempted to predict NBR decision on CBR, 28% were right in their predication about the direction of CBR, 42% somewhat right with differences in the way journalists explain the economic development supporting their prediction, and 30% were wrong. Given that the media plays a big role in the communication of the central bank's decision, it is therefore critical for the bank to keep investing in training of journalists in an effort to reduce miscommunication.

In addition, in an effort to assess if the public can predict the monetary policy decision, another survey was conducted in August 2020, a day prior to MPC meeting. This time around, the targeted audience was the public that follow the bank's twitter account. Of the 130 respondents, 40% anticipated correctly the MPC decision by anticipating a reduction of CBR, 34% said the bank would maintain its rate, 11% anticipated its increase, while 15% indicated that they were not sure about what the MPC decision will be.

With the development of technology in Rwanda, we have used text mining techniques to analyse big data created from twitter about the sentiments of the public from communication following MPFSS. Sentiment analysis is the phenomenon of extracting sentiments or opinions from views expressed by users over a particular subject, area, or product online. The advancement in text mining algorithms provides for a powerful procedure to analyse the content of documents using a computer-based approach. The use of these techniques to analyse monetary policy documents is documented in recent literature (Bholat et al. 2015; Shirota et al. 2015; Bruno 2016; Kahveci and Odabas 2016; Luangaram and Wong-Wachara 2017; Park et al. 2019; Shapiro and Wilson 2019).

In this analysis, we have used data from twitter through a developed twitter application programming interface (API), about the MPFSS released in August, 2020. We have extracted 1345 tweets from the NBR tweet account but restricted to the

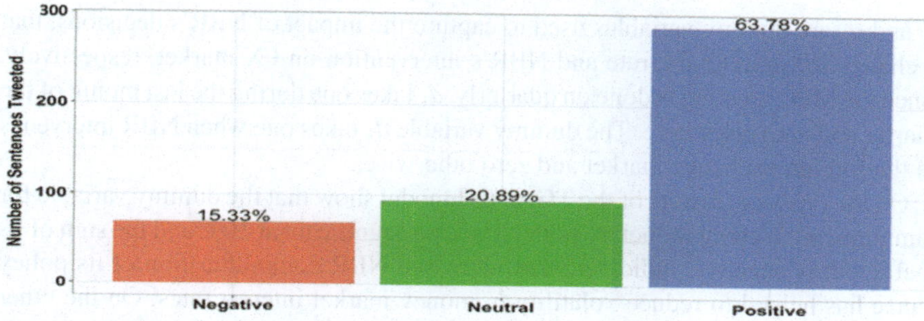

Fig. 5.9 Public sentiment on September 2020 MPFSS

ones written in English only. After preprocessing and preparing the unstructured text data for further analysis, we used the emoticon dictionary, acronym dictionary, and a special lexical dictionary (SentiWordNet) to attribute the emotions and sentiments to the extracted tweets. To obtain prior polarity of word, we used the WordNet dictionary which has assigned to each word the related pleasantness score ($\in$ R) between -1 (Negative) and 3 (Positive). Words with polarity <0.5 are considered as negative, those with polarity higher than 0.8 as positive, while the rest is considered as neutral.

Findings from this analysis are presented in Fig. 5.9 and show that 63.8% of NBR twitter followers expressing positive sentiment about MPFSS released in September 2020, 15.3% expressed negative sentiment, and the rest was neither positive nor negative. This is a clear indication on how the public view NBR communication following MPFSS and the findings can contribute to improve the way NBR communicates to increase the proportion of the followers with positive sentiment on the message communicated by NBR.

There are two empirical studies published in NBR economic review, which assess the impact of NBR communication on the volatility of interest rates (and/or exchange rates) using GARCH model (Karangwa et al. 2017; Nyalihama et al. 2018).

The model is specified as:

$$Y_t = \mu + \varepsilon_t \tag{5.1}$$

where the time series Y_t is the first difference of interbank rate/exchange rate and ε_t is the error term.

To ensure that the value of the variance σ_t^2 depends both on the past values of the shocks captured by the lagged squared residual terms (ε_{t-j}^2), and on its own past values, the following asymmetric GARCH model (i.e. TARCH model) is used:

$$\sigma_t^2 = \mu_0 + \sum_{i=1}^{p} \gamma_i \sigma_{t-i}^2 + \sum_{j=1}^{p} \mu_j \varepsilon_{t-j}^2 + \beta_1 d_{1t} + \beta_2 d_{2t} \tag{5.2}$$

d_1 and d_2 are dummy variables used to capture the impact of NBR's decisions, that is change in central bank rate and NBR's intervention on FX market, respectively. Since the MPC meeting is done on quarterly, d_1 takes one during the last month of the quarter and zero elsewhere. The dummy variable d_2 takes one when NBR intervenes on the foreign exchange market and zero otherwise.

On the one side, results of the TGARCH model show that the dummy variable for communication about monetary policy stance is significant at 10% and the sign of its coefficient is negative, indicating that increased NBR communication of its policy stance has helped to reduce volatility in money market interest rates. On the other side, results of the EGARCH model show that the dummy variable of exchange rate is also significant at 10%, with a negative sign indicating that over the past years, the interventions of the NBR on the foreign exchange market have helped to smooth out excessive volatilities in the exchange rate and those interventions have had a significant impact in terms of stabilizing the exchange rate in Rwanda. Using the same methodology with a larger sample period that comprises the most recent data, results from the study of Nyalihama et al. (2018) are almost similar to what Karangwa et al. (2017) found. The results show that the effect of NBR's communication on reducing interest rates volatility is relatively stronger, whereas the effect of NBR's actions or signal on stabilizing exchange rates are somehow moderated relative to Karangwa et al. (2017) results.

References

Bholat D, Hansen S, Santos P, Schonhardt-Bailey C (2015) Text mining for central banks. Available at SSRN 2624811

Blinder AS (1998) Central banking in theory and practice. MIT Press, Cambridge, MA

Blinder AS (2008) Monetary policy by committee: Why and How? Eur J Polit Econ 23(1):106–123

Born B, Ehrmann M, Fratzscher M (2013) Central Bank communication on financial stability. Econ J 124:701–734

Bruno G (2016) Text mining and sentiment extraction in central bank documents. In: 2016 IEEE international conference on big data (big data). IEEE, pp 1700–1708

Calvo GA (1978) On the time consistency of optimal policy in a monetary economy. Econometrica 46(6):1411–1428

Cecchetti SG (1999) Legal structure, financial structure, and the monetary policy transmission mechanism. Federal Reserve Bank New York Econ Policy Rev 5(2):9–28

Cecchetti SG, Schoenholtz K (2019) Improving U.S. monetary policy communications. CEPR Discussion Papers 13915, C.E.P.R. Discussion Papers

De Haan J, Jansen D-J (2007) The importance of being vigilant: has ECB communication influenced Euro area inflation expectations? CESifo Working Paper 2134

Filardo A (2008) Transparency and communication in monetary policy: a survey of Asian Central Banks. Bank for International Settlements, Basel

FINSCOP (2020) Financial inclusion in Rwanda. Access to Finance, Kigali

Haan D, Jakob FA, Waller S (2004) The transparency and credibility of the European Central Bank. J Common Mark Stud 42(4):775–794

Haldane A, McMahon M (2018) Central Bank communications and the general public. In: AEA papers and proceedings, vol 108, May 2018, pp 578–83

Issing O (2005) Communication, transparency, accountability: monetary policy in the twenty first century. Federal Reserve Bank St. Louis Rev 65–83

Kahveci E, Odabas A (2016) Central bank's communication strategy and content analysis of monetary policy statements: the case of Fed, ECB and CBRT. Procedia-Soc Behav Sci 235:618–629

Karangwa M et al (2017) Impact of Central Bank communication on effectiveness of monetary policy in Rwanda. NBR Econ Rev 11

Knutter R, Mohr B, Wagner H (2011) The effects of Central Bank communication on financial stability: a systematization of the empirical evidence. University of Hagen Discussion Paper, p 463

Kryvtsov O, Petersen L (2013) Expectations and monetary policy: experimental evidence. Bank of Canada Working Paper 2013-44

Kydland, Prescot (1977) Rules rather than discretion: the inconsistency of optimal plans. J Political Econ 85(3)

Luangaram P, Wong-Wachara W (2017) More than words: a textual analysis of monetary policy communication. PIER Discussion Papers 54

Mishkin FS (2000) What should central banks do? Homer Jones Lecture, Federal Reserve Bank of St. Louis, 30 March 2000

Mishkin FS (2004) The economics of money, banking, and financial markets, 7th edn. Pearson, Addison Wesley, Boston

Nier E (2009) Financial stability frameworks and the role of Central Banks: lessons from the crisis. IMF Working Paper 09/70

Nyalihama C et al (2018) Central Bank communication as a policy tool under the price based monetary policy. NBR Econ Rev 13

Park KY, Lee Y, Kim S (2019) Deciphering monetary policy board minutes through text mining approach: the case of Korea. Bank of Korea Working Paper

Powell JH (2019) Speech, challenges for monetary policy, at the challenges for monetary policy symposium, sponsored by the Federal Reserve Bank of Kansas City, Jackson Hole, Wyoming. August 23, 2019

Shapiro AH, Wilson D (2019) Taking the feds at its word: direct estimation of central bank objectives using text analytics. Federal Reserve Bank of San Francisco Working Paper 2019-02

Shirota Y, Hashimoto T, Sakura T (2015) Topic extraction analysis for monetary policy minutes of Japan in 2014. In: Industrial conference on data mining. Springer, pp 141–152

Tsuji C (2016) Did the expectations channel work? Evidence from quantitative easing in Japan, 2001–06. Cogent Econ Financ 2016(4):1210996

Woodford M (2005) Central Bank communication and policy effectiveness. NBER Working Paper No. 11898 Issued in December 2005

Appendix to Chapter 1

Appendix 1.1: MFIs balance sheet (in FRW million)

		2015	2016	2017	2018	2019
1	Total assets	208,953.78	222,736.28	244,253.35	279,521.57	320,730.62
2	Cash in vaults	2,970.61	2,769.20	3,603.05	4,232.61	4,811.54
3	Cash in banks	74,369.83	67,437.77	78,597.34	86,592.42	101,488.95
4	Treasury bills and placements	461.91	1,018.21	2,095.91	3,311.86	5,457.07
5	Loan portfolio (net of provisions)	111,726.73	128,394.53	132,077.17	158,447.34	178,384.56
6	Gross loans	116,579.46	134,054.23	138,284.42	164,007.50	183,569.83
7	Non-performing loans	9,224.91	12,010.25	11,291.96	10,596.48	10,444.54
8	Provisions	4,852.73	5,659.69	6,207.25	5,560.16	5,185.27
9	Other assets	19,424.69	23,116.56	27,879.88	26,937.33	30,588.50
11	Liabilities	143,978.20	144,234.42	156,778.28	181,087.36	206,314.14
12	Total deposits	117,293.31	114,459.67	124,134.69	144,459.41	170,192.44
13	Current accounts	86,792.59	80,228.25	82,629.41	93,888.75	111,091.07
14	Saving accounts	24,572.30	26,145.09	31,687.23	36,840.80	48,434.44
15	Short-term deposits	5,334.29	7,420.79	7,326.15	9,878.72	8,697.89
16	Long-term deposits	594.12	665.55	2,491.90	3,851.14	1,969.04
17	Borrowings and short-term liabilities	17,395.87	17,703.50	18,911.27	21,995.16	14,973.74
18	Other liabilities	9,289.02	12,071.24	13,732.32	14,968.95	21,147.96
19	Equity	64,975.58	78,501.86	87,475.08	98,098.05	114,416.48
20	Earnings	17,099.49	23,252.69	19,089.48	22,998.35	31,254.44

(continued)

T. K. Rusuhuzwa, *Monetary Policy in Rwanda*, Frontiers in African Business Research, https://doi.org/10.1007/978-981-33-6746-3

(continued)

		2015	2016	2017	2018	2019
21	Retained earnings/accumulated losses	10,255.14	13,438.85	16,663.99	15,686.13	19,246.36
22	Net profit/loss of period +/− (From January)	6,844.35	9,813.84	2,425.49	7,312.22	12,008.08
23	Paid up capital	24,865.11	28,928.80	35,235.57	38,507.50	40,877.08
24	Other equity	23,010.98	26,320.36	33,150.03	36,592.19	42,284.95
	Total liabilities and equity	208,953.78	222,736.28	244,253.35	279,521.57	320,730.62

Source NBR, MFIs department

Appendix 1.2: Public notice N°26/2020 OF JUNE 19th, 2020 regarding the issue of Treasury Bills

1. On **Thursday, 25 June 2020**, the National Bank of Rwanda will invite tender bids for Treasury Bills with the following characteristics:

- Negotiable Rwanda Government Treasury bills securities worth 5.0 billion Rwandan Francs, having 28 days maturity, expiring on 23 July 2020.
- Negotiable Rwanda Government Treasury bills securities worth 4.0 billion Rwandan Francs, having 91 days maturity, expiring on 24 September 2020.
- Negotiable Rwanda Government Treasury bills securities worth 6.0 billion Rwandan Francs, having 182 days maturity, expiring on 24 December 2020.
- Negotiable Rwanda Government Treasury bills securities worth 6.15 billion Rwandan Francs, having 364 days maturity, expiring on 24 June 2021.

The bids are open to commercial banks, non-banking enterprises, and individuals.

2. The competitive bids will be considered according to the lowest rate offered. The amounts to be distributed will be considered on the basis of the bids received. The non-competitive bids will be served at the weighted average rate resulting from the competitive bids.
3. Competitive bids must involve a number of bills equivalent to a multiple integer of 50 million Rwandan francs and must indicate the amounts and corresponding return rates. As for the non-competitive bids, they must involve a number of bills equivalent to a multiple integer of 100.000 Rwandan francs.
4. Bidding will be done electronically not later than **10:00 a.m**. on **25th June 2020.** Only authorised commercial bank's treasurers and brokers are allowed to use CSD platform to bid on behalf of their respective bank clients.
5. Mode of auction: Multiple rates for competitive bids and the weighted average rate for non-competitive bids.

6. The auction results will be communicated to the bidders on **Thursday, 25th June 2020 at 3:00 p.m.**
7. Settlement will take place on **Friday, 26th June 2020** by debiting the successful bidders' account or, if need be, via the intermediary banks through which they will be specified.
8. The repayments will be affected the next working day following the maturity date on **24th July 2020; 25th September 2020; 29th December 2020** and **25th June 2021** with maturities of **28, 91, 182,** and **364** days, respectively, by crediting the corresponding accounts.
9. The BNR may, upon deeming the exercise unproductive, decide to nullify the auction.

Kigali, 19 June 2020.

Appendix 1.3: Outstanding T-bill by type of investors in FRW billion

	2012	2013	2014	2015	2016	2017	2018	2019
Banks	55.53	145.63	152.07	210.61	173.73	243.62	232.12	318.65
Institutional investors	38.47	10.47	11.71	11.9	64.92	59.83	110.93	71.83
Retailers	1.25	0.4	0.14	0.03	0.14	0.2	0.17	0.35
Total	95.3	156.5	163.9	222.5	238.8	303.7	343.2	390.8

Appendix1.4: Outstanding T-bill by type of investors (shares in%)

Holder	2012	2013	2014	2015	2016	2017	2018	2019
Banks	58.30%	93.10%	92.80%	94.60%	72.80%	80.20%	67.60%	81.50%
Institutional investors	40.40%	6.70%	7.10%	5.30%	27.20%	19.70%	32.30%	18.40%
Retailers	1.30%	0.30%	0.10%	0.00%	0.10%	0.10%	0.10%	0.10%
Total	100.00%	100.00%	100.00%	100.00%	100.00%	100.00%	100.00%	100.00%

Appendix 1.5: Outstanding T-bonds by type of investors in FRW billion

Holder	2008	2009	2010	2011	2012	2013
Banks	11.51	11.51	13.04	12.95	8.32	6.92
Institutional investors	2.67	2.67	1.89	2.05	1.1	1
Retailers	0.08	0.08	0.08	0	0.58	0.58
TOTAL	14.3	14.3	15	15	10	8.5

Holder	2014	2015	2016	2017	2018	2019
Banks	24.36	46.26	60.91	65.81	76.12	134.51
Institutional investors	23.33	51.22	85.94	102.43	129.65	228.71
Retailers	0.81	2.53	5.65	11.77	24.23	36.06
Total	48.5	100	152.5	180	230	399.3

Appendix 1.6: Outstanding T-bonds by type of investors (shares in%)

Holder	2008 (%)	2009 (%)	2010 (%)	2011 (%)	2012 (%)	2013 (%)	2014 (%)	2015 (%)
Banks	80.70	80.70	86.90	86.40	83.20	81.40	50.20	46.30
Institutional investors	18.70	18.70	12.60	13.60	11.00	11.80	48.10	51.20
Retailers	0.60	0.60	0.50	0.00	5.80	6.80	1.70	2.50
Total	100.00	100.00	100.00	100.00	100.00	100.00	100.00	100.00

Holder	2016 (%)	2017 (%)	2018 (%)	2019 (%)
Banks	39.90	36.60	33.10	33.70
Institutional investors	56.40	56.90	56.40	57.30
Retailers	3.70	6.50	10.50	9.00
Total	100.00	100.00	100.00	100.00

Appendix to Chapter 2

Appendix 2.1. Monetary aggregates developments (in billion FRW)

	M1	M2	M3	CIC	Demand deposits	Term deposits	Foreign deposits	CPS
1968	1.6	1.6	1.6	1.0	0.6	0.03	0	0.2
1969	1.9	1.9	1.9	1.1	0.8	0.0	0	0.2
1970	2.2	2.3	2.3	1.2	1.0	0.1	0	0.4
1971	2.5	2.6	2.6	1.4	1.1	0.1	0	0.7
1972	2.6	2.7	2.7	1.4	1.2	0.1	0	0.5
1973	4.0	4.2	4.2	2.0	2.0	0.1	0	0.9
1974	5.1	5.3	5.3	2.6	2.5	0.2	0	1.9
1975	5.6	5.8	5.8	2.7	2.8	0.3	0	1.7
1976	7.4	7.8	7.8	3.1	4.3	0.4	0	2.1
1977	8.1	10.2	10.2	3.9	4.2	2.1	0	4.2
1978	8.9	11.2	11.2	4.4	4.5	2.2	0	4.9
1979	11.2	14.1	14.1	5.2	6.0	2.9	0	4.3
1980	12.0	15.1	15.1	5.7	6.3	3.1	0	6.3
1981	11.8	15.0	15.0	6.1	5.6	3.2	0	7.9
1982	11.4	16.2	16.2	6.3	5.2	4.7	0	8.4
1983	12.3	18.1	18.1	6.7	5.6	5.8	0	9.0
1984	13.3	19.9	19.9	7.0	6.3	6.5	0	10.9
1985	14.6	23.3	23.3	7.2	7.4	8.7	0	14.1
1986	17.2	26.5	26.5	7.7	9.5	9.3	0	14.1
1987	17.7	29.2	29.2	8.2	9.5	11.5	0	14.0
1988	18.2	31.4	31.4	8.4	9.8	13.2	0	17.2

(continued)

T. K. Rusuhuzwa, *Monetary Policy in Rwanda*, Frontiers in African Business Research, https://doi.org/10.1007/978-981-33-6746-3

(continued)

	M1	M2	M3	CIC	Demand deposits	Term deposits	Foreign deposits	CPS
1989	15.9	30.1	30.1	7.7	8.2	14.1	0	18.7
1990	16.7	31.7	31.7	8.6	8.1	15.0	0	15.6
1991	18.0	33.5	33.5	8.8	9.2	15.5	0.0	12.9
1992	22.5	37.7	37.7	10.3	12.2	15.2	0.0	15.6
1993	24.8	39.4	39.4	11.4	13.4	14.6	0.0	17.9
1994	30.1	36.0	38.4	13.9	16.1	5.9	2.4	16.6
1995	40.3	47.5	62.6	17.3	7.2	23.0	15.2	28.7
1996	45.8	54.7	68.9	20.9	8.9	24.9	14.1	29.0
1997	56.8	74.2	90.2	22.6	34.2	17.4	15.9	45.3
1998	52.9	73.5	92.0	20.9	20.6	32.0	18.5	55.0
1999	58.5	78.6	97.3	21.4	37.2	19.2	19.5	60.8
2000	60.3	84.8	111.8	22.6	38.6	24.1	26.6	70.9
2001	69.0	102.6	130.7	25.8	33.6	43.2	28.0	76.5
2002	75.4	114.9	144.3	28.0	39.5	47.4	29.4	85.8
2003	98.8	138.2	178.0	33.6	65.1	39.4	39.8	120.2
2004	100.6	155.2	206.2	40.3	60.3	54.5	51.0	131.5
2005	129.9	202.6	246.2	47.0	82.9	72.7	43.7	165.7
2006	154.7	261.8	321.0	52.7	101.9	107.1	59.2	211.3
2007	215.0	357.0	425.7	63.2	151.7	142.0	68.6	258.6
2008	248.5	384.1	466.4	80.9	167.7	135.5	82.3	341.0
2009	267.1	429.5	526.6	77.0	190.1	162.4	97.0	357.3
2010	330.6	516.7	615.9	90.5	240.1	186.1	99.2	397.1
2011	381.9	645.2	780.4	102.8	278.7	263.3	135.6	506.1
2012	426.2	725.3	889.9	107.0	319.2	299.1	164.6	682.6
2013	495.5	834.0	1028.2	116.6	378.9	338.5	194.2	758.0
2014	574.8	982.1	1223.9	118.53	456.2	407.3	241.8	906.3
2015	757.2	1226.2	1482.1	142.63	614.6	469.0	255.9	1178.6
2016	733.7	1266.1	1594.7	145.85	587.9	532.4	328.5	1285.4
2017	810.1	1393.2	1791.7	162.73	647.3	583.1	398.5	1464.2
2018	953.9	1557.1	2071.1	183.58	770.3	603.3	514.0	1622.2
2019	1147.5	1879.7	2391.3	214.02	933.5	732.2	511.6	1826.4

Source NBR, statistics department

Appendix to Chapter 3

Annex 3.1: **Payment System Development**

See (Tables 3.1.1 and 3.1.2).

Annex 3.2: **Modelling and forecasting at National Bank of Rwanda (NBR)**

In its effort to improve the decision-making process about monetary policy stance, NBR invested in building the capacity of its staff in modelling and forecasting. Since 2009, NBR has adopted several modelling and forecasting tools, of which near-term as well as medium-term forecasting models. By 2011, two non-structural econometric models were developed and used to perform near-term forecasting (NTF) activities, namely autoregressive moving average models (ARMA) and short-term inflation forecast (STIF). The bank also started to conduct market expectations surveys to supplement insights from NTF models. These methods help to perform short-term

Table 3.1.1 Payment system developments

	Number of automated teller machines (ATMs)	Number of point of sale (POS) terminals	Number of debit cards	Number of credit cards	ATM transactions
2011	167	227	115,200	516	1, 976,376
2012	292	666	389,269	418	5,753,163
2013	333	946	487,498	845	7,774,053
2014	354	1,152	638,869	2,540	7,488,707
2015	380	1,718	657,904	3,485	7,505,815
2016	400	1,885	746,458	3,668	8,183,116
2017	406	2,104	754,806	3,679	9,408,701
2018	383	2,801	883,755	3,638	9,585,002
2019	383	3,477	555,243	3,687	10,061,164

Source NBR, payment system department

T. K. Rusuhuzwa, *Monetary Policy in Rwanda*, Frontiers in African Business Research, https://doi.org/10.1007/978-981-33-6746-3

Table 3.1.2 Mobile payment developments

Mobile payment				
Period	Number of subscribers	Number of agents	Number of transactions	Value in FRW million
2010	231,000	290	829,379	8,355
2011	639,673	1,387	3,420,885	51,024
2012	1,440,541	3,085	22,191,674	161,808
2013	2,538,651	8,745	57,147,777	330,378
2014	6,480,449	25,482	104,773,115	691,477
2015	7,663,199	40,467	168,612,455	1,093,497
2016	9,735,694	59,952	205,687,966	1,040,459
2017	9,079,983	83,531	251,361,153	1,384,686
2018	11,067,077	107,858	299,941,137	1,808,944
2019	15,923,248	98,359	378,847,720	2,349,788

Source NBR, payment system department

horizon of 1–6 months ahead. Multivariate models, specifically vector autoregressive (VAR) models as well as quarterly projection model (QPM) are used for medium-term projections. To take into account sector-specific information and capture sectoral inflationary pressures as well as current price dynamics, a disaggregated approach is used by applying ARMA or VAR models on inflation components, including core inflation, energy inflation, and fresh food inflation. Following is the ARMA model used to forecast inflation in Rwanda.

Generally, the analysis of economic data aims at predicting or forecasting the future values of economic variables or describe the relationship between variables. The forecast of economic variables is mainly done using two approaches: Use of structural econometric models and pure time series. Structural econometric models that describe the relationship between a variable of interest and a number of other variables. The relationship between those variables is estimated using a sample of data and serves as basis for forecasting future values of the dependent variable. Though the estimated relationship gives economic content to the future values of the variable of interest, it requires to have predicted future values of independent variables.

The use of a pure time series is built on the relationship between a variable of interest to its past values for forecasting its future. The use of a pure time series requires understanding the properties of the stochastic process that generated the realizations of the variable of interest. Those properties, particularly the stationarity, allow understanding how observations of the variable of interest are related overtime so that the dynamic properties of the series can be used to generate forecasts for the future period.

In this paragraph, we present the key features of ARMA model used to forecast inflation in Rwanda.

Table 3.2.1 Null hypothesis is that Y has a unit root

Exogenous: Constant

Lag length: 2 (Automatic based on SIC, maxlag = 14)

		–	t-Statistic	Prob.*
Augmented Dickey-Fuller test statistic		–	−3.050464	0.0322
Test critical values	1% level	–	−3.465780	–
	5% level	–	−2.877012	–
	10% level	–	−2.575097	–

*MacKinnon (1996) one-sided p-values

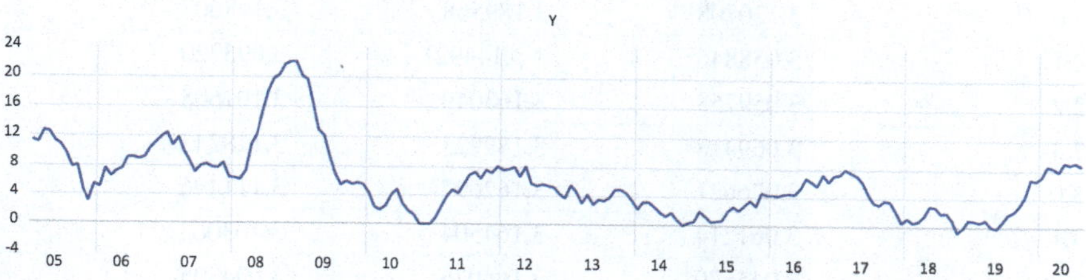

Fig. 3.2.1 Inflation development

Let y_t denotes the inflation rate in Rwanda at period t. If y_t follows an ARMA(p, q) process, it can be expressed as follows:

$$Y_t = \mu + \phi_1 Y_{t-1} + \phi_1 Y_{t-2} + \ldots + \phi_p L^p + \theta_1 \varepsilon^{t-1} + \theta_2 \varepsilon_{t-2} + \ldots + \theta_q \varepsilon_{t-q} + \varepsilon_t \tag{A.3.1}$$

With $E(\varepsilon_t) = 0$; $E(\varepsilon_t^2) = \sigma^2$; $E(\varepsilon_t \varepsilon_s) = 0$; $s \neq t$.

Characteristics of ARMA process will be a combination of two models: AR and MA. In particular, an ARMA(p, q) process will have both autocorrelation and partial autocorrelation functions which decline geometrically. As indicated in Table 3.2.1, inflation is stationary and we can build an ARMA (p, q) model using the variable y_t (Fig. 3.2.1).

Before estimating the parameters of the model, the determination of p and q, information criteria are determined using information criteria. Eviews provides support to choose the best models using information criteria, by simply loading and running "testarma" program and its sub-program "sub arma.prg" as follows: File/open/programs/program files/views 10/example files/sample programs/equation/testarma. We illustrate this using monthly data on inflation in Rwanda. Schwarz indicates that p = 2 and q = 1 (Table 3.2.2).

The following is the estimated ARMA (2,1) inflation model for Rwanda. As it can be observed, the model is stable (all inverted roots lie in a unit root circle) and all coefficients are statistically significant (Table 3.2.3).

Table 3.2.2 Identification of the ARMA(p, q) model

ARMA order	Akaike	Schwarz	Hannan-Quinn
0,0	5.904943	5.922159	5.911918
0,1	4.759556	4.811201	4.780481
0,2	4.253008	4.321868	4.280907
0,3	3.799947	3.886022	3.834821
1,0	3.182221	3.233867	3.203146
1,1	3.143232	3.212093	3.171132
1,2	3.114483	3.200558	3.149357
1,3	3.086265	3.189556	3.128115
2,0	3.120708	3.189568	3.148607
2,1	3.058846	* 3.144921	3.093720
2,2	3.059758	3.163049	3.101608
2,3	3.069418	3.189923	3.118242
3,0	3.076621	3.162697	3.111496
3,1	3.061214	3.164504	3.103063
3,2	3.045570	3.166076	3.094395
3,3	*3.033724	3.171445	*3.089523

*Indicates best model

To ensure that the estimated model is adequate for forecasting inflation, diagnostic checking is done using a set of tests on residuals such as normality and autocorrelation tests. Residuals from the estimated model are both normally distributed (Jarque-Bera = 2.4, p = 0.30) and homoscedastic (F-statistic = 0.23 and $nR^2 = 0.24$ with probabilities equal to 0.63). We use the estimated model to perform in sample and out sample forecasts. The graph below shows how closed are the current values of inflation (y) and the forecasted values of inflation (yf). In the period under review, the average error of estimation (y-yf) is −0.02 with 1.1 as standard deviation. Using the model, we have estimated inflation in September to be 8.6% versus 8.8% realized (Fig. 3.2.2).

Furthermore, in the preparation of adoption of price-based monetary policy, NBR put in place the basic requirements of a forward looking monetary policy framework, including the development of forecasting and policy analysis system (FPAS) in collaboration with the International Monetary Funds (IMF). In 2013, the first version of quarterly projection model (QPM) for Rwanda in line with FPAS practices was developed in-house. After recruiting and training more staff in modelling and forecasting, NBR and IMF developed a joint project to operationalize FPAS at NBR between 2014 and 2015.

With the improved version of the QPM, trained staffs were able to generate the first medium-term inflation forecasts for Rwanda. To ensure that FPAS is used to support the decision-making process on monetary policy stance by the MPC, a review of MPC processes alongside a new communication strategy was done and a new MPC

Table 3.2.3 Estimation of ARMA model

Dependent variable: Y				
Method: ARMA maximum likelihood (OPG−BHHH)				
Sample: 2005M01 2020M08				
Included observations: 188				
Convergence achieved after 28 iterations				
Coefficient covariance computed using outer product of gradients				
Variable	Coefficient	Std. Error	t-Statistic	Prob.
C	6.326819	1.202913	5.259580	0.0000
AR(1)	1.797043	0.091195	19.70552	0.0000
AR(2)	−0.821810	0.086807	−9.467063	0.0000
MA(1)	−0.627324	0.125466	−4.999946	0.0000
SIGMASQ	1.163310	0.116110	10.01901	0.0000
R-squared	0.945260	Mean dependent var		6.138298
Adjusted R-squared	0.944063	S.D. dependent var		4.622246
S.E. of regression	1.093204	Akaike info criterion		3.058846
Sum squared resid	218.7022	Schwarz criterion		3.144921
Log likelihood	−282.5315	Hannan-Quinn criter.		3.093720
F-statistic	790.0178	Durbin-Watson stat		2.096966
Prob(F-statistic)	0.000000	–		
Inverted AR Roots	0.90−0.12i	0.90+0.12i		
Inverted MA Roots	0.63			

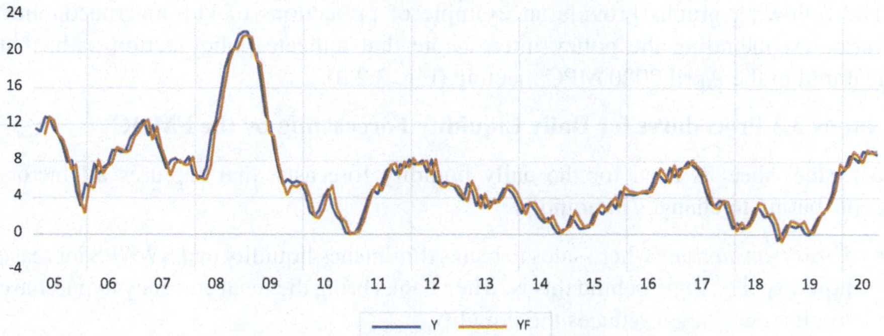

Fig. 3.2.2 In sample inflation forecast using ARMA model

calendar aligned to the data cycle adopted. A forecasting cycle of 6 weeks was introduced. FPAS has at its core, a Quarterly Projection Model (QPM) which comprises six blocks: agricultural and non-agricultural GDP; inflation block; monetary policy;

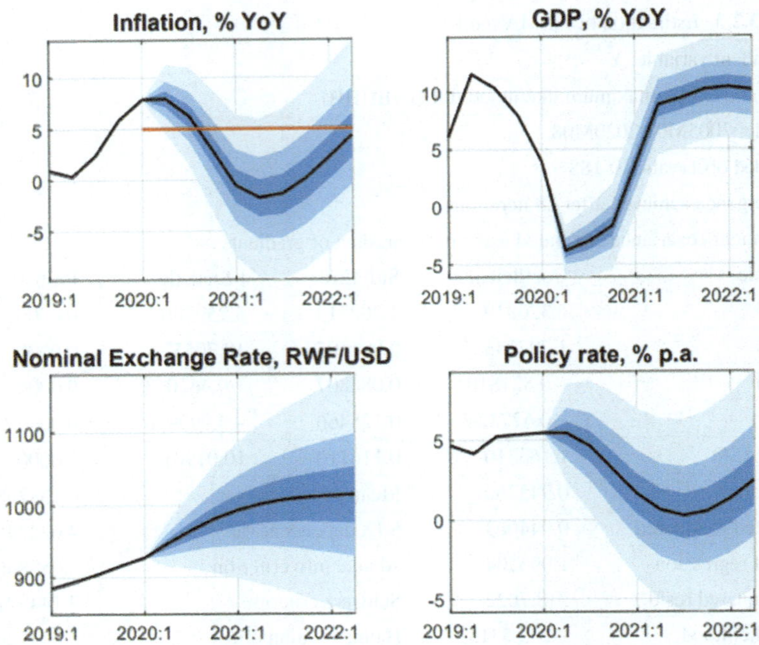

Fig. 3.2.3 Projections of key macroeconomic variables to support MPC decisions

exchange rate framework; fiscal block; and aid. For details, see, for example, Luisa Charry, Pranav Gupta and Vimal Thakoor (2014).

The medium-term macroeconomic projections are key input to MPC decisions. The following graphs provide an example of projections of key macroeconomic variables, including the policy interest rate that indicate policy action path, that featured in the April 2020 MPC meeting (Fig. 3.2.3).

Annex 3.3 Procedures for Daily Liquidity Forecasting by the FMOC

An excel sheet is used for the daily liquidity forecasts, that captures all factors contributing to changes in liquidity.

- *Forex transactions* where sales to banks diminishes liquidity and SWAPS increase liquidity. The logic behind this is, when banks bring the local currency to purchase foreign currency it reduces the liquidity.
- *Government domestic operations through Ordinateur Tresorier du Rwanda (OTR) and Line Ministries.* Revenues in OTR such as taxes, new issuance of government securities diminishes liquidity. Expenditures in both OTR such as salaries of government workers, repayment of government securities, coupon payment, and line ministries such as local governments' and public institutions' invoices reduces liquidity.

Table 3.3.1 Liquidity projections (in billion FRW)

	Monday	Tuesday	Wednesday	Thursday
	3/4/2019	3/5/2019	3/6/2019	3/7/2019
Forex operations				
Purchases of FX to banks (+)	–	–	–	–
Sales of FX to banks (−)	–	–	–	–
Swaps (+)	–	–	–	–
Swaps _reverse (−)	–	–	–	–
Government operations (OTR)				
Revenues (−)	–	–	–	–
of Which T-bond reopening	–	–	–	–
T- bond new issuance	–	–	–	–
Expenditures (+)	–	–	–	–
Line ministries				
Expenditures (+)	–	–	–	–
Commercial banks net (OMO)				
Repo repayments (+)	–	–	–	–
Central bank bill issuance (−)	–	–	–	–
Central bank bill repayment (+)	–	–	–	–
Reverse repo repayment (−)	–	–	–	–
Currency in circulation				
Withdrawals (−)	–	–	–	–
Deposits (+)	–	–	–	–
Net impact on liquidity				
Opening balance (excess + /shortage −)				
Projected closing balance of excess reserves				

- *Commercial banks operations with the central bank.* Government securities repayment such as repo and central bank bill repayment upsurges liquidity and the reverse of this reduces the liquidity.
- *Currency in circulation (CIC).* Withdraws of bank's deposits add to lessen liquidity, while deposits from banks increase their liquidity in NBR (Table 3.3.1).

Appendix to Chapter 4

Appendix A: IRF of Exchange Rate Pass-Through

See (Figs. 4.1, 4.2 and 4.3).

Appendix B: Diagnostic Tests

See (Table 4.1).

Appendix C: VAR Lag Selection, Estimation, Diagnostics, and IRFs

See (Tables 4.2, 4.3, 4.4, 4.5 and Fig. 4.4).

T. K. Rusuhuzwa, *Monetary Policy in Rwanda*, Frontiers in African Business Research, https://doi.org/10.1007/978-981-33-6746-3

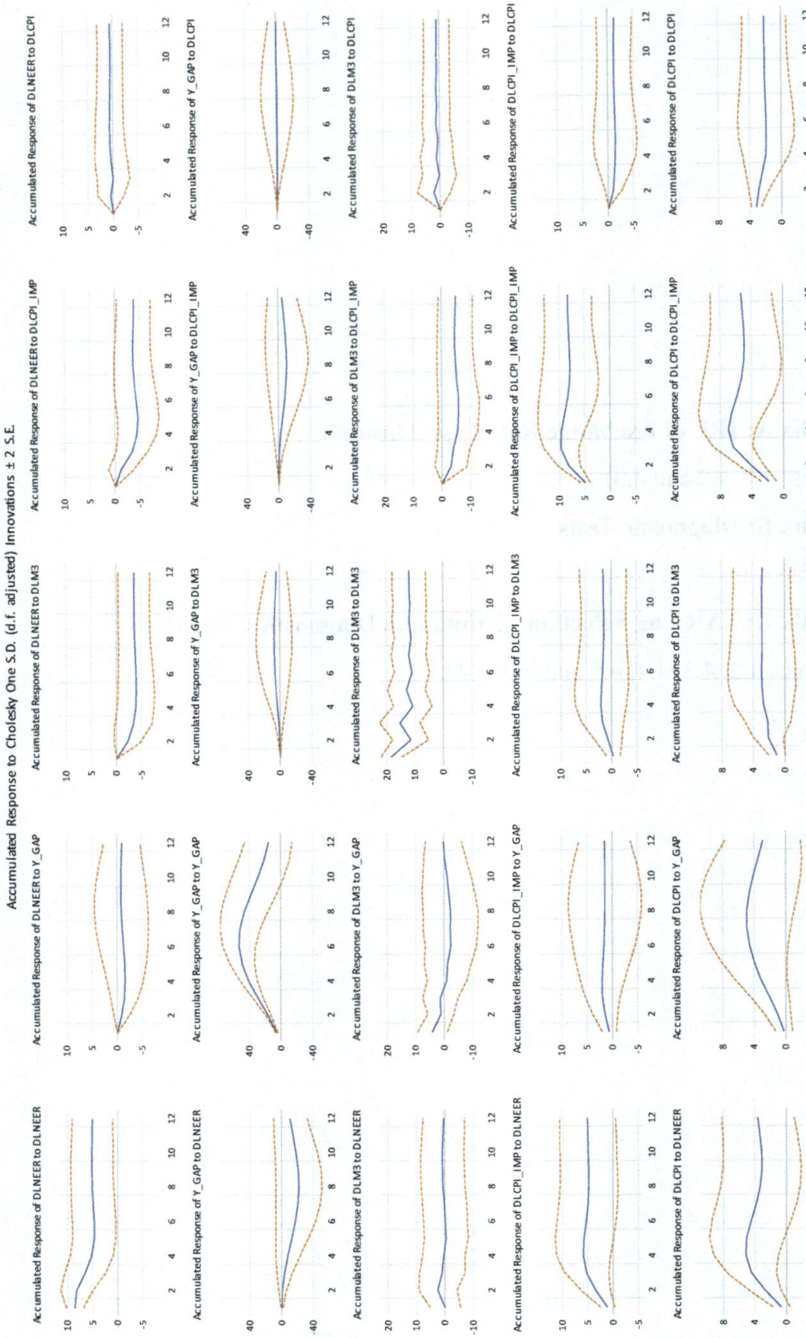

Fig. 4.1 Model 1 IRF

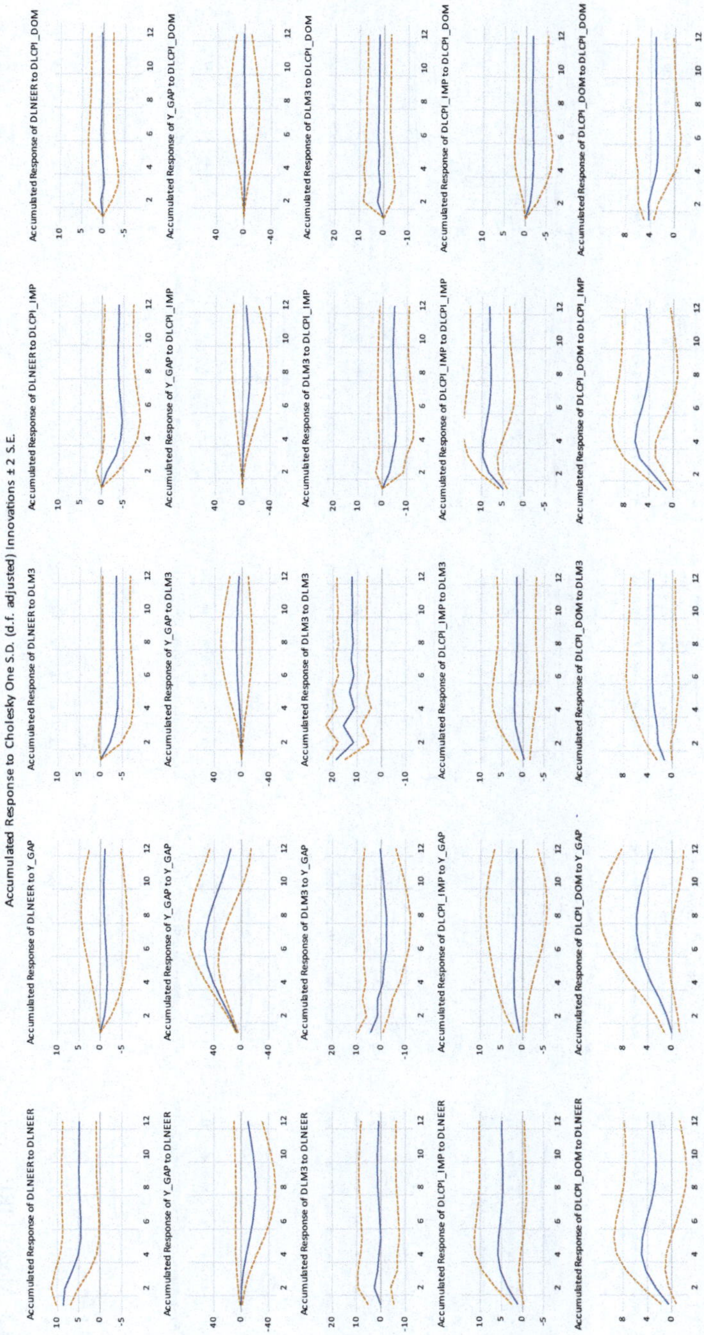

Fig. 4.2 Model 2 IRF

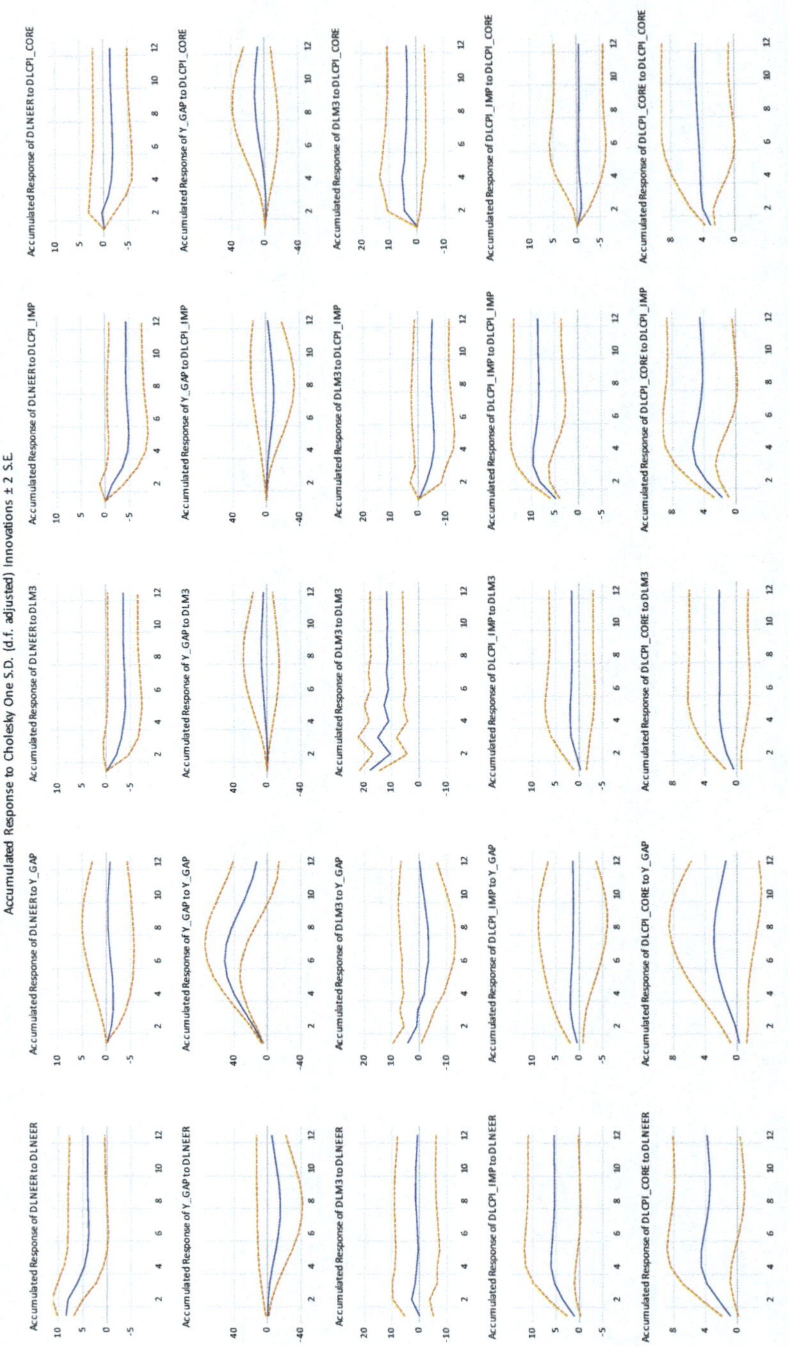

Fig. 4.3 Model 3 IRF

Table 4.1 Unit root tests

Variables	Level		First differences	
	Lag	ADF	ADF	Conclusion
Y	1	−2.74	−2.88***	I(1)
P	1	−2.64	−4.89*	I(1)
M3	0	−1.8	−10.3*	I(1)
T-bill rates	0	−2.9	−7.45*	I(1)
Repo rates	0	−0.96	−7.9	I(1)
Deposit rate	0	−0.32	−7.9	I(1)
Lending rates	2	−0.06	−8.01	I(1)
E	1	−2.06	−3.08**	I(1)
Cps	0	−2.97	−9.03*	I(1)

*significant a 1%; **: significant at 5% and ***: significant at 10%

Table 4.2 VAR lag order selection criteria

Endogenous variables: lry lp lm tb lne

Exogenous variables: C OIL

Lag	LogL	LR	FPE	AIC	SC	HQ
0	126.1943	NA	1.52e-09	−6.115488	−5.684544	−5.962162
1	290.5240	268.1170	1.01e-12	−13.44863	−11.94033*	−12.91199
2	327.9223	51.17653*	5.78e-13*	−14.10117*	−11.51551	−13.18121*
3	350.7444	25.22443	8.15e-13	−13.98655	−10.32352	−12.68327

*significant at 5%

Table 4.3 Roots of characteristic polynomial

Endogenous variables: lry lp lm tb lne

Exogenous variables: C OIL

Root	Modulus
0.983234	0.983234
0.869303	0.869303
0.634919 −0.037241i	0.636010
0.634919 + 0.037241i	0.636010
−0.070706	0.070706

No root lies outside the unit circle

VAR satisfies the stability condition

Table 4.4 VAR residual heteroskedasticity tests

Joint test		
Chi-sq.	df	Prob.
182.2901	180	0.4383

Table 4.5 VAR residual normality tests

Orthogonalization: Residual Correlation (Doornik-Hansen)			
Null Hypothesis: residuals are multivariate normal			
Component	Jarque-Bera	df	Prob.
1	1.072675	2	0.5849
2	0.669157	2	0.7156
3	1.268359	2	0.5304
4	10.72069	2	0.0047
5	1.410507	2	0.4940
Joint	15.14139	10	0.1270

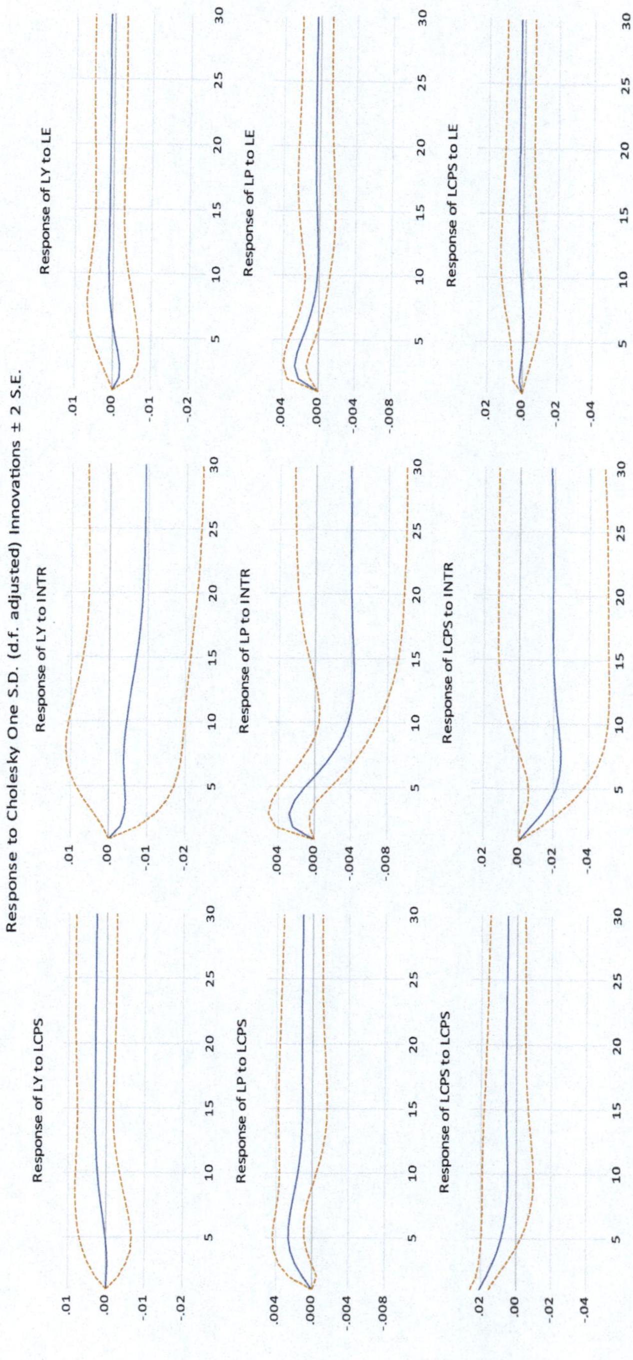

Fig. 4.4 Impulse responses using interbank rates

Appendix to Chapter 5

Appendix 5.1: A Summary of the Uptake of NBR Communication Channels

Activity	Channels	August 2019	February 2020	Difference
MPFSS	YouTube	113 viewers	226 viewers	There was an increase of 113 viewers from August 2019 to February 2020
	Twitter	500 Engagements	1,875 Engagements	There were 1,375 more engagements on our Twitter page from August 2019 to February 2020
	Facebook	61 people followed the Governor's presentation.	259 people followed the Governor's presentation.	We had 198 more people that followed the Governor's presentation from August 2019 to February 2020
	Slido App	–	207 joined the conversation 193 engaged with us 44 questions were asked 129 liked using the app	This is a new App that was introduced for engagement purposes

(continued)

T. K. Rusuhuzwa, *Monetary Policy in Rwanda*, Frontiers in African Business Research, https://doi.org/10.1007/978-981-33-6746-3

(continued)

Activity	Channels	August 2019	February 2020	Difference
MPC & FSC Announcements	All our media channels	201 Total engagements	413 Total engagements	We saw 212 more engagements between August 2019 and February 2020
Media houses coverage	TVs, Radios, Print Newspapers, Online media houses (Igihe, umuseke…)	12 media house reported about the bank's work 416 times. These included MPC & FSC decisions, Cashless campaign and day to day activities of the bank	12 media house reported about the bank's work 314 times so far. These included MPC&FSC decisions, Cashless campaign and day to day activities of the bank	(This is still ongoing)
Media interviews	TVs, Radios, Print Newspapers, Online media houses	10 Interviews were conducted. Management and in other instances the Chief Economist were interviewed by different media houses on MPC decisions, Cashless campaign, and other issues related to the state of the economy	17 Interviews were conducted. Management spoke with different media houses on MPC decisions, Cashless campaign, and other issues related to the state of the economy	7 more interviews were conducted between August 2019 and February 2020
BNR in conversation talk show	YouTube	–	238 Followed the conversation live on our YouTube channel	–
Bank's social and digital media platforms growth	Twitter	35,000 Followers	52,500 Followers	There was an increase of 15,500 people between August 2019 and February 2020
	Facebook	500 Followers	1,376 Followers	876 more followed our Facebook page between August 2019 and February 2020

(continued)

(continued)

Activity	Channels	August 2019	February 2020	Difference
	YouTube	65 subscribers	203 Subscribers	138 new subscribers between August 2019 and February 2020
	Instagram	103 Followers	523 Followers	420 new followers on our Instagram page between August 2019 and February 2020
Annual report	Twitter	309 Engagements	473 Engagements	We saw 164 more engagements regarding the annual report for the period between August and February
Media interviews	TVs, Radios, Print Newspapers, Online media houses	10 Interviews were conducted. Management and in other instances the Chief Economist were interviewed by different media houses on MPC decisions, Cashless campaign, and other issues related to the state of the economy	17 Interviews were conducted. Management spoke with different media houses on MPC decisions, Cashless campaign, and other issues related to the state of the economy	7 more interviews were conducted between August 2019 and February 2020

Appendix 5.2: Questionnaire Used During MPFSS

Section 1: General Information

N	Questions	Answers
01	Are you representing any institution?	1. Yes 2. No
02	If yes, name the institution	–
03	Encircle the type of your institution	1. Private (Finance) 2. Private (Non-Finance) 3. Public 4. Multilateral 5. Other (specify)
04	Write the position you hold in your institution	–

(continued)

(continued)

N	Questions	Answers
05	Encircle the number of times you have or your institution has participated in the monetary policy statement presentations	1. First time 2. Two times 3. Many times
06	Encircle the way through which you learned about the monetary policy statement	1. Invited by BNR 2. Media 3. SMS 4. Invitation and Media 5. Invitation and SMS 6. Media and SMS 7. Invitation, Media and SMS 8. Other (Specify)

Section 2 Appreciation of The Monetary Policy Statement

N	Questions	Answers
07	Please rank in order of satisfaction the content of today's monetary policy statement	1. Excellent 2. Very good 3. Satisfactory 4. Inadequate
08	Generally, the presentation time for today's monetary policy statement was	Short 2. Long 3. Enough
09	If the presentation time was short or long, what time do you think is appropriate (in minutes)?	–
10	Mention any elements, if any, which can be considered in future so as to improve the monetary policy statement.	–
11	The time for questions and discussions in today's monetary policy statement was:	1. Short 2. Long 3. Enough
12	If the time for questions and discussions was short or long, what time do you think is appropriate (in minutes)?	–
13	To what extent do you think BNR has achieved its mandate?	1. Excellent 2. Very good 3. Satisfactory 4. Unsatisfactory
14	For your institution or activities, do you use information released in the past Monetary Policy Statements?	1. Yes 2. No
15	If yes, rank between 1 and 5 your level of satisfaction with respect to the usefulness of the information. [RANKING: 1 means extremely satisfied and 5 means not satisfied]	1. Extremely satisfied 2. Very satisfied 3. Moderately satisfied 4. Slightly satisfied 5. Not satisfied

Appendix 5.3: Findings from MPFSS Survey

Are You Representing Any Institution?

	Yes	No
2014 February	150	7
2014 August	167	15
2015 February	177	24
2015 August	116	14
2016 February	60	60
2017 February	188	18
2017 August	142	11
2018 February	137	8
2018 August	31	2
2019 February	66	3
Average	123.4	16.2

Number of Times You Participate in MPFSS

	2014 Feb	2014 Aug	2015 Feb	2015 Aug	2016 Feb	2016 Aug
First time	24	40	57	22	110	24
Second time	15	28	24	25	3	57
Many times	120	114	120	84	7	120

	2017 Feb	2017 Aug	2018 Feb	2018 Aug	2019 Feb
First time	57	24	26	10	22
Second time	23	14	19	2	11
Many times	67	115	100	21	36

Order of Satisfaction About MPFSS Content

	2014 Feb	2014 Aug	2015 Feb	2015 Aug	2016 Feb	2016 Aug
Excellent	89	79	109	49	75	25
Very good	59	85	85	68	26	76
Satisfactory	11	19	7	13	19	19

	2017 Feb	2017 Aug	2018 Feb	2018 Aug	2019 Feb
Excellent	130	67	84	15	54
Very good	62	70	53	16	8
Satisfactory	14	19	8	2	7

Views on Time Allocated to the Presentation of MPFSS

	2014 Feb	2014 Aug	2015 Feb	2015 Aug	2016 Feb	2016 Aug
Short	4	11	3	12	3	2
Long	6	6	11	9	11	9
Enough	149	165	106	180	109	180

	2017 Feb	2017 Aug	2018 Feb	2018 Aug	2019 Feb
Short	24	9	5	2	9
Long	0	4	7	3	4
Enough	182	140	133	28	132

Views on Time Allocated to Questions and Answers After Presentation of MPFSS

	2014 Feb	2014 Aug	2015 Feb	2015 Aug	2016 Feb	2016 Aug
Short	6	16	5	45	4	6
Long	12	17	7	60	10	5
Enough	141	149	189	60	106	56

	2017 Feb	2017 Aug	2018 Feb	2018 Aug	2019 Feb
Short	45	45	9	5	9
Long	120	45	4	10	4
Enough	30	45	140	16	32

To What Extent BNR has Achieved its Mandate

	2014 Feb	2014 Aug	2015 Feb	2015 Aug	2016 Feb	2016 Aug
Excellent	42	42	64	164	40	64
Very good	103	113	115	33	69	115
Satisfactory	14	27	19	4	7	19
Not satisfied	23	0	3	0	4	3

	2017 Feb	2017 Aug	2018 Feb	2018 Aug	2019 Feb
Excellent	56	32	33	11	33
Very good	116	97	88	16	25
Satisfactory	32	23	18	5	7
Not satisfied	2	4	6	1	4

Do You Use Information Released in MPFSS?

	2014 Feb	2014 Aug	2015 Feb	2015 Aug	2016 Feb	2016 Aug
Yes	83	78	119	164	87	87
No	18	45	11	37	43	33

	2017 Feb	2017 Aug	2018 Feb	2018 Aug	2019 Feb
Yes	189	75	84	89	88
No	17	25	17	15	12

Level of Satisfaction About the Usefulness of MPFSS

	2014 Feb	2014 Aug	2015 Feb	2015 Aug	2016 Feb	2016 Aug
Extremely satisfied	79	89	108	109	15	106
Very satisfied	84	59	85	85	95	85
Moderately satisfied	1	10	6	5	10	4
Slightly satisfied	0	1	2	0	3	2
Not satisfied	0	0	0	2	0	2

	2017 Feb	2017 Aug	2018 Feb	2018 Aug	2019 Feb
Extremely satisfied	32	29	84	14	34
Very satisfied	84	86	53	13	32
Moderately satisfied	18	18	8	8	2
Slightly satisfied	3	2	0	0	0
Not satisfied	16	1	0	0	0

The manufacturer's authorised representative in the EU is Springer Nature Customer Service Centre GmbH, Europaplatz 3, 69115 Heidelberg, Germany. If you have any concerns regarding our products, please contact ProductSafety@springernature.com

Printed and bound by CPI Group (UK) Ltd, Croydon, CR0 4YY
30/09/2026
02225307-0014